W9-BRT-724

Michigan's Best BEER GUIDE

Michigan's Best BEER GUIDE

Kevin Revolinski

Thunder Bay Press

HOLT, MICHIGAN

Michigan's Best Beer Guide
by Kevin Revolinski

Copyright © 2013 Kevin Revolinski

All Rights Reserved.

No part of this book may be used or reproduced in any form without written permission from the publisher, except in the case of brief quotations embodied in critical reviews and articles.

Published by
Thunder Bay Press
Holt, Michigan 48842

First Printing, November 2013

17   16   15   14   13   1   2   3   4   5

ISBN: 978-1-933272-38-2

Library of Congress Control Number: 2013952281

Cover Photo: Kevin Revolinski
Except where credited, Interior Photos: Preamtip Satasuk

Book, Map and Cover Design: Julie Taylor

Printed in the United States of America

TABLE OF CONTENTS

ACKNOWLEDGEMENTS

I know full well that my part in this book is just laying down the highway miles and then pulling together all the work of so many others. From the fantastic brewers of Michigan, the local restaurants and bars and producers, the tourism boards and visitor bureaus out there touting their communities' brewers, to the locals and fellow travelers—many of whom I don't even know by name—who gave me the tips to find hotspots and secrets that supplement the breweries here. I say to all of you: Right on, Michigan! Thanks!

Specifically I have to say thanks to Dave Lorenz of Travel Michigan, Mike Norton of Traverse City, Janet Korn and Experience Grand Rapids, Renee Newman of Discover Kalamazoo, Tracy and Lori at Great Lansing CVB, Crystal and Renee of Detroit Metro CVB, Barb Barden of Livingston County CVB, Sydney Hawkins of Ann Arbor CVB, Terry and Laurel at Kalamazoo House, Pat and Alison at the Marquette County CVB, Mariah at Sault Ste Marie CVB, Judi at Blue Water Area CVB, George Percy and Rob Klepper of Geiger PR. Tip of the hat to Michigan DNR for the State Parks that often were our crash spot for the night. Thanks to Kim and Karl Schneider for being great hosts and sailing companions.

Thanks to Kyle and Bessie Krum for taking us in on our passage via the Chicago route. Another huge thanks to Julie and Amelia at Thunder Bay for eternal patience and speedy quality work. Again!

Thanks to the folks at S.S. Badger and Lake Express for making Michigan a wee bit closer for a commute from Wisconsin.

Thanks to my wonderful wife Preamtip Satasuk for playing the challenging role of navigator with the Gazette and taking all the photos for this book while I was free to take notes, sample beers, and talk smack with brewers and bartenders.

INTRODUCTION

We live in a new Golden Age of Beer. At one time, before the Dark Ages of 1919 to 1933 (Prohibition), many American towns had brewers doing their thing. You couldn't swing a cat without hitting one. When consumption of our veritable holy water became a mortal and legal sin, many were the breweries that went beer belly up. The larger ones survived, a few got by on root beer and soda (Pabst survived with cheese), and for this we can lift a pint. Then over the following few decades, many of the mid-sized survivors closed their doors until by the mid-1970s there were fewer breweries in the entire USA than there are today in the State of Michigan. The few remaining brewers such as Anheuser Busch, Miller, Pabst, Schlitz, G. Heileman, and Michigan's Stroh's Brewing Co. battled it out, and today all the mass-market beer comes from just a few companies, ultimately owned by foreign entities.

But never mind all that: We live in a new golden age. President Carter made homebrewing legal back in 1978. Since the 1980s, we have witnessed a rise in the number of craft breweries. In 1982, Real Ale Co. opened in Chelsea, Michigan, but perhaps the world wasn't ready, because the brewery closed about a year later. Bell's managed to survive its humble beginnings in Kalamazoo, selling its first commercial beer in 1985. Almost 3 decades later it is one of the top ten largest craft brewers by volume. A surge and collapse in the 1990s hinted that opening a microbrewery might be a fad, but such is most definitely not the case today. Michigan's breweries now count well over 100 and the pace of growth shows no sign of slowing. The big producers—Bell's, Founders, Short's, for example—are still growing by leaps and bounds, and the little guys, like the corner brewpubs or regional production breweries, keep opening—and are staying open. Wineries are adding beer to the production. Small towns we may have doubted could ever support one microbrewery 10 years ago, now suddenly have two or three. (Hello, Marquette and Muskegon!) Grand Rapids has taken the title of Beer City USA a couple times already, but you can just hear Kalamazoo, Ann Arbor, and Traverse City in hot pursuit, and Metro Detroit is as good a beer destination as Portland.

Michigan beer is on the rise. Many Michiganders are fortunate to have someone looking out for them with a handcrafted lager or ale. Who in this state should not have their own personal hometown beer? (My condolences to those who don't, but don't worry—this book can help you adopt and probably someone already has one planned anyway.) Designate a driver (or pack your sleeping bag in the trunk), turn the page, and set off on a *pils-grimage* to the breweries of Michigan.

BUT I DON'T LIKE BEER

You'll hear it time and time again when you ask a brewer—pro or homebrewer—why they got into brewing. Many of them will say they were dissatisfied with what was on the market back before the advent of the modern craft-beer revolution. Maybe they took a trip to Germany. Maybe they were inspired by another homebrewer. But in the end, regardless of that original motivation, it becomes a passion for quality beer. I have to admit it took me a long time to become a beer convert. If you had offered me a beer in college, I would likely have gone the choosy-beggar path and ask if you had any vodka or rum instead. I really didn't even like beer. I can already hear the collective gasp of horror, but let me explain: beer was social lubricant, something you sipped at with friends at a cookout, bought for the cute woman at the other end of the bar, or beer-bonged on occasion. I didn't like the taste so much and—oh the humanity—often didn't even finish them. I killed many a houseplant at parties and have gotten hordes of bees drunk at picnics with the remains of a bottle of Something-or-Other Light.

It wasn't until craft beer that I became a Born Again Beer Drinker. Beer experts already know, and mass-market beer drinkers might be leery of the fact, that outside of the mass-produced impersonal brews, beers are as different as people. They have tremendous character and the people who dedicate their lives to brewing are characters as well. Traveling to visit a brewery—what I like to call a pils-grimage—is as much about appreciating the subtleties and variations of beer, as it is about taking a peek into local communities and beer's place in them. What makes Michigan great, and what makes brewing great, is the sense of the little guy. All respects to the giants of the mass-market beer industry, but how cool is it to walk into a local place and see the brewmaster standing at the bar sharing suds with the guy next door?

This book is a compilation of all the places that brew their own beer in Michigan. That means from the big boy Bell's all the way down to the little nanobreweries like the one at Bier Camp. The list continues to grow and even at the moment I closed the book on this first edition of my Michigan brewery road trip guide, at least a dozen more were likely planned to open the very next week. That's the nature of the beast.

Using the very latest cutting-edge state-of-the-art rocket-science-level technology, I established the locations of all of the breweries in the state. OK, actually it was a Sharpie and a free Michigan highway map from the Michigan Department of Transportation (517-373-2090). You can also contact Pure Michigan (Michigan.org, 888-784-7328) to get your own paper or digital travel guide from them at michigan.org/travel-guide. I sat down with the list and divided the state into four zones. Each of those zones is listed in the Where's the Beer At? section and shows the brewtowns alphabetically. If you already know the name of the brewery you are seeking, look for it in the cross-referenced lists at the beginning of Where's the Beer At? Make sense? Worked for me!

WHAT IS BEER?

Beer is produced by fermenting some sort of starch product. In many cases this is barley, wheat, oats, or rye, but even corn, rice, potatoes, and certain starchy roots in Africa have been used. In parts of Latin America, corn is chewed, spit out, and left to ferment and become a sort of corn beer called chicha. I've tried it… before my traveling companion told me about the chewing process. We are no longer on speaking terms. Don't expect MillerCoors or Anheuser Busch to be rolling it out in mass quantities very soon. And since you don't hear anyone advertising "brewed from the finest Senegalese cassava roots" you can guess barley is still the primary grain of choice. (If you've tasted some of those commercial beers though, you've gotta wonder.) There's no distilling for beer—that would make it some kind of liquor, and it's not strictly sugars or fruit juices—which is where your wine comes from.

THE HISTORY OF BEER

MANNA FROM HEAVEN

Yes, beer is pure brewed right here in the Great Beer State of Michigan (as the Michigan Brewers Guild likes to call it) but it wasn't always so. Egyptians loved it long before, Sumerians wrote down recipes for it on stone tablets, and you can imagine the drunken bar brawls over at the Viking lodge. Beer dates way back beyond 5000 BC, which is before writing even. (I think Ernest Hemingway, F. Scott Fitzgerald, and many other writers have also put the one before the other.)

The word itself comes to us by way of Middle English *ber*, from Old English *bEor* which goes to show you just how difficult life must have been without spellchecker. The English version surely comes from *bior* which was Old High German which became Old Low German by the end of a serious night of drinking.

BEER IN MICHIGAN

In 1998, I traveled to Czech Republic to see a bit of the land my forefathers left behind for the sake of Michigan and Wisconsin. I landed in Frankfurt, Germany (cheaper flight!) and drove a rental car to Prague. In fact, as I bundled up in a jacket and faced an unseasonably cold June in Plzen, this is pretty much what struck me: My great grandparents had packed up all they had into small trunks or had a big barn sale perhaps, left behind everyone they knew on this earth—friends, family, perhaps a few creditors—spent much of their remaining money on ocean-liner tickets, braved the long and sometimes dangerous Atlantic crossing, had their names misspelled at Ellis Island and went overland halfway across a continent to settle in the same damn place they left behind. Seriously. Change the highway signs to English and set up some road construction detours and I may as well have been driving down M-66 outside of Battle Creek. But these immigrants' absurd notions of improving their lots worked to our benefit: conditions were perfect here for making the same great German, Belgian, Czech, British, etc. beers of Northern Europe—and so they did.

How serious were the European settlers about beer? Consider this: Michigan became a state in 1837. Commercial brewing goes back at least to 1829. At that time, ales were king. But when political turmoil pushed

Join the Michigan Brewers Guild:

Become a Michigan Beer Enthusiast!

Michigan: The Great Beer State. It's a catchy play on the Great Lakes State nickname, and one made popular by the Michigan Brewers Guild. One can already guess that the organization accepts company members that have Michigan brewing licenses. They also have "Allied Trade" members, which are companies involved in the beer world in some other way, perhaps distribution, equipment, ingredients, etc. But here's the kicker: YOU can be a member too. Join the MBG as a Beer Enthusiast and support Michigan craft beer. As an Enthusiast your annual membership gets you a special t-shirt, VIP status including early admission at all four of the Guild's awesome annual beer festivals (with the purchase of a ticket), VIP brewery tours, special tastings at member breweries, and even some discounts at participating member brewpubs.

Check the Guild's blog, The Mash, for upcoming events. (mbgmash.org)

Follow the Guild on Twitter @MiBrewersGuild and Facebook.com/michiganbrewersguild, or www.MIbeer.com.

a wave of Germans immigrants to the US in the 1840s, the lagers began their gradual takeover of the people's tastes. Bernard Stroh was one of those immigrants in 1849. He started homebrewing (seriously, in his basement like many of you!) and went around door-to-door selling it out of a wheelbarrow. He built a proper brewery and then built a beer empire on that Bohemian pilsner recipe.

PROHIBITION

The Prohibitionists had been on the boil already since the middle of the nineteenth century for religious and social motivations. Voters changed the State constitution to make Michigan a dry state in 1917. Also in that year, the US Congress passed a resolution to shut down sales, transportation, and production of all forms of alcohol. States signed off on it and the amendment went into effect on July 1, 1919. And if you were looking for loopholes, the Volstead Act in October defined alcoholic beverages as containing over one-half percent of alcohol. So do the math here. At best, you'd need about NINE BEERS to drink the equivalent amount of alcohol as a normal picnic beer! Even the most ambitious drinkers weren't going to be getting a buzz.

Brewing was a productive industry in the state and it had just been banned.

The best way to make something attractive? Prohibit it. This also goes a long way to making it profitable on the black market. Stories of Al Capone and bootleggers and the mob in Chicago are widely known. Something as crazy as outlawing beer was doomed to fail, and when Prohibition was repealed by the Twenty-first Amendment in 1933, there was much celebration.

BEER COMMERCIALS

Advertising wasn't a big deal right away. Who needed an ad to know where the brewery was across the street? But as breweries got bigger and started shipping over distances, there was a rise in beer propaganda. It started with newspapers, of course, and went on into the radio age with brewers sponsoring popular shows. Well, despite surviving the dry years on soda or near beer, most of the breweries hit hard times by the late 60s, and some even crawled into the 70s before giving up the ghost. One of the survival strategies of the big guys was to buy up the labels of the sinking ships and thus acquire the loyalists who went with them. So, for example, Stroh's picked up Schaefer's Brewing and by 1982 had bought up the stock of Milwaukee brewing giant Schlitz, making the Detroit brewer the 3rd largest in the country. But by 1985 Stroh's announced the closing of their Gratiot Avenue brewery and demolished it a year later. They bought other brands, including the Augsburger brand in 1989, and sold off Stroh's ice cream to Dean Foods. But the fat lady was singing. Pabst, no longer a physical brewery itself, gobbled up most of Stroh's brands in 1999 (Miller took the rest). But by this time, craft brewing already had strong roots in Detroit and the rest of the state. Changes in Michigan state law in 1992 allowed brewpubs and microbrewery taprooms to serve beer to the public. Before that they were only allowed to sell via distribution. This changed everything.

The history of Michigan brewing continues as we speak, with new brewpubs opening every year and a few unfortunates falling by the wayside. But you can play your part in making history: support your local brewers!

INGREDIENTS

Hops

Malt

Water

Yeast

Other

THE DIVINE PROCESS

The first step in brewing beer is MASHING, and for this you need a malted grain, such as barley, and it needs to be coarsely ground. (Michigan is fortunate to have a growing number of producers of grains and hops for brewing.) The brewer will add hot water to the malt to get the natural enzymes in the grain to start converting the starches into the sugars necessary for fermentation. Think of your bowl of sugared breakfast cereal growing soggy and then making the milk sweet. It's kind of like that, only different.

The next step is SPARGING when water is flushed through the mash to get a sweet liquid we call WORT. The wort is sent to the brew kettle and filtered to remove the barley husks and spent grain. Wort then needs to be boiled to kill off any unwanted microcritters and to get rid of some of the excess water. This generally goes on for about an hour and a half. It is at this stage that any other flavoring ingredients are generally added, including hops.

Once this is all done, the fermentation is ready to begin. A brewer once told me, "People don't make beer, yeast does." Yes, yeast is the magical little element that monks referred to as "God is Good" when they were making their liquid bread in the monasteries. If you wanted to grab a brewsky in the Middle Ages (and believe me you didn't want to drink the water), the best place to stop was the local monastery. The monks made beer, the travelers spent money, the church got along. Everyone happy. How the Church ended up with Bingo instead of beer we may never know. Bummer.

Yeast eats sugars like the little fat boy in *Willie Wonka and the Chocolate Factory* and as we all know from a long afternoon of drinking and stuffing our faces, what goes in must come out. As Kurt Vonnegut once put it and as unpleasant as it may seem, beer is yeast excrement: alcohol and a little bit of gas. Reminds me of a night of Keystone Light, actually.

ALES VS. LAGERS

There are two basic kinds of beer: ales and lagers. It's all about yeast's preferences. Some yeasts like it on top, some prefer to be on bottom. Up until now, yeasts have not been more creative in their brewing positions, but we can always fantasize.

Ale yeasts like it on top and will ferment at higher temperatures (60–70 °F) and so are quicker finishers than lagers (1–3 weeks). Usually ales are sweeter and have a fuller body, which really starts to take this sexual allusion to extremes.

Lagers, on the other hand, use yeasts that settle in at the bottom to do their work and prefer cooler temps of about 40–55 °F. They take 1–3 months to ferment. Lagers tend to be lighter and drier than ales and are the most common beers, often easier to get along with for the average drinker and they don't mind if you leave the seat up. (In fact, you might as well—you'll be coming back a few times before the night is done.) For lager we can thank the Bavarians who—when they found that cold temperatures could control runaway wild yeasts in the warm summer ale batches—moved them to the Alps. The name lager comes from the German "to store."

Ale is the first real beer that was made and it was sort of a mutation of another alcoholic drink called mead. This was made with fermented honey. Remember the mead halls when you read Beowulf in high school? OK, I didn't read it either, but the Cliffs Notes mentioned it some. This is the sweet and potent concoction that put the happy in the Vikings as they ran wild, pillaging and plundering. Someone added a bit of hops, and later some malt, and the hybrid brackett evolved.

THESE ARE NOT YOUR MALTED MILKBALLS

Malting is a process of taking a grain, such as barley or wheat, getting it to start germinating, and then drying it quickly to cut off that process. I like to call this germinus interruptus, but then I like to make a lot of words up, so take that with a grain of barley.

So the malting process is 1: get grain (seeds) wet 2: let it get started 3: roast it in a kiln until dried. And here's where the specialty malts come in. You can roast the malted grains to different shades, a bit like coffee beans, and you can even smoke the stuff for a real twist on flavor (check out Rauchbier). I mean smoke like you smoke bacon, not like you smoke tobacco—don't get any ideas.

Why is barley the most common grain? It has a high amount of those enzymes for beer. So although corn, wheat, rye, and even rice can be used, you'll see that barley is the king of the malts. If you have gluten troubles, this is bad news because barley has it. But fear not: last I read Mike Hall of Northern United Brewing Co. was working on a gluten-free IPA.

I know you're wondering, because I was too: What about malted milk balls? There is a connection, in fact. William Horlick of Racine, Wisconsin, sought to create a food for infants that was both nutritious and easy to digest. He mixed wheat extract and malted barley with powdered milk to form malted milk. Walgreens Drugstores almost immediately started selling malted milkshakes.

WHAT'S HOPPENIN', HOP STUFF?

So why the hops? It's a plant for cryin' out loud; do you really want salad in your beer?? Actually, without refrigeration beer didn't keep all too well. The medieval monks discovered that hops had preservative properties. The sun never set on the British Empire which meant it never set on the beer either. So the Brits hopped the ale hard to get it all the way to India and thus India Pale Ale was born. (No, the color is not really pale, but compare it to a porter or a stout, and the name makes sense.)

The point in the process when you put the hops in makes all the difference, and generally it goes in the boil. Boil it an hour and it's bitter; half an hour and it's less bitter with a touch of the flavor and aroma; toward the end of the boil and you lose the bitter and end up with just the aroma and flavor, making it highly "drinkable." (You will hear people describing beer as very "drinkable" and it would seem to me that this was a given. Apparently not.) There is another way to get the hoppiness you want. Dry hopping— which sounds a lot like what some of yous kids was doin' in the backseat of the car—is actually adding the hops after the wort has cooled, say, in the fermenter, or more commonly in the keg.

But let me tell you this, when I first sipped a beer I only stared blankly at brewers when they asked me, "Now, do ya taste the hops in this one?" How was I to know? I mean, if someone from Papua New Guinea says, "Do you get that little hint of grub worm in that beer?" I really have nothing to go on. Before touring or on your brew tour, if you aren't already hops-wise, ask someone if you can have a whiff of some. I did, and suddenly the heavens parted and Divine Knowledge was to me thus imparted. I could then identify that aroma more accurately and I have to confess I'm still not sure I taste it in those mass market beers.

THERE'S SOMETHING FUNNY IN MY BEER

So you know about the German Purity Law and the limits on what goes into a beer, but obviously there is a whole range of stuff out there that thumbs its nose at boundaries. Some of this is a good thing, some of it not so much. These beyond-the-basics ingredients are called adjuncts.

Let's talk about the type of adjunct that ought to make you suspicious and will elicit a curse or look of horror from a beer snob. In this sense an adjunct is a source of starch used to beef up the sugars available for fermentation. It is an ingredient, commonly rice or corn, used to cut costs by being a substitute for the more expensive barley. Pale lagers on the mass market production line commonly do this. It doesn't affect the flavor and often cuts back on the body and mouth feel of the brew, which is why if

---

Reinheitsgebot! The German Purity Law

Gezundtheit! Actually, it's not a Bavarian sneezing; it's the German Purity Law. Want to know how serious the Germans were about beer? By *law* dating back to 1516, beer had to be made using only these three ingredients: barley, hops, and water. (The law later added yeast to the ingredient list once Louis Pasteur explained to the world the role of the little sugar-eating microorganisms in the process.) But this meant you wheat or rye or oat lovers were out of luck. Barbarians! Bootleggers! Outcasts! Why so harsh on the alternative grains? Because these grains were necessary for breads and these were times of famines and the like. Fortunately, times got better and we have the wide variety of ales and lagers that we see today. Nevertheless, the Germans came to Wisconsin quite serious about beer (see Farm Breweries). In the end, the law was used more to control competitors and corner a market—so much for its pure intentions.

But there's more to beer quality than a list of ingredients anyway; it's the *purity* of those ingredients that makes all the difference. It's also the time, patience and care of the brewer that lifts the brew to a higher level. Am I talking about craft brewing here? I most certainly am!

you drink a mass market beer and then compare it to the same style (but without adjuncts) from a craft brewer you will taste a significant difference.

You may hear beer snobs use the word adjunct when ripping on the mass-produced, non-handcrafted brews, but there are other ingredients which are also adjuncts that we can't knock so much.

Wheat, rye, corn, wild rice, oats, sorghum, honey—many are the options that don't just serve to save a buck or two on the batch ingredients but rather bring something to the beer. Maybe a longer lasting head, a silkier mouth feel or a sweeter taste. And in the case of a wheat beer can one really call wheat an adjunct? Most would say no. Word dicers will say yes. Whatever.

Fruits and spices are also friendly adjuncts. Think of cherry, orange, or pumpkin flavors in certain brews, or spices such as coriander in Belgian wit beers, ginger, nutmeg, or even cayenne pepper. Brewers can add chocolate, milk sugar, or even coffee as in the case of a good coffee stout. By German Purity Law, of course, this is a big no-no, but there's nothing wrong with pushing the envelope a bit for some new tastes. It's not cutting corners, but rather creating new avenues.

BARRELS OF FUN

It's a trend that's gone so widespread that even many of the smallest breweries do at least a little bit of barrel aging. This can be done with a fresh oak barrel (or by throwing oak chips into a beer as it ages) or by using a previously owned barrel. Bourbon barrels are the most common, but chardonnay, brandy, rye, and other barrels can be used as well. The wood and the bourbon, for example, impart an amazing flavor to the beer the longer you leave it sit there. One of the most notable barrel-aged beers in Michigan is New Holland Brewing's Dragon's Milk Ale. It's so successful it's become their flagship beer and they've dedicated a lot of brewery space to its barrel-conditioning.

How long does a beer have to wait? Some brewers suggest one month of aging per alcohol percentage point. So seven months for a 7% alcohol beer. The beer takes on some of the bourbon flavors but also develops a relationship with the charred wood. Just like wine, beer can mellow and age, and some beers might be best drunk fresh, while others just keep getting better over time.

GREEN BEER

It may sound like I'm talking about St. Patrick's Day but this is about local brewers doing their part to work toward a cleaner, energy-efficient future while keeping us well stocked in suds. One of the first brewers to go "green" was Arbor Brewing Company. They have solar panels heating water, providing power, and saving them money.

There are many other ways to make difference. Having a grain silo eliminates the need for bags of malt. Heat exchangers recapture the heat of cooling wort. Cooling water can be used to clean the tanks. Using recycled equipment is another method of minimizing a brewery's impact on the environment. So many have used old dairy equipment in the past, but many more have purchased other brewers' systems.

Keeping the ingredients local is another great contributor to Michigan's economy that also cuts down on the energy required to bring grains in from far away. Bell's Brewery has their own farm dedicated to grain for their brews. Hops farms are on the rise in Michigan as well as specialty malting.

Not only are more and more brewers using local ingredients, but many more are also recycling the spent grain, sending it out to area farmers as feed for farm animals.

The latest trend has been in packaging: the aluminum can. The lighter weight saves energy and money on shipping/transportation, and aluminum doesn't let the beer-spoiling light in like glass does. Plus it's easier to recycle.

And let's not forget, if you are drinking a pint at your local brewpub, there's a bottle or can that was never needed. Pack a growler for carry-out purposes!

TASTING YOUR BEER

Back in the days of youth I suppose savoring the taste of your beer meant you belched after pouring it down your throat. Since you have evolved to drinking craft beers, you may take a bit more time to savor it. Here are a few pointers for savoring the stuff:

Sniff it for aromas. Remember your nose works with your tongue to make you taste things. Kids plug their noses to eat liver for a reason! Get a bit of that beer in your sniffer before you sip by swirling it around in your glass to raise the aroma like you would with wine.

OK, now sip it. Swirl it a bit around on your tongue. Gargling is generally frowned upon, however. Is it watery or does it have a bit of body to it? Squish it against the roof of your mouth with your tongue to appreciate the "mouth feel."

Swallow! Wine tasters can spit it out during a tasting but beer has a finish that you can only get at the back of the tongue where the taste receptors for bitterness are. The most graceful option is to swallow. (Remember what I said about gargling!)

Everyone's tastes are different, of course, and some may prefer a bitter IPA to a sweet Belgian tripel, but the test of a good beer is that bittersweet balance. Now if you want to be good at this tasting business, you need to practice. I know, I know, oh the humanity of it all! But you can suffer all this drinking if it really matters to you. Repeat the process with various craft brews and you will start to see how different all the beers are. Is this one too bitter? Too malty? Is the hops aroma strong, fair to middlin', barely noticeable? Hints of chocolate? Coffee? Caramel? Is it citrusy? Creamy? Crisp? Even smoky? (See "rauch beer" in the glossary.)

Sour Ales

Throw out what you think you know about keeping your brewing equipment all squeaky clean so as not to spoil a brew. Yes, that is extremely important for brewing typical beers, but it's a rule that gets a little bent when making a sour ale. This is not a beer gone wrong, but an actual style of beer that is gaining in popularity in the US and so is worth noting here.

Most commonly associated with Belgium (lambics or Flanders red ales), sour ales are intentionally allowed to go "bad." And by bad, we mean good. Wild yeasts and/or bacteria are purposely introduced to the beer to give it a sour or tart acidity. If you are familiar with Jolly Pumpkin Artisan Ales, then you already know what I'm talking about.

Fruit can be added for a secondary fermentation, but many sours use bacteria such as Lactobacillus or Pediococcus, or a special yeast such as "Brett" (Brettanomyces) which occurs in nature on fruit skins. Brewing such a beer can be challenging in that by introducing these wilder elements into the brewhouse, a brewer increases the risk of infecting other beers that aren't intended to be soured.

Is that butterscotch I'm tasting?!?

Shouldn't be! Beware of diacetyl! This natural byproduct of yeast is actually used in artificial butter flavoring. At low levels diacetyl gives a slippery mouth feel to the brew. A bit more and the butterscotch flavor starts to appear. Brewers need to leave the yeast a couple days or so after the end of fermentation and it will reabsorb the flavor-spoiling agent. The warmer temp of ale brewing makes this happen faster.

Here's something that will sound crazy: a good beer will even taste good when it has gone warm in your glass. (Some will even taste better!) Now try THAT with your crappy picnic beer!

BEER ENGINES AND NITRO

On your exploration of the brewpubs you may find a beer engine. No, I'm not talking about an alternative motor for your car that runs on brewsky. The beer engine looks suspiciously like a tap handle, but not exactly. Normally, beer is under pressure from carbon dioxide—or air you pumped into the keg at a party—which pushes your pint out at the tap. Now this can affect your beer, of course. Air will eventually skunkify it (which is why pubs aren't using it; at a party you will probably finish the keg in one go, so it doesn't matter anyway) and too much CO_2 increases the carbonation of the brew, sometimes beyond what is desirable. There are a couple of tricks that can avoid all this.

The beer engine is one. It is a piston-operated pump that literally pulls the beer up from the barrel or holding tanks. So when it looks like the barkeep is out at the water pump in an old western, he or she is actually using a beer engine. When you use this, the beer gets a cascading foam going in the glass (very cool and hypnotic, really) and a meringue-like head. Look for the tap with the long curved swan-neck spout that delivers the beer right against the bottom of the glass to make that special effect.

In Ireland, the Guinness people came up with an alternative to the barkeep arm-wrestling the pump handle. They put the beer "under nitro." This was not some sort of IRA terrorist plan (talk about hitting the Irish where it hurts!), it means nitrogen. Unlike CO_2, nitrogen does not affect the natural carbonation of the beer and yet it still provides the pressure to get the brew up the lines and into your glass. You'll mostly see Irish-style stouts coming out this way, though a few exceptions are out there.

PRESERVING YOUR BEER

You probably know enough to cool your beer before you drink it, but remember that many craft brews are not pasteurized. Yes, hops are a natural preservative, but let's face it, we are not sailing round the Cape of Good Hope to India eating hardtack and hoping for the best for the ale. This is fine beer, like fine wine, and needs some tender loving care.

If on your brewery tour you pick up a growler, put that thing on ice! If you don't refrigerate unpasteurized beer, you are getting it at less than its best and perhaps at its worst. And if your local grocer thinks stacking bottled six-packs of the unpasteurized stuff in fancy geometric designs on the floor is a good marketing strategy, have a word with that guy. Get that beer to a fridge!

If you are picking some up on a longer road trip, please, take a cooler along. The longer you leave good beer exposed to light and heat, the more likely the taste will deteriorate until you have the infamous beer of Pepé Le Pew.

Living yeast? Treat it like milk!

Louis Pasteur Changed Beer Forever

Well, and milk too I suppose. But really, which one is more important? Louis demonstrated that there wasn't any sort of magic mumbo jumbo going on in the brewing process and that, actually, fermentation was brought about by microorganisms (that'd be the yeast). Prior to this the theory was spontaneous generation, that things just happened, but he figured out it was airborne yeasts that got into the brew kettles. The alcohol, of course, comes as a byproduct as the little buggers went about eating the sugar. (Author Kurt Vonnegut once described alcohol as "yeast excrement," but that's kind of a gross thought, so let's forget it.)

But it wasn't just yeast getting in there—there were other little critters messing up things and making people sick or simply skunking up the beer. Solution? Pasteurize it. (Notice the name is from Louis. I'm just pointing it out in case you are four or five beers in on that case you bought already.) Pasteurization was heating the liquid (milk, beer, etc.) and killing off the nasty bits that would eventually spoil the beverage (or worst case, such as with milk, make the drinker quite sick!)

BREW YOUR OWN

OK, I know what you're thinking: if so many of these brewmasters started in their basements, why can't I? Well, truth is, you can!

Check your local yellow pages under BEER to find a place near you that sells what you need.

A basic single-stage brew kit includes a 6.5 gallon plastic bucket with a lid and fermentation lock, a siphoning tube, bottle brush, handheld bottle capper and caps, and hopefully, instructions. You then need a recipe pack and about 50 returnable-style bottles (not twist-offs). (Grolsch bottles with the ceramic stopper also work great; you only need to buy new rubber rings for the seal.) The kit starts around $50.

A two-stage kit throws in a hydrometer, thermometer, and a 5-gallon glass "carboy" where the brew from the bucket goes to complete fermentation. Now you can watch it like an aquarium. Don't put any fish in it though.

Ingredient kits have all you need for a certain recipe. Simple light ales might start around $25 while an IPA with oak chips can get up around $50. Each makes about 50 bottles of beer. In many cases you are using malt extracts thus skipping the grinding of grain in the wort-making process. As you go deeper into the art you will likely want to do this yourself as well.

If your future brewpub patrons are really slow drinkers or Mormons, this basic kit will do you fine. That said, the pros are by no means always using the state-of-the-art equipment either. Remember Egyptians and Sumerians were already making beer over 5,000 years ago and they didn't even have toilet paper yet. Um… my point is big brewers might have the funds to get the fancy copper brew kettles made in Bavaria and a microbiology lab, while others at least got their start with used equipment that had other original purposes. Old dairy tanks are popular.

But before you get all excited about naming your beers and what the sign on the pub is going to look like, consider Lake Louie Brewing founder/brewer Tom Porter's thoughts on the challenges of starting a brewery.

ON STARTING A BREWERY: TOM PORTER

If you want to start a brewery, use somebody else's money. Because you can go big to start, big enough to make it a profitable minimum, and then if it goes belly up you just tell them, "Sorry, guys, I did the best I could!" I'm on the hook for it, win or lose. It does give you tremendous impetus to not fail. There's no doubt about it. "Hey, you gotta make good beer." That's a given. There's nobody out there making really crummy beer anymore, they all went belly up and we all bought their used equipment. It's a given that the beer is pretty darn good. Yeah, there are different interpretations of style, but it's really all about costs.

I could be in the muffler business, or I could be in the hub cap business; I could be making paper clips for chrissakes, as long as the paper clip quality is as good as everybody else's, it doesn't matter. The reality is you better be darn good on cost control and you better know business, and I didn't. I was an engineer. Engineers sit way in back of a great big company. Someone else goes and sells it, someone else decides if there is profit in it. By the time the paper ever gets to your desk, it's a done deal. I went from the engineering business to having to do the business, the books, the capital decisions, the sales… inventory control. All those things: debt amortization, accounting… ggarrggh, accounting? Man! I never went to accounting classes. I got out of those thinking they were like the plague to me. "A credit is a debit until it's paid?!?" What?!?

My accounting system that started out when I started this brewery is I had a bucket of money. And every time I get some more I put it in the bucket. And when I need it, I take it out of the bucket. When the bucket's empty I got to stop taking money out until I get some more to put in. Well, that system still works here, but there's a WHOLE—SERIES—OF BUCKETS now! There's literally dozens of buckets. It gets hard to remember which one do I put it into and which one do I take it out of. And sometimes you don't notice one's empty. So business and accounting—that's really been my learning curve. I went from going "What's a balance sheet?" to a profit and loss statement, and now I work off cash flow statements and sometimes I split them up. I want to know where the push and pull is of my cash flow, because that's really what makes a good businessman. And I'm learning this because I HAVE to. And it has had NOTHING to do with making good beer. The good beer part is a given. You've gotta have it. If you don't have it, don't even think about it. But having that is not enough. I have a lot of people here coming through the door on tours and such saying, "I'm thinking of starting a brewpub. Gees, I make really good homebrew." And I say, "That's a really good first step." But the second through fortieth steps are… how are your plumbing skills? How're your carpentry skills? Can you pour concrete? Can you weld? And then can you balance a balance sheet every thirty days?

WHERE'S THE BEER AT?

(INTRO TO THE LISTINGS)

The listings for all the commercial brewers in Michigan are divided here into the four zones: 1–Southwest, 2–Southeast, 3–Northern Lower Peninsula, 4–Upper Peninsula. Each section has a map of that portion of the state with the brewtowns marked. Within each zone the communities are listed in alphabetical order with the brewpubs and breweries below the town heading. Watch for a few extra non-brewing but brewing-related attractions and other interesting bits you can read during your journey.

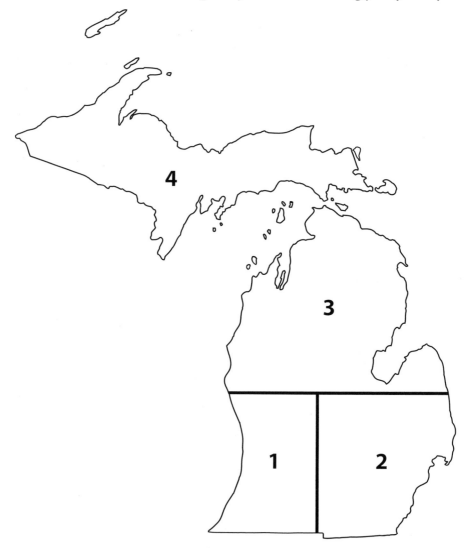

HOW TO USE THE LISTINGS:

OK, this isn't rocket science but let's go over a brief summary of the finer points of the listings.

Brewmaster: So you know who to ask brewing questions.

Staple Beers: Always on tap.

Rotating Beers: Like roulette only with beer, the beers that may come and go, often seasonal brews.

Special Offer: This is something the management of the place you're visiting agreed to give to a patron who comes in and gets this book signed on the signature line of that particular brewer in the back of the book. This is a one-time bonus and the signature cancels it out. You must have a complete book, and photocopies or print-outs don't count. I didn't charge them and they didn't charge me; it's out of the goodness of their hearts, so take it as such and don't get all goofy on them if the keychain turns out to be a bumper sticker or something. And if they are offering a discount on a beer, it is assumed that it is the brewer's own beer, not Bud Light or some such stuff or that fancy import you've been wishing would go on special. The brewer reserves the right to rescind this offer at any time and for any reason. Legal drinking age still applies, of course. Not all brewers are participating and that will be noted on each brewer's page.

Stumbling Distance: Two or three cool things that are very local, very Michigan, or just plain cool. Some may be more of a short car ride away. If you really are stumbling, get a designated driver for those.

And that's about it, the rest should be self-explanatory. Enjoy the ride! Last one all the way through the breweries is a rotten egg. Or a skunk beer.

LISTINGS BY BREWER

LISTINGS BY BREWTOWN

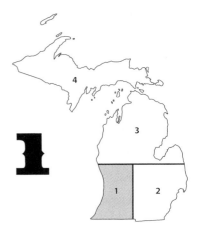

ZONE 1

ROUND BARN BREWERY & PUBLIC HOUSE

Founded: 2002 (Pub opened 2013)
Brewmaster: Chris Noel
Address: 9151 First Street • Baroda, MI 49101
Phone: 269-326-7059
Website: www.roundbarnwinery.com
Annual Production: 1,500 barrels
Number of Beers: 12 on tap, 30 styles annually

Staple Beers:
» AMBER
» BOB'S YOUR UNCLE
» COCOA STOUT
» KOLSCH
» OAKED IPA

Rotating Beers:
» CREAM DREAMS DOUBLE CREAM STOUT
» GRAPE EXPECTATIONS
» HARVEST ALE
» SANTA'S LISP CHRISTMAS PORTER
» VACATION WHEAT
» WEST HIGHLAND SCOTCH ALE

Most Popular Brew: Kolsch

Brewmaster's Fave: Oaked IPA (and IPAs in general)

Tours? By appointment only.

Samples: No.

Best Time to Go: Open daily at 3PM, but at noon Friday–Saturday. Double check the website for seasonal variations. Summertime offers beautiful outside seating.

Where can you buy it? Onsite by the glass and in growlers, and throughout Michigan and Indiana.

Got food? Yes. Also, the winery has a grill during summer months for bistro-style cuisine.

Special Offer: Not participating.

The Beer Buzz: Round Barn started exclusively as a winery and it wasn't until the early 2000s that they took on beer as a sort of side project. Why? Because they were hosting weddings at the winery and the demand was there for suds. They started with a one-barrel system but it soon became clear people wanted more beer. By 2008 they were bottling and the demand—and subsequently the production—has been increasing each year as much as 30%.

Round Barn actually offers three places to try the brews. The address above and hours are for the latest addition: a public house in Baroda. Do check out the awesome white round barn at the Baroda Tasting Room and Estate (10983 Hills Rd, Baroda, 800-716-9463) or visit their tasting room in Union Pier (9185 Union Pier Rd, 269-469-6885) as well.

The brewing facility was originally a tool and die factory, with all the machine grease and grime one might expect. Clean up was no small task, but now it houses a state-of-the-art brew system with shining epoxy floors.

Brewer Chris actually got his degree in history. Well, beer has history, right? He took over brewing in 2011.

Lifetime Beer Club.

Directions: Get to Bridgman off I-94 at Exit 16 and on the town's north side on Red Arrow Hwy, take Lemon Creek Rd east 3.4 miles to Baroda and turn right on First Street. It's 0.3 mile south on the left. Also, Exit 23 for Stevensville gets you to St. Joseph Ave which turns into Stevensville-Baroda Rd then First Street, a total of 5.9 miles south from I-94 to the front door.

Stumbling Distance: *Round Barn Winery & Distillery* at 10983 Hills Road in Baroda has live music every weekend plus other wine, spirits, and beer events throughout the summer. Visit the sister winery *Free Run Cellars* 4.5 miles away in Berrien Springs (10062 Burgoyne Rd).

ARCADIA ALES

Founded: 1997
Head Brewer: Dave Sippel
Address: 103 Michigan Avenue West •
Battle Creek, MI 49017
Phone: 269-963-9690
Website: www.arcadiaales.com
Annual Production: 12,000 barrels
Number of Beers: 14 on tap; 22 styles
with seasonals

Staple Beers:
» ANGLERS ALE
» IPA
» HOPMOUTH DOUBLE IPA
» LOCH DOWN SCOTCH ALE
» SKY HIGH RYE PALE ALE

Rotating Beers: (These come and go, sometimes draft only, sometimes barrel-aged.)
» B-CRAFT BLACK IPA
» CANNONBALL GOLD IPA
» CEREAL KILLER BARLEYWINE
» COCOA LOCO TRIPLE CHOCOLATE STOUT
» HOPMOUTH DOUBLE IPA
» IRISH RED
» JAW JACKER AMBER-WHEAT ALE
» LONDON PORTER
» NUT BROWN ALE
» WHITSUN ALE

Most Popular Brew: IPA

Brewmaster's Fave: Sky High Rye

Tours? Yes, scheduled tours on weekends for about $5 which includes a pint glass and 3 sample pours.

Samples: 4 oz. pours of all taps for about $15.

Best Time to Go: Happy hour is 2–6PM Monday–Friday with $1 off beers. See their anniversary below.

Where can you buy it? On tap in 10, 16, 20 oz. pours and growlers. Cans and bottles in Michigan and 7 other states: IL, KS, KY, MO, NJ, OH, PA.

Got food? Yes, wood-fired oven pizzas, house-smoked cheeses, and BBQ, hummus, soup, sandwiches, and salads.

Special Offer: $1 off your first pint during your signature visit.

The Beer Buzz: Tim and Marty Suprise were fans of English ales and wanted to start a brewery. They bought a used system from Shipyard Brewing in Portland, Maine, a British kit just the right size for a brewpub and thus popular in the 1990s when a brewpub boom began. The brewery is located in an old Chevrolet dealership and inside you'll find cement floors, an industrial ceiling painted black and featuring sounds pads to cut crowd noise. There's a long bar to one side and the windows along the opposite wall look in on the brewing facility. Award certificates and medals adorn the back wall and there's a real dartboard. The styles remain focused on the UK, relying on UK malts but Pacific Northwest hops, and using a single yeast strain and open fermentation. Free Wi-Fi on site. In early December each year, Arcadia celebrates its anniversary. Bring your kilt. There will be haggis and Irish/Celtic bands. Also, see Arcadia Ales' second location in Kalamazoo!

Brewer Dave Sippel came to Arcadia from Victory Brewing Co. in Downingtown, PA. Raised outside of Indianapolis, Dave began homebrewing when he was in high school, then went on to study brewing, business, and graphic design at Indiana University. While in school, he worked as an Assistant Brewer at the Bloomington Brewing Company, then moved on to brew at Upland Brewing Company (also in Bloomington) after graduation. At Victory, Dave moved through various positions, doing it all: Senior Brewer, Packaging Manager, Brewmaster, and Process Engineer. Now with Arcadia, Dave is once again at the brewing helm and happy to be back in the Midwest.

Check out their new production facility and pub soon in Kalamazoo.

Directions: From I-94, take I-194/M-66 north into Battle Creek. Stay on M-66 as it crosses Dickman Rd on an overpass, and then go left (northwest) on Michigan Ave. Drive 2.5 blocks and the brewery is on the left.

Stumbling Distance: If you are looking for a liquor store with a decent Michigan craft beer selection, try *Mega Bev* (5570 Beckley Rd, 269-979-9463, megabev.com).

THE LIVERY

Founded: 2005
Brewmaster: David Sawyer (call him "Sawyer")
Address: 190 5th Street • Benton Harbor, MI 49022
Phone: 269-925-8760
Website: www.liverybrew.com
Annual Production: 600 barrels
Number of Beers: 80 styles annually

Staple Beers:
» ANVIL AMERICAN IPA
» MCGILLIGAN'S AMERICAN IPA
» STEEL WHEELS OAT MALT STOUT (DRY-HOPPED)
» STEEP CANYON BOHEMIAN PILSNER
» STRING OF PONIES IPA

Seasonal and Specialty Beers (too numerous to list!):
» BARLEY LEGAL ENGLISH-STYLE PALE ALE
» BIER MUNRO
» CHERRY BOMB
» FREAK SHOW BEGLIAN INDIA RED ALE (DEC–MAR)
» KILT TILTER SCOTCH ALE
» THE LIVERATOR DOPPELBOCK (10% ABV)
» MAILLOT JAUNE FRENCH FARMHOUSE ALE (SUMMER)
» OKTOBERFEST (SEP–NOV)
» SILVER QUEEN HELLES LAGER
» TELEWHACKER AMERICAN BROWN ALE (DEC–MAR)
» TRIPPEL WEIZENBOCK
» UMAMI WHEAT WINE
» Various REAL ALES and SOUR ALES and BARREL-AGED BREWS

Livery Pub Series
» BASKET CASE IMPERIAL CHOCOLATE RYE OATMEAL MILK STOUT
» BLACK DYNOMYTE
» DANIMAL (HOPPY AMERICAN RED ALE)
» DYNOMYTE AMERICAN OAT IPA
» HIGH 5 MICHIGAN IPA

Most Popular Brew: McGilligan's and some other IPA rivals such as Bier Munro.

Brewmaster's Fave: If he had to pick, he'd pick McGilligan's but he loves the sour ales. Barrel-Aged Cherry Bomb, for one.

Tours? Free tours the last Sunday each month (maybe the second last).

Samples: Platters of 5 plus a specialty beer for $13–$15.

Best Time to Go: Live music on weekends (with cover charge). Check site/call for current hours. A firkin release the last Friday of every month.

Where can you buy it? Growlers and draft on site. Throughout Michigan, Milwaukee, and Madison, WI.

Got food? Yes, housemade brats, burgers, locally sourced salads, nothing deep-fried. Beer is used in soups, sauces, and marinades, and the corned beef is braised in stout. The café serves pizzas.

Special Offer: $1 off your first pint on your signature visit.

The Beer Buzz: Fans of hoppy IPAs will be especially pleased with the variety of recipes for them here. Sour ales and "über lambics" are a specialty as well but the styles go way beyond those. The list of beers is ambitious and adventurous. How about a barrel-aged wheat wine with 2 different yeast strains? The Livery Pub Series beers are limited releases and they never leave the pub, not even in growlers. Danimal, a hoppy red ale, is brewed in honor of a dearly departed friend of the brewers, Dan Wissman.

Previous brewer Steve Berthel used to race bicycles (note the beer Maillot Jaune means "yellow jersey" in French) and started up this brewery in a 1905 former horse livery. The floor in the café was originally dirt and you can see where the elevator used to raise and lower horses with counterweights. If you look closely at some of the wooden posts you can even see where the horses used to rub against them. When Steve left to pursue other interests, his assistant, Sawyer, took on the head-brewer role.

Sawyer, originally from Traverse City, got started on a Mr. Beer kit. He moved to Grand Rapids where he worked at The Hideout before landing here in 2010. He likes to do SMaSH beers (single malt and single hops recipes) as well as beers with herbs. He continues to build his own reputation at The Livery while keeping many of Steve's classics in production. The brewery added fermentation space in 2013 to increase their capacity by at least 30%.

The entertainment venue is upstairs with open wood-beam ceilings and a mezzanine seating area; the café is downstairs. In summer there is a beer garden with tents and picnic tables with bar service and live music. Free Wi-Fi on site and lots of parking in a lot out back. A production facility offsite helps keep up with demand.

Directions: From I-94 take Exit 33 and go west on Main St. Take a right on 5th St and the brewery is on the left at the corner of 5th and Park St.

Stumbling Distance: *The Ideal Place* (212 Territorial Rd, 269-934-0460, theidealplace.com) offers good American bistro eats right out the front door from here, with 10 craft taps plus bottles. *Lark and Sons Hand Car Wash & BBQ* (440 W Main St, 269-926-9833) is a must. Exactly what the name says, with smokers out back. For a stellar beer bar just five minutes away in St Joseph: *The Buck Burgers and Brew* (412 State St, St Joseph, 269-281-0320, eatatthebuck.com). 60 beers on tap, great food, and perhaps 2 custom-made Livery brews in the house.

TAPISTRY BREWING CO.

Founded: 2013
Head Brewer: Nathan Peck
Address: 4236 Lake Street • Bridgman, MI 49106
Phone: 269-266-7349
Website: www.tapistrybrewing.com
Annual Production: 2,200 barrels
Number of Beers: 20 on tap; 30+ beers per year

Staple Beers:
» CHOCOLA JAVA STOUT
» DUBBEL STANDARD
» ENIGMA DOUBLE IPA
» PECKS ROBUST PORTER
» REACTOR IPA
» SKIPJACK PALE ALE

Rotating Beers:
» ALTERNATER ALTBIER
» BAT COUNTRY BROWN ALE
» BEATNIK AMERICAN BLONDE
» BRIDGMAN BITTER
» BURN THE WITCH WEIZENBOCK
» DRIFTER IN THE DARK
» GRETEL DUNKELWEISS
» HANSEL HEFEWEIZEN
» REVOLVER AMERICAN RED ALE
» RYEM OR REASON PALE ALE
» SIXTEEN TONS BARLEYWINE
» SUMMER HAZE

Most Popular Brew: Skipjack Pale Ale (but Summer Haze in summer)

Head Brewer's Fave: Sixteen Tons Barleywine or Reactor IPA

Tours? Yes, by appointment.

Samples: Yes, five 5-oz. pours for about $8.

Best Time to Go: Open daily 11AM–11PM.

Where can you buy it? Here on tap and to go in growlers and kegs, and draft accounts in the tri-county area and as far as Marshall and Grand Rapids.

Got food? Yes, a simple menu of a few sandwiches/panini, plus snacks, meat and cheese trays, and the like.

Special Offer: $1 off your first pint during your signature visit.

The Beer Buzz: Owners Joe Rudnik and Greg Korson met years ago through Joe's wife. They were all working at Pfizer when they discovered they had craft beer in common, and became good friends. Once a year they'd make a pilsgrimage to a major beer destination—Traverse City, Detroit, etc.—and spend a weekend hitting all the breweries. Joe got into homebrewing and then the two of them were convinced they could begin their own brewery. Greg had the finance background and Joe was an engineer and weld inspector. So they left their corporate jobs to do this.

In the heart of downtown Bridgman, Tapistry occupies two buildings: an old, painted brick hardware store is the taproom. Joined to it next door is a steel building with a brick front, which is the production facility. The taproom shows a high ceiling and open duct work and local art on the walls. But perhaps the loveliest artwork is the long stainless steel strip along the wall with 20 taps hanging from it.

Brewer Nate previously worked at Sand Creek Brewing in Wisconsin (he's a Packer fan). Assistant brewer Michael Ludwig spent time with Jolly Pumpkin up north. Joe brings recipes from his years of homebrewing. Everyone contributes to the fabric of the brewery. They play a lot with their beers; they might take their porter and add various ingredients, jalapeno, for example. They keep three yeast strains to alternate into their line up and they even change their water profiles. For their ESB they duplicate the water chemistry of Burton-on-Trent. They keep a one-barrel pilot system on hand for various one-offs, so you can expect a constant variety among those 20 taps. Enjoy the beer garden out back in season.

Free Wi-Fi. Mug Club. Find them on Facebook and Twitter @TapistryBrewing.

Directions: From I-94 take Exit 16 and head north on Red Arrow Hwy/ Old US-12 about 0.9 mile and turn right (east) on Lake St. The brewery is 0.4 mile on the right.

Stumbling Distance: *Warren Dunes State Park* features towering natural wonders on Lake Michigan. You should really see them. (Warning: they don't allow alcohol.) *Waco Beach* is also nice. *Olympus Restaurant* (9735 Red Arrow Hwy, 269-465-5541) offers some solid, reasonably priced diner food. *Tapistry* makes a nice hat-trick with *Greenbush* and *Round Barn* breweries just a few minutes down the road in either direction.

PATCHWORK BREWING

Founded: July 15, 2011
Brewmaster: Brooke Rosenbaum
Address: 103 North Phelps • Decatur, MI 49045
Phone: 269-436-8052
Website: www.patchworkbrewing.com
Annual Production: 70–80 barrels
Number of Beers: 6 on tap, 11 per year

Beers:
» ALE MARY HONEY PALE
» BLACKBERRY WHEAT
» CHARLIE MCCARTHY'S CHOCOLATE STOUT
» IRA'S REVENGE DOUBLE INDIA DARK ALE (9.6% ABV!)
» KING ARTHUR'S ROUND TABLE PORTER
» LAKE OF THE WOODS BELGIAN
» LIQUID BREAKFAST OATMEAL STOUT
» NEWTOWN WOODS IPA
» OLD SWAMP DOUBLE IPA
» PUMPKIN WHEAT
» REDLIGHT BARLEYWINE
» SUMMER WHEAT

Most Popular Brew: Ira's Revenge

Brewmaster's Fave: Old Swamp Double IPA

Tours? Not really—you can see it all from the counter.

Samples: Yes, 6 six-ounce samplers for about $10.50.

Best Time to Go: Double check the hours, but closed Tuesday and Wednesday. Hours Thursday 3–9PM (8PM Sunday–Monday, 10PM Friday–Saturday), with happy hour at 5–7 on weekdays. Acoustic open mic night is on Thursdays.

Where can you buy it? Only here on tap or to go in growlers.

Got food? Yes, fresh and local organic ingredients. Ciabatta pizzas are the specialty, but the rest of the menu changes with the seasons. Appetizers, soups (beer cheese soup!), salads, and sandwiches. Kids' menu available.

Special Offer: Get a sampler flight for half price during your signature visit.

The Beer Buzz: Brewer Brooke got into homebrewing because she thought it would save money. But then she ended up sharing all her beer. She had always wanted to open a bar and restaurant, but when she discovered that it'd be easier to get a microbrewery license than a liquor license, the direction changed a wee bit. She enjoys cooking and brewing quite a bit and likes to develop new recipes and explore flavor combinations. When asked about the scarcity of her gender in the brewing industry, she just shrugs: "I'm surprised there aren't more female brewers."

The brewery occupies what was a vacant 1902 men's shoes and clothing store. They remodeled and put in a pressed-tin ceiling, a new wood floor, and a small bar. This place is as much a café as a brewery, and it is totally family friendly (unlike a neighboring business, a topless bar). Once a weekend someone walks in and says "Where's the girls?"

And for those of you who remember the dummy Charlie McCarthy and wonder why his name shows up on a beer here, his ventriloquist master Edgar Bergen was a Decatur native.

Directions: From I-94 just north of Decatur take Exit 56 for M-51. Turn south and take M-51 6.3 miles. As it comes into Decatur it becomes Delaware St and intersects with Phelps St. The brewpub is on the right on the corner of that intersection.

Stumbling Distance: If you want some outdoor activity, take a 2–6 hour paddle down the Dowagiac River. 11 miles southwest of Decatur, *Doe-Wah-Jack's Canoe Rental* (52963 M-51, Dowagiac, 269-782-7410, www.paddledcri.com) can set you up.

SAUGATUCK BREWING COMPANY

Founded: 2005
Head Brewer: Ron Conklin
Address: 2948 Blue Star Highway • Douglas, MI 49406
Phone: 269-857-7222
Website: www.sbrewing.com, saugatuckbrewing.com
Annual Production: 4,000 barrels
Number of Beers: 16 on tap, 7 bottled

Staple Beers:
» ESB Amber
» Neapolitan Milk Stout (Chocolate, Vanilla, Strawberry)
» Oval Beach Blonde Ale
» Pier Cove Porter
» Singapore IPA

Rotating Beers:
» De Wylde Berry Wheat (Summer)
» Brewer's Reserve Series

Most Popular Brew: Singapore IPA

Brewmaster's Fave: Hop in Ur Rye

Tours? On Saturdays at 2PM. $5 for the tour, samples, and a pint glass or empty growler.

Samples: Six 5-oz. samples for about $12.

Best Time to Go: Happy hour is 4–6PM Monday–Friday. Live music on the patio on Thursday and Saturday.

Where can you buy it? Half and full gallon growlers on site. Bottles throughout Michigan and in select stores in Chicago.

Got food? Yes, burgers, sandwiches, wraps, salads, surf and turf, beer-battered fish and chips, brisket, stout cake. Appetizers include soft pretzels, hummus, cashew-crusted Brie. Items are paired with beers.

Special Offer: Get two $1 pints during your signature visit

The Beer Buzz: Founder and brewer Barry Johnson started this brewery in the warehouse across the street in 2005, operating as a Brew-Your-Own facility for homebrewers that wanted to go beyond the pail. In June of '08 they made the move to this 25,000 square-foot place, which was once a tool manufacturer but had been vacant for 10 years, and added their own 10-barrel brew system to supply their Irish-style Lucky Stone Pub and to distribute a bit. The kitchen opened, and soon after they also added banquet facilities—the Singapore Room—which accommodates over 200 people and has a stage for performances.

Founder and Brewer Barry is now "retired" so brewing is a team effort led by Ron. The IPA doesn't refer to a city-nation in Asia, but rather is named after a former logging town, now a ghost town, at the mouth of the Kalamazoo River.

Homebrewers in the area take note: Saugatuck still offers brew-on-premise with a full barrel kettle and fermenters. The cost for a batch is about $250.

Free Wi-Fi on site. They have a Pint Club.

Directions: From I-196 take Exit 36 and head north on Blue Star Highway about 0.5 mile and the brewery is on the right at the intersection with Enterprise Rd.

Stumbling Distance: *Phil's Bar and Grille* (215 Butler St, Saugatuck, 269-857-1555, philsbarandgrille.com) isn't far for some more good food and beer selections, including fish tacos, gorgonzola ale dip, wings, burgers, pizzas, etc. Holland is just another 15 minutes north for more breweries.

BELL'S BREWING CO. (PRODUCTION BREWERY)

Opened: 2003
Brewmaster: Larry Bell, President/Founder
Address: 8938 Krum Avenue • Galesburg, MI
Phone: 269-382-2338
Website: www.bellsbeer.com
Annual Production: 200,000+ barrels
Number of Beers: 20+ beers for distribution

Staple Beers:
» Amber Ale
» Kalamazoo Stout
» Lager Of The Lakes
» Midwestern Pale Ale
» Oarsman Ale
» Porter
» Third Coast Beer
» Two Hearted Ale

Rotating Beers:
» Best Brown Ale
» Cherry Stout
» Christmas Ale
» Consecrator Doppelbock
» Expedition Stout
» Hell Hath No Fury Ale
» Hopslam Ale
» Java Stout
» Oberon
» Octoberfest
» The Oracle Dipa
» Smitten Golden Rye Ale
» Special Double Cream Stout
» Third Coast Old Ale
» Winter White Ale

Most Popular Brew: Oberon or Two-hearted

Tours? Free guided tours are usually offered and at times an observation deck is open for self-guided views. But the schedule changes constantly so check their website. Large groups should email ahead: tours@bellsbeer.com.

Samples: No.

Best Time to Go: See Tours.

Where can you buy it? In 19 states, roughly from North Dakota down to Florida, plus Puerto Rico and D.C. Use their Beer Finder on the website.

Got food? No.

Special Offer: Not participating.

The Beer Buzz: What happens what your beer gets super popular? To paraphrase Roy Scheider in *Jaws*: you're gonna need a bigger brewery. On 32 acres east of Kalamazoo in Comstock (Galesburg), Bell's built a production facility in 2003—and expanded it five times in less than 10 years. In 2012, a 200-barrel brewhouse came online inside this 100,000 square-foot building and it operates in tandem with the previous 50-barrel operation. Canning is in the works as well as more and more fermentation space, adding to the 400-barrel fermentation tanks (fourteen of them, so far). Bell's is already one of the top ten craft breweries in the USA by volume. Bell's even grows some of its grains for a few beers on an 80-acre farm about 1.5 hours north of Kalamazoo. They use a very environmentally sound and functional method of planting called no-till.

There is no tap room here or gift shop. You'll need to visit the Eccentric Café in Kalamazoo for that. For your troubles you will also find a number of specialty beers brewed only at that location.

Directions: From Bell's Eccentric Café in Kalamazoo, you can just get back on East Michigan heading east for 6.3 miles, heading out of town, until Van Bruggen Street. Turn right and follow it to the end, it becomes Krum Ave as you turn left. Bell's facility is the really big brewery-looking building on the right. Use the curving parking lot out front.

Stumbling Distance: Nothing much to see out here after the brewery. Head back to Kalamazoo and explore their beer culture.

ODD SIDE ALES

Founded: 2010
Brewers: Chris Michner and Kyle Miller
Address: 41 Washington • Grand Haven, MI 49417
Phone: 616-935-7326
Website: www.oddsideales.com
Annual Production: 800 barrels with capacity up to 3,000
Number of Beers: 15 on tap, plus root beer

Staple Beers:
» CITRA PALE ALE
» JACKALOPE AMBER

Rotating Beers:
» MAYAN MOCHA STOUT
» PEANUT BUTTER CUP STOUT

Blondes and fruitier brews in the summer, spiced beers for the holidays, and random "weird ones" such as MUSHROOM STOUT

Most Popular Brew: Citra Pale Ale

Brewmaster's Fave: Citra Pale Ale

Tours? No.

Samples: Yes, 6 five-ounce samplers for about $9.

Best Time to Go: Open Monday–Thursday 1–10PM, Friday–Saturday 12–12, and Sunday 1–10ish. Live music on Fridays and Saturdays.

Where can you buy it? Only right here, on tap or in growlers or howlers (32-oz.) to go, and soon some small-scale bottling to be available at the pub for starters.

Got food? Yes, chips and popcorn. Bring your own food or order-in.

Special Offer: $1 off your first pint during your signature visit

The Beer Buzz: The name comes from the fact that the brewery is on the odd-numbered side of the road, they originally had an odd number of taps, and they brew beers that are a bit on the odd side (see Mushroom Stout above). In college, Chris and Kyle were roommates. Instead of buying cheap beer, they decided they'd just make their own. After graduation, they kept at it with weekly brewing nights. Chris was working as an accountant and decided he wanted to open a brewery and he brought Kyle in to help. The brewery was quickly successful and in 2012 they opened a 15-barrel production facility in a warehouse space offsite. Now Kyle does the brewing here and Chris is in charge of the production brewery.

Beginning back in about 1900, this building—now a collection of shops called Harbourfront—was the Story and Clark piano factory, and you can see a piano just inside the bar. The factory/warehouse feel remains with the old hardwood floors laid out in a diagonal pattern and the ceiling showing the wood beams and joists. Seating is a collection of heavy benches and tables at the center of the room and some smaller tables around the edges. A short bar has a few perches and the bar top is decorated with patterns laid out with varying shades of grain under the epoxy surface. The colorful club mugs hang above the back bar. Brewing equipment and old barrels spread into the tap room. See how many jackalopes you can spot here.

Free Wi-Fi. Parking is in a big lot behind the building and the entrance to the arcade of shops is there; the brewery is just inside.

Directions: From US-31 through Grand Haven, turn west on Franklin Avenue. Go 0.7 mile, turn right on 1st Street, go one block, and then turn left. The parking lot on the right is directly behind the building.

Stumbling Distance: If you're in town in the morning, *Morning Star Café* (711 Washington Ave, 616-844-1131, morningstarcafe.org) is the best bet in town for breakfast—though you may have to wait a spell for a seat. *Seaway Party Store* (815 Taylor Ave, 616-842-7650, seawaypartystore.com) has the best beer selection in town.

THE B.O.B. BREWERY

Founded: 1997
Brewmaster: John Svoboda
Address: 20 Monroe Avenue NW • Grand Rapids, MI, 49503
Phone: 616-356-2000
Website: www.thebob.com
Annual Production: 800 barrels
Number of Beers: 8–10 on tap throughout the building, dozens of styles each year

Staple Beers:
» Blondie
» Crimson King Amber
» Full On IPA
» Hopsun Belgian Wit
» Summer Wheat / Stout Space Boy Stout

Rotating Beers:
» Bobinator Bock
» Hop Zeppelin Black IPA
» London Calling Porter
» Mango Chipotle Ale
» Oktoberfest
» Papaya Peach Ginger Ale
» ...and many more!

Most Popular Brew: Full On IPA

Brewmaster's Fave: He's a seasonal drinker. In summer it's the wheat, for example. Not a hophead, more of a malt guy.

Tours? Yes, call ahead for an appointment.

Samples: Yes, beer flights $5 for 4 five-oz. glasses.

Best Time to Go: Depends on what you're here for. The brewery bar itself in the basement has its own hours (check website). Other establishments in the complex have different hours.

Where can you buy it? Only here on tap and in growlers to go.

Got food? Yes, plenty of options, and cooking with beer or beer pairing is common throughout the cuisine.

Special Offer: Mug club prices for the book holder during your signature visit. You must go to the brewery bar or the first floor to show them the book (or see John if he's there).

The Beer Buzz: You can't miss this big brick complex of fun. The various establishments here are all part of the Gilmore Collection. Get the "G Card" for some weekly specials throughout the building on Wednesdays (5–8) and Sundays (8–10), some of which may blow your mind. (A ten-cent beer? Yeah, it's happened.) Be aware that during special events there may be a cover charge just to get into the building.

Ownership is local and the developer took this Big Old Building—get it? The B.O.B.?—and turned a former grocery warehouse into a collection of great restaurants, clubs/bars, and even a comedy club.

Brewer John has a science background from college and got started with homebrewing. Back in 1993 he worked as an assistant brewer at an incarnation of Grand Rapids Brewing (not the original one, nor the current one). When the head brewer position opened up here in 2008 , he took over.

Directions: On the corner of Fulton St and Monroe/Market Ave in downtown Grand Rapids. On US-131, take Exit 85A and take a left up Market Ave (becomes Monroe) just 3 short blocks. Or take Exit 85B, take a right on Pearl St, cross the river, take a right on Monroe, and continue 3 blocks to Fulton.

Stumbling Distance: Just stumble up and down the stairs. You've got *Dr. Grin's Comedy Club*, nightclubs *Crush, Eve*, restaurants *Gilly's* or *Judson's*, plus *Bobarinos, Monkey Bar*, and soon a biergarten and piazza (summer 2014). Just down the street, go to the *Grand Rapids Art Museum* (101 Monroe Center St NW, 616-831-1000, artmuseumgr.org) or check out *Rosa Park Circle* where there is always something going on pretty much any time of the year.

BREWERY VIVANT

Founded: 2010
Brewmaster: Jacob Derylo
Address: 925 Cherry St, SE • Grand Rapids, MI 49506
Phone: 616-719-1604
Website: www.breweryvivant.com
Annual Production: 4,000 barrels with hopes to hit 5,000
Number of Beers: 12 on tap, 30–40 styles per year

Staple Beers:
» Big Red Coq (Hoppy Belgo-American Red Ale)
» Farm Hand (Farmhouse Ale)
» Solitude (Inspired By Belgian Abbey Brewing)
» Triomphe (Belgian IPA)

Rotating Beers: (just a few examples of many)
» Belgian Wit
» Contemplation (With Michigan Honey And Hops)
» Helter Spelter (With Spelt, A Relative To Wheat)
» Hubris Quadrupel
» Maple Amber Ale
» Nitro Stout
» Trebuchet (Double IPA)
» Tripel
» Zaison (Imperial Saison)
» Wood-aged beers as well

Most Popular Brew: Farm Hand and Triomphe

Brewmaster's Fave: Ancho Rauchbier

Tours? Yes, on Saturdays at 2 and 3:30PM, $5 for the tour, samples, and 10% off your beer afterward.

Samples: Yes, 5 oz. tasters: Vivant flight (3 staples plus 1) $8, Cambier flight (choose 4) $10, Around the World (all taps) $18–20. ("Cambier" is what Belgians call brewers.)

Best Time to Go: Friday/Saturday nights are packed, Sunday is laid back. Happy Hour runs weekdays 3–6PM. Open 3–11PM weekdays, until midnight on weekends, and for lunch Saturday–Sunday.

Where can you buy it? Throughout MI and the greater Chicago area in 4-pack 16-oz. cans, and here on tap and in growlers and pitchers.

Got food? Yes, rustic dishes which go well with beer. Bavarian pot roast, wild game stew, escargot, frites, artisanal cheeses, moules frites, beer cheese with pretzel rods, a burger, duck confit nachos, desserts, and more.

Special Offer: Buy an appetizer or entrée and get a sampler flight of 4 for $1 during your signature visit.

The Beer Buzz: Step inside this neighborhood brewpub and right away you know this wasn't originally a beery sort of place. The vaulted ceiling, the stained glass behind a pointed arch—it seems more like a church. From 1915–1980, this was a funeral home, and this was the chapel. This is an historic district of Grand Rapids, and while the owners felt it appropriate to keep as much of the old look as possible, they also turned it "green," making this the first LEED-certified microbrewery in the US. The stained glass windows are original and because of the nature of a funeral home, show no particular religious denomination. Along with a horseshoe-curving bar at the back arch, the room has beer-hall-style community tables made of reclaimed barn wood, a few tables up the center, and some booths around the perimeter.

The brewery's rooster logo comes from owners Jason and Kris Spaulding's travels through Northern France and Belgium; it is the symbol of Wallonia, a French-speaking region of southern Belgium. During that trip the couple targeted farmhouse breweries. The experience made an impression and deep impact on the beers they brew, and the food they serve. The brewers they met "brewed by feel, more than by science." Jason and Kris would ask, "What style is this?" and the response was elusive, "Do you like it?" The brewery takes the same artistic approach. No rules or limits other than a commitment to using only French or Belgian yeast strains.

Jason and Brewer Jacob used to be at New Holland Brewing. Jacob (despite the Swedish name) comes from an Italian family that liked to make wine a lot. "His passion and his appreciation for wine help with our styles," says Jason. Jacob's interest in fermentation evolved to beer. (His uncle owned a homebrew supply shop.) In 1998 he joined New Holland Brewing and worked his way up to assistant brewer.

Vivant uses a 20-barrel system, and unlike some brewers who look for continual growth, they are aiming to use their space to its maximum and be content with that. They employ about 45 people between the brewery and restaurant, and hope to reach 5,000 barrels and produce that each year.

Free Wi-Fi. Parking is on the street or in a lot shared with Maru Sushi.

Directions: The best way to get here from downtown Grand Rapids is to take Fulton St heading east and take the soft right on Lake Dr heading southeast. Take a right (south) at Diamond St and right away take another right (west) on Cherry St. The brewery is on the right (north side) midway down the first block.

Stumbling Distance: Dueling gourmet food: *The Green Well* (across the street, 616-808-3566, thegreenwell.com) or *Grove* (right next door, 616-454-1000, groverestaurant.com). Locally sourced, creative menus.

ELK BREWING

Founded: Proposed 2013
Address: 700 Wealthy St SE • Grand Rapids, MI 49503
Website: www.elkbrewing.com

Directions: Exit 84 from US-131 puts you on Wealthy St. Go east from there about 1 mile. Or from downtown Grand Rapids, take Ionia Ave south to Wealthy and turn left (east) as well.

Grand Rapids: Beer City USA

If you are into homebrewing, it is likely you have heard of Charlie Papazian. In 1984 he published *The Complete Joy of Homebrewing*, a book highly regarded by DIY beer crowd. He also founded the Great American Beer Festival and the Association of Brewers (now the Brewers Association). That's some street cred. So it's not surprising that when he started an online poll to annually vote for a national beer capital, people took notice. Beer City USA voting takes place every May. In 2012, Grand Rapids, Michigan, managed to make it to the finish line and share the title with longtime reputable brewtown Asheville, North Carolina. In 2013, however, Grand Rapids took the title of Beer City USA all for itself. Ann Arbor and Kalamazoo, not surprisingly, also made a showing.

FOUNDERS BREWING CO.

Founded: 1997
Head Brewer: Jeremy Kosmicki
Address: 235 Grandville Avenue SW • Grand Rapids, MI 49503
Phone: 616-776-1195
Website: www.foundersbrewing.com
Annual Production: 71,000 barrels and rising
Number of Beers: 16 on tap, over 60 styles in a year

Staple Beers:
» CENTENNIAL IPA
» DIRTY BASTARD SCOTCH ALE
» PALE ALE
» PORTER

Rotating Beers:
» ALL DAY IPA
» BACKWOODS BASTARD
» BREAKFAST STOUT
» CURMUDGEON
» DEVIL DANCER
» DOUBLE TROUBLE IPA
» HARVEST ALE
» IMPERIAL STOUT
» KBS (IMPERIAL STOUT, WITH COFFEE AND CHOCOLATES, AGED IN BOURBON BARRELS)
» RED'S RYE
» RUBAEUS
» THE BACKSTAGE SERIES

Most Popular Brew: Centennial IPA or Dirty Bastard Scotch Ale

Tours? Yes, on select Saturdays at 11:15AM and 12:30PM by online reservation only: Foundersbrewing.com/tours. The 30–50 minute tour is limited to 12 people, costs $10, and includes a Founders pint glass and a 16 oz. pour of a Class 1 beer in the taproom.

Samples: Yes, for $1.50 to $4 each.

Best Time to Go: Open 11AM–2AM Monday–Saturday, 3PM–2AM on Sunday. Expect live music on Thursday and Saturday, and perhaps a DJ or some jazz on Sunday. Cheap pints on Monday nights. Open mic on Tuesday.

Where can you buy it? Here on tap and in growlers and bottles, and in 24 states mostly from about the Mississippi to the East Coast.

Got food? Yes, deli sandwiches. And breakfast, if you count the Breakfast Stout.

Special Offer: Not participating.

The Beer Buzz: Centennial, Dirty Bastard, Kentucky Breakfast Stout. These are familiar names to anyone familiar with Michigan craft brewing.

The founders of Founders, Mike Stevens and Dave Engbers, quit their day jobs to take on the dream of starting a brewery. That's no simple matter, with big loans, business planning often being a much bigger challenge than just making good beer. As they came closer and closer to failing, they realized good beer wasn't enough: they needed the bold sort of brews that grabbed craft beer fans by the collar and said, "Drink Me!" The brewers

were excited about what they were making and that translated to great beer and a turnaround that set them on the road to the enormous success they celebrate today. While their mantra is not to brew beer for the masses, there is nevertheless a massive following of people who appreciate the complex unapologetic styles coming out of Founders. They continue to be rated very highly among beer websites and have numerous medals from World Beer Cup and Great American Beer Festival.

In 2007 they moved to the current location, an old trucking depot across from the city bus station. That's right, all buses lead to Founders. Inside you'll find a massive open warehouse sort of space with exposed wood beams, heavy wood tables, and a long curvy bar along the back wall. A stage for live music is at one end, and behind it under glass you can see part of the brewery. Straight in from the front door is the window to the kitchen where you can order food (after 3PM, or table service before that). There's a pool table, music playing, and an outdoor patio.

One of those passionately followed beers, where people mark calendars and stand in line at liquor stores, is KBS: Kentucky Breakfast Stout, bourbon-barrel aged for a year and ringing in at 11.2% abv. Watch for the brewery's huge block party mid- to late June.

Directions: From US-131 take Exit 185A for Cherry St and turn right on Grandville, or Exit 184B (a left lane exit) for Wealthy St and go left to Grandville and turn right. If you're already downtown, take either Cherry St or Wealthy St to just west of US-131 and Grandville runs between them (Cherry to the north, Wealthy to the south of the brewery).

Stumbling Distance: Check out *Pyramid Scheme* (68 Commerce Ave SW, 616-272-3758, pyramidschemebar.com) for some live music but also great Michigan beers (often various Short's brews are on tap) and some pinball. The Ionia Ave/Fulton St brewpub crawl isn't far off either.

GRAND RAPIDS BREWING CO.

Founded: December 2012 (December 1892)
Head Brewers: Jacob Bremer, Stu Crittenden and Corey Nebbeling
Address: 1 Ionia Avenue SW • Grand Rapids, MI 49503
Phone: 616-458-7000
Website: www.grbrewingcompany.com
Annual Production: 3,500 barrels
Number of Beers: 8–10 on tap plus guest beers; up to 30 styles annually

Staple Beers:
» Brewers' Heritage Hefeweizen
» Campau's $90 Pale Ale
» The Fishladder IPA
» The John Ball Brown
» Rosalynn Bliss Blonde
» Senator Lyon Stout
» Silver Foam American Lager

Rotating Beers:
» Maibock
» Old Kent Belgian Dubbel
» Original 6 Dunkelweiss
» Veit & Rathaman's Beglian Pale Ale
» plus some Sour Ales and Barrel-Aged Beers to come

Most Popular Brew: The Grassfields IPA

Brewmaster's Fave: Jake: Hefeweizen; Stu: The John Ball Brown

Tours? Yes, email Jacob@grbrewingcompany.com to make an appointment.

Samples: Yes, 6 three-oz. samplers for $6.

Best Time to Go: Open at 3PM weekdays, 11AM weekends, until midnight. Happy hour is 3–6PM weekdays.

Where can you buy it? Only here by the glass or growler.

Got food? Yes, house-made and Sobie sausages with pretzel buns, soups, salads, burgers and melts, a few large plates (flank steak, chicken, etc.), poutine, fried Michigan pickle slices, Michigan Cheddar Cheese Clouds, Scotch egg, hand-netted smelts.

Special Offer: A free order of kale chips during your signature visit.

The Beer Buzz: The original Grand Rapids Brewing Co. was a collaboration of six back in December 1892 on a site just a few blocks from here. After surviving just barely on soda during Prohibition, it never recovered. A shopping-mall brewpub used the name in the 90s and failed in 2010. Mark Sellers, of BarFly Ventures (the entity behind HopCat, the world-famous beer bar and brewery at the opposite end of this block), bought the name and opened this Grand Rapids Brewing exactly 120 years after the first opened its doors. Set in an 1884 wholesale grocery building, this is Michigan's first USDA-certified all-organic brewery. The brewery consumes nearly all of the organic hops produced in Michigan.

Renovations removed the drop ceiling, exposed the brick walls and cast-iron columns. The brewery also occupies the neighboring building which connects into the main bar and offers a second bar and space for the brewhouse. Check out the old fire door painted red and hung above the bar. The tap handles are the staves of old beer barrels. A third bar was scheduled to open during summer 2013, in a back room opening up to the outside.

The heavy tables and chairs were made in Grand Rapids, which is famous for its furniture making history. The railings and table legs are old pipes, and the bricks of the bar are also recycled. In fact, "green" is a major initiative for GRBC, well beyond the organic ingredients. Have a look out back at all the trash receptacles. Only one small residential-sized bin is for true garbage. The rest is composting, recycling, spent grain headed to area farms and a local bakery, and fry oil destined for bio-fuel vehicles. 90% of all "waste" here isn't actually wasted. Some of the grain goes to cattle at Grassfields farm, which in turn helps produce the meat and cheese for the restaurant. It's a circle of life for sure.

Beer City Series

Many of the Grand Rapids area brewers agree to brew the same recipe (with their own tweaks on it) occasionally throughout the year. Grand Pumpkin was a previous fall brew, for example, available at several of the breweries. Another example of beer bringing people together.

The 7-barrel system is in the basement and the kettle uses city steam, piped in under the sidewalks, to boil the wort. Brewer Stu was a production brewer at the now-defunct Michigan Brewing Co. Brewer Jake started as a homebrewer and got a job as a bartender/server at HopCat, working his way through the ranks to get here. Brewer Corey left his head brewer job at the Blue Heron in Marhsfield, WI to return to his native home.

A mural of the original GRBC adorns a wall in the bar. At its peak in 1908, GRBC rolled out half a million barrels per year. The beer names refer to some of the original cooperating breweries or other local elements. City founder Louis Campau bought all the land in Grand Rapids for $90. Senator Lyon was a GR native and strong advocate for the brewing industry (plus there's a play on words with Sri Lanka's Lion Stout). You can see the fish ladder in the Grand River which allows spawning fish to get over the dams. Veit & Rathman's Eagle Brewery was one of the city's first and merged with 5 others to form the original GRBC.

Since the moment it opened, the place has been packed. If you plan on eating there, consider making reservations. Free Wi-Fi onsite. Mug club. Facebook.com/GRBrewingCo

Directions: The brewery is on the corner of Ionia Ave and Fulton St in downtown. You can take Business US-131/Division St into downtown and go west on Fulton St two blocks.

Stumbling Distance: Many places are within walking distance, including *Stella's Lounge* (stellasgr.com, 53 Commerce Ave SW, 616-742-4444) known for its burgers, drinks, and quirky interior (and arcade games) and, of course, *HopCat* in this book. *The Amway Grand Plaza Hotel* (amwaygrand. com, 187 Monroe Ave NW, 800-253-3590) and *JW Marriott* (ilovethejw. com, 235 Louis Campau St. NW, 888-844-5947) are riverside and good bets.

HARMONY BREWING COMPANY

Founded: 2012
Brewers: Barry and Jackson VanDyke
Address: 1551 Lake Drive SE • Grand Rapids, MI 49506
Phone: 616-233-0063
Website: www.harmonybeer.com
Annual Production: 110 barrels
Number of Beers: 6–7 on tap

Possible Beers:
» CROSSROADS RYE PA
» DOUBLE IPA (11% ABV)
» GRUIT (WITH HEATHER FLOWERS)
» QUASAR BELGIAN AMBER
» STAR STUFF BELGIAN DUBBEL

Brewers' Faves:
Barry: Star Stuff
Jackson: Crossroads Rye PA

Tours? Yes, if someone's free to show you around, but it's a 5-minute job.

Samples: Yes, 5 five-ounce beer for about $8.

Best Time to Go: Open daily from noon to midnight. Happy hour runs 2–6PM weekdays, or all day on Sunday and Monday.

Where can you buy it? Only here over the bar in a glass or a growler.

Got food? Yes, a full menu and full bar with some wines. Soups and salads, and some very good wood-fired oven pizzas.

Special Offer: Happy hour prices on beer for the book holder during your signature visit.

The Beer Buzz: Harmony Brewing is a family affair: brothers Barry and Jackson, and sister Heather are part owners. They bought an old wreck of a house with a liquor store in front in Grand Rapids' Eastown neighborhood and spent two years making it into a brewpub. (For a time, it was actually a Miller Beer distribution center right after Prohibition.)

With 10 years first as homebrewers, Barry and Jackson do the brewing. As Barry says, he and his brother do not brew on the same day "to avoid fighting." They brew using repurposed yogurt processing tanks from Wisconsin. There is no fixed number of beers; the brewers love experimenting and the wide variety is whimsical. A local homebrewer might bring in a sample and if it appeals to the brewers, it could show up on tap. While some wise geeks may have already known, the name Star Stuff comes from a Carl Sagan quote. Beer cocktails are popular here, such as the Beergarita, an IPA with tequila, lime and triple sec.

The place feels like a coffee shop with a neighborly vibe, bright interiors, and a family friendly atmosphere. And in truth the "harmony" name suggests the owners' hopes to create a community space and to use local farmers' ingredients as much as possible. The brewpub's Black Squirrel University, a weekly event hosted in the upper room on Tuesday nights, brings in locals to present on topics of their interest and expertise.

In summer there is a patio out on the walk. Free Wi-Fi. Mug club.

Directions: From US-131 through Grand Rapids, take Exit 84 for Wealthy St and go east 2 miles. Turn right on Lake Dr and the brewpub is there on your left.

Stumbling Distance: If you like some spicy Caribbean food, check out *Chez Olga* (1441 Wealthy St. SE, 616-233-4141, chezolga.com). The way funky building alone is worth a stop. Breakfast all day? *Eastown Café* (410 Ethel Ave SE, 616-233-0797) is delicious and affordable.

THE HIDEOUT BREWING CO.

Founded: 2005
Brewers: Mike Humphrey, Heather LaRowe, Andrew Dehaan, James Julius
Address: 3113 Plaza Drive NE • Grand Rapids, MI 49525
Phone: 616-361-9658
Website: www.hideoutbrewing.com
Annual Production: up to 1,000 barrels
Number of Beers: 26 on tap

Staple Beers:
» Aviator Pale Ale
» Cement Shoe Stout
» Gangster IPA
» 9 am Hazelnut IPA
» Polish Potato Ale
» Purple Gang Pilsner
» Smuggler's Hazelnut Stout
» Silky Smooth Cream Ale
» Tommy Gun Red

Rotating Beers:
» Backway Double IPA
» Beer City Pale Ale
» Belgian Rye Angle
» Black Lager
» Citrus IPA
» Clove Anise Pilsner
» Colson Rice
» Hefeweizen
» Not Black Cat Belgian Black
» Oatmeal Stout
» Pants IPA
» Prohibition Pale Wheat
» Promiscuous Pilsner
» Pumpkin Milk Stout
» St. Valentine's Day Red
» Sour Ales
» Triforce IPA

… So Much More: Pickle Beer, Sriracha Beer, You Name It

Most Popular Brew: Smuggler's Stout or Gangster IPA

Brewmaster's Fave: 3 out of 4 brewers choose Trigger Man IPA. (Heather likes the Coconut Almond Brown Ale.)

Tours? Sure, if someone's free, they'd be happy to show you around.

Samples: Yes, 5 three-ounce samplers for about $5.

Best Time to Go: Open Monday–Thursday noon–1AM, Friday–Saturday noon–2AM, Sunday 12–12. Busiest on Friday and Saturday nights.

Where can you buy it? Here at the bar, to go in growlers, and a few local bars (maybe HopCat).

Got food? Yes, but just soft pretzels, chips and salsa, cheese and cracker plates. Carry-in food is OK, and local pizzerias deliver here.

Special Offer: Not participating

The Beer Buzz: This place can be tricky to find (it is The Hideout after all), but worth the effort. Tucked away on Grand Rapids' northeast side, the brewery has a Prohibition Era theme—the old photos hang on the walls and beer names hearken back to the dark days of dry. In 2012, ownership changed and brewer Rob Wanhatalo left for The Mitten Brewing Co.

New owners Nick Humphrey and Scott Colson have only increased the production and charm of this place. Despite the gangster theme and beer names, this brewery is also known affectionately by some as the Island of Misfit Toys or the Candy and Coffee Brewery. Why? Just have a look at the incredible range of try-anything-once brew recipes. Brewing here is a team effort. While the four people listed above may be the primary brewers, everyone is pitching ideas and pitching yeast at one point or another. Owner Nick brews from time to time, as does his wife Theresa.

The tap room features a U-shaped concrete-top bar in the center, and a sort of loft area above with shuffleboard, darts, and a large-screen TV. The outdoor beer garden is nice in summer and a good place to pitch some horsehoes; a fireplace keeps patrons warm inside in winter.

Free Wi-Fi. Mug club. Facebook.com/hideoutbrewing

Directions: Take I-96 across the north side of Grand Rapids and take Exit 33 at Plainfield Ave. Go northeast on Plainfield (Michigan 44 Connector) and take the first right on Lamberton Lake Dr NE. Then take the very next right on Plaza Dr NE. Follow this 0.4 mile and The Hideout is on your right (next to WXMI-TV).

Stumbling Distance: *Wing Doozy* (3916 Plainfield Ave NE, 616-608-3067, wingdoozy.com) sells never-frozen wings and hand-cut fries to die for. *Fred's Pizza* (3619 Plainfield Ave NE, 616-361-8994, fredspizza.com) delivers to the pub and you can order online.

HOPCAT

Founded: 2008
Head Brewers: Bobby Edgecomb and Ernie Richards
Address: 25 Ionia Avenue SW • Grand Rapids, MI 49503
Phone: 616-451-4677
Website: www.hopcatgr.com
Annual Production: 400 barrels
Number of Beers: 48 beers on tap (about 6 of their own); 40–50 styles per year

Most Often Recurring Beers:
» DICTATOR CUBAN COFFEE STOUT
» HOPPOPATAMUS IPA
» THE JERK (GHOST PEPPERS WITH LEMON, LIME, ORANGE ZEST)
» OIL RIGGER ANNIVERSARY RELEASE (IMPERIAL STOUT)
» SAGE AGAINST THE MACHINE (HONEY SAGE PALE ALE)
» ZUGSPITZE HEFEWEIZEN

Rotating Beers:
» ALL BEERS COME AND GO, AND RARELY REPEAT.

Most Popular Brew: Hoppopatamus IPA

Brewmaster's Fave: Hoppopatamus IPA

Tours? Yes, email Jacob@grbrewingcompany.com to make an appointment.

Samples: $1 samples.

Best Time to Go: Happy hour 2–4PM, Monday–Friday, and from 4–6PM there's "Burger & Beer" for about $6.

Where can you buy it? Only here on draft, and growlers are only for house-brews (unless a law changes some day). Other brewers' bottled beers are available to go.

Got food? Yes, sandwiches, burgers, and wraps, salads, appetizers such as warm pretzels, fresh mussels, wings, Crack Fries, beerbar cheese with pita chips, cheese ale soup, and a few bigger plates such as fish and chips, mac and cheese. Late night menu runs 10PM–2AM.

Special Offer: A free order of Crack Fries during your signature visit.

The Beer Buzz: BeerAdvocate.com rated HopCat the 3rd best beer bar in the world. While this place is first a beer bar—offering a wide selection of brews from Michigan and the rest of the world (especially Belgium)—it is also a brewery. HopCat, a creation of BarFly Ventures, occupies a restored 19th century building with an interior that shows some old school class with exposed brick, a wood ceiling, and cast-iron columns. They've got tables up front, communal beer-hall-style benches and tables along the wall, and a few booths farther back. There's also an oft-overlooked little space upstairs (beyond the restrooms in back). An outdoor patio is available in season. After 8 PM, no one under 21 is allowed, so not a night out for the kiddies, and though there are a couple of TVs in here, it's not a sports bar either. It's about beer. Really good beer. (Well, OK, the food's not bad either!)

Brewers Bobby and Ernie both had other jobs here at HopCat, and though they now do the brewing here and assist at Grand Rapids Brewing Co. up the block, they still bartend as well. Ernie has a background in biochemistry. The batches are small and change frequently and as you can see from the number of styles they do each year, there is a lot of play going on here. For a Thanksgiving specialty beer they performed "fatwashing" on a turkey (boil, create stock, freeze, skim fat) so they could get the flavor into a cranberry version of Sage Against the Machine. HopCat has a full calendar each month, including beer dinners and ale events. Free Wi-Fi.

Check out the other HopCat in East Lansing!

Directions: HopCat is one block south on Ionia Ave from the intersection of Ionia Ave and Fulton St in downtown. You can take Business US-131/Division St into downtown and go west on Fulton St two blocks and turn left on Ionia at the sister brewery Grand Rapids Brewing Co.

Stumbling Distance: You're at the opposite end of the block from sister brewer *Grand Rapids Brewing Co.*, and just another block further from *The B.O.B. Brewery*, both in this book.

JADEN JAMES BREWERY

Founded: 2003 (2010 brewery)
Brewer: Chris Diemer
Address: 4665 Broadmoor • Grand Rapids, MI 49512
Phone: 616-656-4665
Website: www.jadenjamesbrewery.com
Annual Production: 50 barrels
Number of Beers: 7 and 2 ciders

Staple Beers:
» CREAM ALE
» IPA
» PORTER
» RUSSIAN STOUT

Rotating Beers:
» BLACK IPA
» LAZY LEMON WHEAT
» OKTOBERFEST

Most Popular Brew: Russian Stout

Brewmaster's Fave: Oktoberfest or Cream Ale

Tours? No.

Samples: Yes, $1.50 for each five-ounce sampler.

Best Time to Go: The winery is open Monday through Saturday 11AM–7PM. Thursday has a happy hour from 4–7PM.

Where can you buy it? The beer is only here, on tap or in growlers.

Got food? Chips and salsa, cheese and crackers, sub sandwiches. The shop sells local Amish and other Michigan cheeses.

Special Offer: $1 off one pint of Jaden James beer during your signature visit.

The Beer Buzz: Winemaker Bob Bonga has won awards for his wines, and this brewery is actually first Cascade Winery. You can sample the wines for free, and purchases a few bottles. But it's not uncommon for a wine person to visit with a beer person in tow. "We get so many couples that one comes with a long face," says Bob. "When they find out we have beer, it becomes a happy face." So adding the tiny brewery made perfect sense. The winery started in another place in 2003 and moved to this more spacious location in 2008. They added the brewery a couple years later. Business is still growing. In addition to the beer and wine, they also make hard ciders.

Brewer Chris started brewing on a generic kit he got as a Christmas gift, but the batches weren't so great. He didn't brew again until he got a first edition of Charlie Papazian's book *The Complete Joy of Home Brewing*; he wasn't going to go any further until he finished it. He started with extracts, but wasn't satisfied with the brews. Then in 1999 he made his own equipment, started using all grain, and never looked back. His first professional brewing job was when he took over here in 2011. He calls his Cream Ale a go-to American version of a Helles.

Free Wi-Fi. Facebook.com/jjbrewery

Directions: Broadmoor Ave is also M-37 which passes north to south through Grand Rapids. From M-6/Paul B. Henry Freeway, take Exit 15 and head north 2.1 miles and the winery/brewery is on the left (west) side of the divided highway which may require a U-turn if you are coming from the south.

Stumbling Distance: You are only 3.5 miles from *Schmohz Brewing* (2600 Patterson Ave SE) also in this book, and the rest of Grand Rapids is a beer lover's dream as well.

THE MITTEN BREWING CO.

Founded: 2012
Brewers: Rob "Wob" Wanhatalo, Max Trierweiler, and Chris Andrus
Address: 527 Leonard St NW • Grand Rapids, MI 49504
Phone: 616-608-5612
Website: www.mittenbrewing.com
Annual Production: 600 barrels
Number of Beers: 5 on tap

Staple Beers:
» Eighty-Four Double IPA
» The Iron Man IPA
» Peanuts And Crackerjack Porter

Rotating Beers:
» Black Betsy Stout
» English Dark Mild
» Hefeweizen
» Kissing Bandit Blonde
» '68 Rye PA
» Seasonals such as Pumpkin Beer or Imperial Stout Aged in a Heaven Hill Barrel

Most Popular Brew: Peanuts and Crackerjack Porter or The Iron Man IPA

Brewmaster's Fave: Eighty-Four Double IPA

Tours? A tour is just a 10-minute look around, but if someone is available, yes.

Samples: Yes, 4 four-ounce samplers for $4.

Best Time to Go: Open from lunch to midnight all days but Sunday, when they close around 8, and Monday, when they are closed. (Check their website.)

Where can you buy it? Only here by the glass, pitcher, or growler, but with hopes of some area draft accounts some day.

Got food? Yes, gourmet pizzas with dough that is fermented 48 hours, peanut baskets. Gluten-free and vegan available.

Special Offer: 10% off of one Specialty Pizza on your signature visit

The Beer Buzz: As this is a vintage baseball-themed brewery/pizzeria, it's only appropriate that it opened in 2012, a year the Detroit Tigers were in the World Series. Just inside the front door are some seats from the old Tiger Stadium. But while much of the decoration is baseball paraphernalia, this building was once a firehouse that dated back to 1890. It took seven months to tear out layers of old drywall and plaster to expose the brick walls, and they polished the concrete floor and opened up the rafters above. The office upstairs was the hayloft for the horses (yes, horses) that would pull the fire wagons. During renovations, an old pulley system was found in the wall. When the fire alarm went off, a counterweight used to drop and lift the stable doors; the horses were trained to step forward immediately to take their harnesses. Look up at the rafters and you can still see the original lumberyard's name, John Dregge & Co. A couple of vintage fire extinguishers and a fireman's hat rest on the back bar next to the tap handles made from old baseball bats. The fireman's pole is still standing.

Owner/brewers Max and Chris started homebrewing in 2007, and Chris really took to the science of it. The double IPA is named for the last year the Tigers won the World Series, but the 84 also relates to the beer's specs: 8.4% ABV, 84 IBU, 1.084 original gravity, and an 84-minute boil. The porter is made with 20-pounds of organic peanut butter. Brewer Rob came here from another Grand Rapids brewer, The Hideout.

With 5 TVs, this is a good place to see baseball games—all the Tigers games, for sure. Chris' wife Shannon did the awesome bar top, transferring old newspaper articles and images into the glue under the seal. Very cool. Max's great aunt's Prohibition-era cider barrels stand by the side door. For a gourmet pizza and a craft beer, you can't go wrong here.

There is a parking lot out back. Free Wi-Fi. Facebook.com/mittenbrewingco

Directions: From US-131 through Grand Rapids, take Exit 87 and turn west on Leonard St. Drive 0.2 mile and the brewpub is on the right on the corner of Leonard and Quarry.

Stumbling Distance: *Graydon's Crossing* (graydonscrossing.com, 1223 Plainfield NE, 616-726-8260) is just west of here past the highway. "Have you seen our beer menu??" You should.

PERRIN BREWING COMPANY

Founded: 2012
Brewers: Nate Walser, Sam Sherwood, Brian Thorson
Address: 5910 Comstock Park Dr • Comstock Park, MI, 49321
Phone: 616-551-1957
Website: www.perrinbrewing.com
Annual Production: 5,000–6,000 barrels
Number of Beers: Up to 18 on tap

Staple Beers:
» BLACK LAGER
» EXTRA PALE ALE
» GOLDEN ALE
» IPA
» RASPBERRY BLONDE

Rotating Beers:
» AUBURN WHEAT
» CHOCOLATE PORTER
» DOUBLE IPA
» I2D2 IPA
» IMPERIAL STOUT
» NUT BROWN ALE
» ROGUE RYE
» RYE WINE
» SCHWARZBIER
» STRONG PALE ALE
» ALSO SOME BARREL-AGING AND SOUR ALES

Most Popular Brew: Golden Ale or IPA

Brewmaster's Fave: Extra Pale Ale

Tours? In the planning. Check the website.

Samples: $1–2 each, flights of 5 or 15.

Best Time to Go: Open daily 11AM–11PM, but Sunday 12–8PM.

Where can you buy it? 12/16 oz glasses, pitchers, growlers, and in Western Michigan stores in 12- and 22-oz. bottles.

Got food? Yes, burgers, dogs, and sandwiches, fried with chili and beer cheese, ale-battered onion rings, hummus.

Special Offer: Get 10% off merchandise purchases during signature visit

The Beer Buzz: Just northwest of Grand Rapids in Comstock Park, this may be every brewer's dream of what could be done with ample start-up funding. Randy Perrin and Jarred Sper, two successful businessmen, sold their previous companies and had the capital to go state-of-the-art with a 30-barrel brewing system; a water filtration system with carbon filters and reverse osmosis that allows the brewers to adjust water chemistry to match that of faraway places; a keg filler that kicks out 65 per hour; and a bottling line that can fill and cap 360 bottles in one minute.

The brewery is hard to miss with its grain tower, hops vines, and a parking lot out front. The long industrial building has an equally long taproom and eatery inside as you enter. The interior shows polished concrete floors, high ceilings and some reclaimed wood. A concrete bar lies at one end of the room with three tanks behind it. A second room in the front of the building is connected by a garage door and similar doors actually open on the front of the building making this a nice open-air section. A private party area is up one floor, a reservable mezzanine with leather-back chairs that overlooks the taproom. Along the wall separating this area from the brewhouse are large windows so that the beer curious can look in on production. Food is prepared in a kitchen that looks like a carnival's food truck at the far end from the bar. This is not a sports bar but three TVs and two projection screens are on hand for important games/events. Current beers are posted on menus and chalkboards, and prices follow a tier system of 1–5, Tier 5 being the most expensive specialty beers.

Brewer Nate made a name for himself developing Centennial, Dirty Bastard, and Kentucky Breakfast Stout over at Founders before leaving in 2005 to do consulting work until he found a home here. Sam worked at Founders and Waldorff Brew Pub. Brian migrated from the West Coast where he won awards for a sour ale and an IPA. Combined they have over 30 years of brewing experience. The plan here is to make a variety of styles and distribute a bunch of it. The brewery hopes to bring back the old-school steel beer cans, the ones you needed a church key (can opener) to get into.

Wi-Fi on site. Shuffleboard. No mug club, but a $75/yr VIP club. Facebook.com/perrinbrewing

Directions: Head north on US-131 and take Exit 89 on the left to I-96/M-37 (Muskegon) and stay left to keep on I-96. In 0.2 miles (really soon after) keep left and follow M-37 North/Alpine Ave exit and take it curving north (right), crossing over the Interstate. Drive north and turn right (east) on 7 Mile Rd and take the 2nd right on Comstock Park Dr. The brewery is right there on the left.

Stumbling Distance: *Fricano's Pizza* (fricanospizza.com, 5808 Alpine Ave NW, 616-785-5800), a franchise version of the legendary Grand Haven original, serves the same thin-crust pizza recipe that made it famous. Don't expect fancy; this is as casual as it gets. Paper plates!

SCHMOHZ BREWING CO.

Founded: 2004
Beer Engineer: Chas Thompson
Address: 2600 Patterson SE • Grand Rapids, MI, 49546
Phone: 616-949-0860
Website: www.schmohz.com
Annual Production: 1,200 barrels
Number of Beers: 12–14 on tap, 24 styles per year

Staple Beers:
» Amber Tease Ale
» Bonecrusher Stout
» Hopknocker IPA
» Pail Ale
» Treasure Chest Esb

Rotating Beers:
» 120 NA
» Barley Wine
» Bloody Red Ale
» Cirrus Wheat
» John T. Pilsner
» Kiss My Scottish Arse
» Mad Tom's Robust Porter
» Pickle Tink Ale
» Razzmanian Devil
» Schwartz

Most Popular Brew: Hopknocker IPA or Treasure Chest ESB in house; Hopknocker IPA in retail.

Tours? Yes, if Chas is available.

Samples: Yes, five samplers for about $5

Best Time to Go: Open Monday–Tuesday 2pm–10pm, Wednesday–Thursday 2pm–midnight, Friday–Saturday noon–midnight. Drink specials every weekday, happy hour on Friday 12–3pm.

Where can you buy it? Right here on tap, in growlers and bottles to go, and regionally distributed in Michigan in 6-pack bottles. (See the website for where.)

Got food? Free popcorn. Otherwise you can carry-in or order from menus from nearby establishments that deliver.

Special Offer: Not Participating

The Beer Buzz: Founder Jim Schwerin, a Michigan Tech alumni, decided in college that he wanted to open a brewery. As is the trick in any business, money was elusive. If the banks won't work with you, what then? Why friends, of course. He put together his business plan and funding and in 2004 he found this place—former home of the now defunct Robert Thomas Brewery. The brewery, with its metal siding, looks like something out of an industrial park. But inside is a hopping bar scene with a pool table (or ping pong), darts, pinball, and a big-screen TV. At the back end is the bar with its counter wrapped in copper.

So what got Brewer Chas into brewing? "I was thirsty," he says. He took up brewing in college. His 120 NA is the only craft-brewed nonalcoholic beer in Michigan. Some of the brewery's spent grain goes to a local bakery.

Free Wi-Fi. Mug club. Facebook.com/SchmohzBrewery

Directions: From I-96 on Grand Rapids' southeast side, take Exit 43. Go west on 28th St SE/M-11. Drive about 0.6 mile and go right (north) on Patterson and Schmohz is another 0.2 mile on your right.

Stumbling Distance: You don't even have to stumble over to *JT's Pizza* (616-942-1552, 6716 Old 28th St SE, jtspizza.com)—they deliver here. A place recommended for either great seafood or a sports bar is *Spinacher's Restaurant and Lounge* (616-957-1111, 4747 28th St SE, facebook.com/SpinnakerRestaurantLounge). Go get some of that spent-grain bread at *Great Harvest Bread Co.* (616-942-0606, 850 Forest Hill Ave SE, grandrapidsbread.com)

OSGOOD BREWING

Founded: 2013
Brewmaster: Ron Denning
Address: 4051 Chicago Drive SW • Grandville, MI 49418
Phone: 616-432-3881
Website: www.osgoodbrewing.com
Annual Production: 750 barrels
Number of Beers: 6

Staple Beers:
» BIG SPRING STOUT
» JOURNEY IPA
» NOTLEY PORTER
» OAKESTOWN AMBER ALE
» SOL SEEKER (AMERICAN WHEAT ALE)
» 358 PALE ALE

Most Popular Brew: Big Spring Stout

Brewmaster's Fave: Journey IPA with Big Spring a close second

Tours? Not yet, but coming soon.

Samples: Yes, a three- and a six-glass flight of 4-oz. samples for $4 and $8.

Best Time to Go: Open Monday–Wednesday 4–10PM, Thursday 4–midnight, Friday 4–1AM, Saturday noon–1AM, closed Sunday (check the website). Live music on weekends.

Where can you buy it? Only here on tap and in growlers, some draft accounts.

Got food? Yes, including gourmet salads and pizzas.

Special Offer: 15% off the book holder's food purchase during the signature visit.

The Beer Buzz: Back in 2005, the brother-in-law of founder/brewer Ron Denning suggested Ron start brewing. Apparently open to suggestion, Ron started on a stovetop in his kitchen (he still has a bottle from that first batch). He gained experience and better and better equipment until he felt confident it was time to go pro. This is the dream for most brewers, but the stars aligned for Ron. Grandville was in the middle of a downtown beautification and development project. Four lanes were reduced to two, power lines were buried, and the community sought to revitalize business. Ron's wife's family had lived in Grandville for generations, and Ron himself has been a teacher of Tech Ed at the local high school. They are committed to their town and saw that a brewpub fit with the new vision for downtown.

Wood floors and the wood tones of the interior make the brewpub feel like it has been here a while. The fermenters are visible behind glass. The 1949 building has been home to Elder's Electric and Elder's Appliance. In 1997 they remodeled and built an addition (you can still see the division) and split the two businesses into separate spaces. When Elder's Appliance moved out in 2012 and freed up the space, Ron had a home for his brewery.

The brewery name comes from Osgood Tavern, the first bar in Grandville, opened in 1837 by Kent County's first D.A., Hiram Osgood. You see, back then, lawyering wasn't enough to pay the bills, so the tavern kept him afloat. The first church services in Grandville were held in the dining hall of that tavern.

Free Wi-Fi. Mug Club. Facebook.com/OsgoodBrewing and Twitter @OsgoodBrewing

Directions: From I-196 southwest of Grand Rapids, take Exit 70 for M-11 and rolls directly into Wilson Ave. Continue 0.3 mile and turn right on Chicago Dr and it's on the right. If you are coming from the west on I-196, take Exit 70A, turn right on M-11, and another quick right on Wilson Ave. Turn right on Chicago and it's on the right.

Stumbling Distance: From here, downtown Grand Rapids is about a 10-minute drive.

57 BREW PUB & BISTRO

Founded: 2012
Brewmaster: Victor Aellen
Address: 1310 W Washington St. • Greenville, MI 48838
Phone: 616-712-6226
Website: www.57brewpub.com
Number of Beers: 8 on tap

Beers:
» Blueberry Ale
» Dark Knight Stout
» 57 Chevy Imperial IPA
» Mayan Midnight Mocha Stout
» Raspberry Blonde
» Red Shedman's Imperial
» Victory Double IPA
» Wayne's Green Tractor
» Yellow Jacket Stinger Honey Ale
» some bourbon-barrel aging as well

Tours? By appointment.

Samples: Yes, beer flights.

Best Time to Go: Open daily from 11AM (noon on Sundays).

Where can you buy it? Here on tap (12- and 16-oz. pours) or to go in growlers and kegs.

Got food? Yes, a full menu with appetizers, soups and salads, sandwiches and burgers, wood-fired pizza and entrees.

Special Offer: Not participating.

The Beer Buzz: With two honored chefs in the kitchen, the restaurant here has a lot going for it. Brewer Vic comes from a wine background. His family has one of the largest in Maryland. He spent a combined 30 years in the chemical industry and financial services, before finally settling into brewing beer. Pub Club. Facebook.com/57BrewPub

Directions: From US-131 north of Grand Rapids, take M-57 east 15.4 miles to Greenville and the brewpub is on the left.

Stumbling Distance: Best beer selection in town is at *Jorgi's Marketplace* (6403 S Greenville Rd/M-91, 616-225-9570).

WALLDORFF BREWPUB & BISTRO

Founded: 2006
Head Brewer: Brett Hammond
Address: 105 E State St. • Hastings, MI 49058
Phone: 269-945-4400
Website: www.walldorffbrewpub.com
Number of Beers: 9 on tap

Staple Beers:
» AMBER WAVES
» BEE STING HONEY RYE
» BISTRO BLONDE
» COBAIN'S DOUBLE DARK IPA
» HOPNOXXXIOUS PA
» STATE STREET STOUT

Rotating Beers:
» BELGIAN TART CHERRY (BELGIAN SOUR ALE
   WITH MICHIGAN CHERRIES)
» DOUBLE DRY-HOPPED BROWN ALE
» IMPERIAL STOUT
» JAVA CRÈME BRULÉE OATMEAL STOUT
» SUNDANCER WHEAT
» PLUS SOME BOURBON-BARREL AGED VARIETIES

Tours? Maybe, if he's around and not busy.

Samples: Yes, 4 five-ounce samplers for about $5 or 9 for about $8.

Best Time to Go: Open Monday–Thursday 11AM–9PM, Friday–Saturday 11AM–11PM, and Sunday noon–8PM. Hours are seasonal and it may be open later in summer. Live music some weekends, trivia on Wednesday.

Where can you buy it? Here on tap or in growlers or some bottles to go.

Got food? Yes, a full menu including sandwiches, soups, salads, and wood-fired oven pizzas. Try the fried pickles, fried ravioli, and schnitzel sliders. There's beer in some soups. The gouda/spinach crab dip is a favorite. After dinner time they switch to a latenight menu.

Special Offer: Not participating.

The Beer Buzz: The Walldorff building dates back to the 19th century, and most recently before it was a restaurant/brewpub, it held a furniture store. The Walldorff today is actually two buildings connected through a knocked out section of the old brick wall. In 1868, part of this was a funeral parlor. The old hardwood floors remain and the brick is exposed throughout. Old malt bags hang from the ceiling the way other bars dangle sports team banners. The bar top is copper and the old back bar has a couple wooden pillars, and in the bar area there are a couple of TVs on for sports. The third floor has a banquet room and in the stairwell leading up to it, a bunch of quotes are written on the wall. Patrons often linger here a moment on their way to the restrooms in the basement level. The brewery and restaurant put an emphasis on getting ingredients from local producers. Much of the hops, for example, are from Hop Head Farms in Hickory Corners.

Free Wi-Fi. No Mug Club, but Pub Club with lifetime membership. Facebook.com/walldorff

Directions: Coming to Hastings by either M-37 or M-43 brings you to the center of town where the two highways meet and join to go west. At this intersection of Broadway and State St, go east on State St two blocks and the brewery is on Jefferson and State.

Stumbling Distance: This is a good midway point between Battle Creek or Lansing area and Grand Rapids (about 40 minutes). *Yankee Springs Recreation Area* (2104 S Briggs Rd, Middleville, 269-795-9081) is about 15 minutes west of town for great hiking, camping, and picnicking. From mid-July to mid-August, pick your own at *Kendall's Blueberries* (2124 Coburn Rd, 269-945-3735, kendallsblueberries.com).

BIG LAKE BREWING

Founded: 2013
Brewmaster: Travis Prueter, Nic Winsemius
Address: 977 Butternut Avenue, Suite 4 • Holland, MI 49424
Phone: 616-796-8888
Website: www.facebook.com/biglakebrewing
Annual Production: 200 barrels
Number of Beers: 6 on tap; plus 2 ciders and 2 wines on tap

Staple Beers:
» CHINOOK STRONG ALE
» BIG LAKE IPA
» LEROY BROWN
» RYECOE RYE IPA

Rotating Beers:
» CITRA WHEAT
» LOCKED OUT PALE ALE
» STOUT

Most Popular Brew: Leroy Brown or Ryecoe

Brewmaster's Fave: Travis: Ryecoe, Nic: Citra Wheat

Tours? Sometimes, but by appointment. But if they aren't busy they are always happy to chat.

Samples: Yes, six 4-oz. samplers for about $6.

Best Time to Go: Closed Monday and Tuesday. Open 5PM Wednesday–Friday, noon Saturday–Sunday.

Where can you buy it? Here on tap and to go in growlers.

Got food? No, but food-friendly. Bring your own or order in.

Special Offer: Not participating.

The Beer Buzz: What is it that drives engineers to beer? Or is it just that beer makes a more attractive offer? All three owners—Greg MacKeller, Travis Prueter, Nic Winsemius—have engineering backgrounds, but they haven't quit their day jobs just yet. Brewers Travis and Nic both got their start homebrewing when they were at Michigan Tech but oddly enough, they didn't meet each other there. They met at work in Holland, which is also where they met Greg. When Greg was in the Navy he lived down in New Orleans and used to dream of owning a bar. Travis and Nic were brewers. You see where this is going, right? They put together a five-year plan. They wanted to take this low and slow. No debt; they'd self-fund it. And so they bought their own system.

The perfect location had to be something within their budget but close to food for carry-in. Large enough for their needs but with room for expansion. This 3,000 square-foot space in a strip mall was open, and as a bonus, the landlord was enthusiastic about helping them out a bit. And with a huge residential area around them, they immediately had a customer base, making this a neighborhood brewery with a laid-back local atmosphere. In addition to their craft beer, they also produce hard cider and wine. You can see sports on TVs here, and board games are available. Watch for live music.

Mug Club. Free Wi-Fi.

Directions: From US-31 get off on the exit for Lakewood Blvd and turn right (west). Follow Lakewood Blvd about 1.4 miles and watch for a gentle right turn that keeps you on West Lakewood for another 0.3 mile. Take the next right on River Ave and stay on it as it become Butternut Ave. You will cross Riley Ave at an angle and see a strip mall on the right behind a large parking lot. This is the place.

Stumbling Distance: The brewery is in a strip mall, so there are several eateries right next door. *Thai Palace*, *Santa Fe Market* (authentic Mexican), *Peppino's Pizza*, *Turks* (bar food, great pork chops, craft brews on tap). Menus for each are in the taproom.

NEW HOLLAND BREWING CO. (PRODUCTION BREWERY)

Founded: 1997
Brewmaster: Brett VanderKamp
Head Brewer: Jason Salas
Address: 690 Commerce Ct • Holland, MI 49424
Phone: 616-510-2259
Website: www.newhollandbrew.com.com
Annual Production: 22,000 barrels
Number of Beers: 25–27 beers per year

Staple Beers:
» Dragon's Milk Ale (Oak-Barrel Aged)
» Full Circle Kölsch-Style Beer
» Mad Hatter IPA
» Monkey King Saison Farmhouse Ale
» The Poet Oatmeal Stout
» Sundog Amber Ale

Rotating Beers:
» Agribrew
» Cabin Fever Brown
» Four Witches Black Saison
» Golden Cap Saison
» Hopivore Michigan Wet-Hopped Harvest Ale
» Ichebad Pumpkin Ale
» White, Black, Rye, Farmouse, Oak-Aged versions Of Mad Hatter IPA

Cellar Series:
» Envious (with local pears, raspberries, aged in oak)
» Blue Sunday Sour...

High Gravity Series:
» Beerhive Honey Ginger
» Black Tulip Tripel Ale
» Charkoota Rye Smoked Doppelbock
» El Mole Ocho Mexican Spiced Ale
» Imperial Hatter
» Night Tripper Imperial Stout
» Pilgrim's Dole Wheatwine

Most Popular Brew: Dragon's Milk and Mad Hatter IPA

Brewmaster's Fave: Dragon's Milk stands out, but favorites change with the season

Tours? Scheduled on Saturdays at 12, 1, 2, and 3. Brewery tours are $10 and include samples throughout and a pint glass to take home. The tour lasts just over an hour. A distillery tour for $5. Make a reservation for either online.

Samples: During a scheduled tour, yes.

Best Time to Go: Check the tour schedule (Saturdays) and make a reservation.

Where can you buy it? In bottles (six-packs and bombers) at retailers and bars throughout Michigan, parts of the Midwest and the East Coast. Use their beer finder on the website to find the closest place to where you are.

Got food? No.

Special Offer: Free beer tour for one person with advanced reservations and with book to be signed upon arrival.

The Beer Buzz: Set out in an industrial park, this is where New Holland Brewing does its large-scale production (see the New Holland pub listing as well). With a flagship beer that is barrel-aged, parts of this place may seem more like a distillery (and, in fact, they do have a whole line of distillates as well!).

Brett VanderKamp (a geology and art major) and Jason Spaulding (now owner/founder of Brewery Vivant) used to homebrew together in college. They both went to Siebel in Chicago to get brewer certification and took the risk, founding New Holland Brewing Co. in 1997. The risk paid off and the brewery grew rapidly. The brewpub opened downtown in 2002. When the production brewery moved to this new location in October 2006, the previous brewery got leveled. Now it's the Hope College soccer field.

Beers are diverse and many. The core brand Mad Hatter IPA gets played with a lot to create variations and hybrids. The Cellar Series are some oak-aged brews, and a High Gravity Series highlights more potent beers.

The brewing and distilling systems are a bit of history. Just after World War II, the brewhouse was built in Germany. The distillery was commissioned in 1934 in New Jersey and sat in storage for more than 60 years before New Holland found it on the web, bought it, and had it worked on by some coppersmiths in Kentucky before firing it up once again.

Their brewery's signature beer Dragon's Milk Ale has a rabid and devoted following. It is aged in oak barrels for 90 days, and the barrels are only used twice. It's rather unusual for a brewery to have such a time-intensive brew produced in such large quantities. The Dragon's Milk Ale cellar takes up 6,000 square feet of space (in the 23,000 square foot facility).

Directions: From US-31 get off on the exit for Lakewood Blvd and turn right (west). Follow Lakewood Blvd about 1.4 miles and watch for a gentle right turn that keeps you on West Lakewood for another 0.3 mile. Take the next right on River Ave and then 0.3 mile later take the soft right into 136th Ave. Continue 0.6 mile and turn right on Manufacturers Dr. Turn left onto Commerce Ct 0.2 mile later. The brewery is on the left.

Stumbling Distance: Check out *Big Lake Brewing* just a few minutes away from here in Holland Township. Then head into downtown for a meal at the *New Holland Brewpub*. Watch for *Homebrewers United*, a September team-brewing event at the production brewery in the parking lot. All raw materials are provided by New Holland and the 20 teams of brewers take their batches home.

NEW HOLLAND BREWING CO. (PUB)

Founded: 2002
Brewmaster: Steve Berthel
Address: 66 E 8th St. • Holland, MI 49423
Phone: 616-355-6422
Website: www.newhollandbrew.com
Annual Production: 1,000 barrels
Number of Beers: 28 on tap, 3–7 pub-only specialties, 3 casks

Staple Beers:
» Dragon's Milk Ale (Oak-Barrel Aged)
» Full Circle Kölsch-Style Beer
» Golden Cap Saison
» Mad Hatter IPA
» The Poet Oatmeal Stout
» Sundog Amber Ale

Rotating Beers:
» Cabin Fever Brown
» Four Witches Black Saison
» Hopivore Michigan Wet-Hopped Harvest Ale
» Ichebad Pumpkin Ale
» White, Black, Rye, Farmouse, Oak-Aged Versions Of Mad Hatter IPA

Cellar Series:
» Envious (with local pears, raspberries, aged in oak)
» Blue Sunday Sour

High Gravity Series:
» Beerhive Honey Ginger
» Black Tulip Tripel Ale
» Charkoota Rye Smoked Doppelbock
» El Mole Ocho Mexican Spiced Ale
» Imperial Hatter
» Night Tripper Imperial Stout
» Pilgrim's Dole Wheatwine

Most Popular Brew: Dragon's Milk Ale or Mad Hatter IPA

Tours? Not here, except on rare occasions and by prior arrangement. See the New Holland production brewery pages for scheduled Saturday tours.

Samples: Yes, four-ounce samplers for $1.50–$2 each.

Best Time to Go: Open Monday–Thursday 11AM–12AM, Friday–Saturday 11AM–1AM, Sunday 11AM–10PM. Watch for live music; from May through December on weekends, less often in winter. Tuesday offers specials on growlers. May is tulip time in town; it ain't called Holland for nothing. Loads of tourists. Artisan Bloody Mary bar on Sundays.

Where can you buy it? Here on tap, and in growlers, 12-oz. and 22-oz. bottles. For sale in 14 states (the spirits are in 7).

Got food? Yes, pizza, sandwiches, soups, salads, some entrees such as ribeye or salmon, and kids' and dessert menus. Many recipes include beer and dishes have beer pairing suggestions on the menu. Try the beer float with Dragon's Milk. Oh my.

Special Offer: The book owner can drink beer at mug club prices during the book signature visit.

The Beer Buzz: Technically, this is a "tasting room" in a brewery, but most will see this as a spectacular brewpub. New Holland Brewing opened originally in an old mirror manufacturer's plant in 1997. They only served snacks and such at first, but then expanded the menu as it became more popular. When this location went up for sale, they moved in here after over 6 months of retrofitting the place. The production brewery continued on that original site until the move to the current facility in 2005.

Right inside the front door of this corner pub in downtown Holland you enter into a gift shop/beer fridge/spirit sales area and are met by the hostess. The bar area is to the right; more dining seating is to the left. J.C. Penney occupied this building in the 1920s, and until the pub opened, this had been a hardware store. The floor is the original hardwood and the pressed-tin ceiling is intact. Tall windows let in a lot of light, a few TVs show some sports.

Patrons get to try a wide range of New Holland beers and spirits here, while the brewers themselves get to come for six-week turns to test their legs, push their creativity, and interact more with their fellow brewers. Test batches, limited batches, and even vintage beers (from the cellar dating back 6 or 7 years and listed under "The Library") may appear on the menu.

The mug club tops 600 members, each one with a personalized etched Mason jar, and those are sorted out on the wall behind the bar. All the way to the back of the bar you can see the copper brewhouse. Frankenstill (they started distilling in 2006) is also on display on the mezzanine floor where there's more seating. A patio is out front on the walk, another is out back and features live music and Beer-B-Q in season. Until very recently, Sundays were dry in Holland. The brewery helped push for that to change and the sour ale, Blue Sunday, was named for the state of things prior to that. Come here and be very happy.

Head brewer Steve "Bert" Berthel is a well known figure in the Michigan brewing scene and was one of the founders of The Livery. He took the lead here at the pub in 2013.

Free Wi-Fi. Facebook.com/newhollandbrewpub

Directions: From US-31 on Holland's east side, get off at Chicago Dr and head west. Follow it 0.8 mile and take the slight right curve onto 8th St, still heading west for 0.6 mile, and the pub is on the left on the corner of 8th and College.

Stumbling Distance: *Our Brewing Co.* is a couple doors down the street. Watch for Hatter Days in June, a sort of anniversary for the brewery. Don't miss *Big Red*, the lighthouse, and a nice beach on Lake Michigan over at *Holland State Park* (2215 Ottawa Beach Rd, michigan.gov/Holland). No beer allowed, unfortunately, so come to the pub afterward.

OUR BREWING COMPANY

Founded: November 2012
Brewmaster: Trevor Doublestein
Address: 76 E. 8th Street • Holland, MI 49423
Phone: 616-994-8417
Website: www.ourbrewingcompany.com
Annual Production: 250–300 barrels
Number of Beers: 18 on tap, endless styles

Staple Beers:
» FOREIGN MARKET ALE (FENUGREEK AND PALM SUGAR)
» ST. CELIAC'S BELGIAN TRIPEL (GLUTEN-FREE WITH SORGHUM)
» STRAIGHT UP MILK STOUT
» TOASTED COCONUT PORTER

Rotating Beers:
» AS YOU LIKE IT PORTER
» BELGIAN-STYLE DUBBEL
» BLACK IPA
» HARVEST ALE
» HOLIDAY STOUT SERIES: ANDES MINT, HEATH, COFFEE, ETC.
» MAI TAI FARMHOUSE
» MAPLE COFFEE STOUT
» ROOT BEER BROWN
» SEA FOAM STOUT
» SOMETHING NEW EVERY WEEK!

Most Popular Brew: Stouts and Belgians

Brewmaster's Fave: Stouts and bigger beers

Tours? If he's free, sure.

Samples: Yes.

Best Time to Go: Open noon to midnight all week. Happy hour is in the planning as well as an industry night. Watch for live music on Saturday nights.

Where can you buy it? Right here on tap or to go in growlers.

Got food? No, but there's free popcorn, and you can bring your own in or order off menus for delivery. Coming soon: an iPad set up to take direct orders and payment to 3 local restaurants for delivery.

Special Offer: Half off your first pint during your signature visit

The Beer Buzz: The brewery owners' surname is Doublestein? You couldn't make that up. Trevor and Lisa previously lived in Petoskey but chose this 1904 building in Holland as the site of their brewery. The tap room has an old-school look with the original brick exposed, a pressed tin ceiling, and hardwood floors. Behind the galvanized steel-top bar is a chalkboard with what's on tap, and the mugs of mug club members hanging from pegs. Find plenty of space at the bar or the tables and tall cocktail tables around the room. One wall has a big brewery logo painted on it. There's an electric fireplace for some winter coziness, outdoor seating for the summer, and three TVs for when the game's on. Shuffleboard is in back and a few board games are available.

Brewer Trevor was a general contractor before this, just homebrewing on the weekends for about five years, when he decided, "Life is short. I'd rather be doing something I enjoy." He and his wife Lisa planned for this place for two years before they made it a reality. Trevor's background was helpful as they did a lot of restoration work, carpet removal, drop ceiling installation, and removed layers of old dry wall and plaster to get down to the brick walls and pressed-tin ceiling. Six 1.5-barrel fermenters do the magic in the basement and Trevor does batches from a half barrel on up to a three-barrel. He did 50 styles just in the first two months they were open. The beer cellar actually extends under the sidewalk and Trevor has plans to do some barrel aging.

The "Our" in the name is intended to give it a community feel, and to stress that, Trevor does "suggested brews," drawing upon ideas put forth by his clientele. Locals are enthusiastic about their new beer—the mug club sold out before the place opened, before many of them had even tried a beer. He expects to dabble in wines, ciders, and maybe even meads in the future.

Free Wi-Fi. Mug club may be sold out.

Directions: From US-31 on Holland's east side, get off at Chicago Dr and head west. Follow it 0.8 mile and take the slight right curve onto 8th St, still heading west for 0.6 mile, and the pub is on the left just before College Ave.

Stumbling Distance: *8th Street Grill* (20 W 8th St, 616-392-5888, 8thstreetgrille.com) just a few doors down has 28 craft beers on tap.

PIKE 51 BREWING CO. (HUDSONVILLE WINERY)

Founded: June 2012
Brewmaster: Jeff Williams
Address: 3768 Chicago Drive • Hudsonville, Michigan 49426
Phone: 616-662-4589
Website: www.pike51.com
Annual Production: 300+ barrels
Number of Beers: 9 on tap, up to 16 eventually

Staple Beers:
» Everlasting Light
» Dark Star
» For Whom The Stout Tolls
» The Knight's Brown (Imperial Brown)
» The Kush IPA
» Marvin's Weizen

Rotating Beers:
» Ticket To Rye'd

Most Popular Brew: Everlasting Light, The Kush IPA, Dark Star

Brewmaster's Fave: The Kush IPA

Tours? Maybe, if the brewer is around; nothing fancy or formal.

Samples: Yes, $1.50 each.

Best Time to Go: Open Monday–Thursday 3–11PM, and Friday–Saturday noon–11PM.

Where can you buy it? Here on tap and in growlers to go. HopCat sometimes offers it on tap back in Grand Rapids.

Got food? No, but there is a food truck parked outside.

Special Offer: Not participating.

The Beer Buzz: Pike 51 was actually the former name of Chicago Drive which is where you'll find this little brewery sharing space with Hudsonville Winery. Brewer Jeff whips up 3.5-barrel batches about twice a week. Previously, Jeff was a homebrewer working in construction. When he lost his job, he approached his friends over at HopCat in Grand Rapids and they took him on as head brewer until he was ready to branch out on his own in nearby Hudsonville. (It was a much better commute for the Hudsonville resident; just a mile from home.)

The trouble was that Hudsonville was a dry town. It wasn't until 2008 that this law was overturned. Immediately a pizza joint and Hudsonville Winery opened, bringing some business into this bedroom community. The winery specializes in fruit wines, offering over 30 varieties, but also produces a few reds and whites. Bottle sales topped 40,000 in 2011.

The beer has a long way to go to catch up with that quantity, but it is attracting more and more people to the place. And as wine people traveling with beer people can tell you, it is great to find a place that both types of people can enjoy together. For the record, up to 5 wine samples are free.

Facebook.com/Pike51

Directions: Head west from Grand Rapids on I-196. Take Exit 69B for Chicago Dr (M-121) and take this 5.6 miles and make a U-turn just past 37th Ave to get to Hudsonville Winery/Pike 51 Brewery on the south side of the road.

Stumbling Distance: Looking for something to eat? Give *Vitale's Pizza* (5779 Balsam Dr, 616-662-4447, vitaleshudsonville.com) a try. (It's much more than just pizza.) Don't miss *White Flame Brewing* here in town (and on the next page).

WHITE FLAME BREWING CO.

Founded: January 28, 2012
Brewmaster: Bill White
Address: 5234 36th Ave. • Hudsonville, MI 49426
Phone: 616-209-5098
Website: www.whiteflamebrewing.com
Annual Production: 450 barrels
Number of Beers: 5 for starters, up to 12 on tap

Beers:
» Black Sheep Black IPA
» Eagle Eye Rye PA
» Golden Boy
» Pale Otter Porter (P.O.P. Porter)
» Super G IPA
» Ugly Stick Oatmeal Stout
» White Shoes Pale Ale

Rotating Beers:
» Andy's Double Tap Pale Ale (With Honey)
» Hawaii 5-O Hawaiian Coffee Stout
» Hooterville Wheat
» Red Shoes Pale Ale (with Habanero Peppers)
» plus some bourbon-barrel aging, sours, and more.

Most Popular Brew: Super G IPA

Brewmaster's Fave: Super G IPA and Andy's Double Tap

Tours? No.

Samples: Yes, 5 four-ounce samplers for about $6.

Best Time to Go: Open Tuesday–Thursday 4–10PM, and Friday–Saturday 4–midnight. Live music most Thursdays.

Where can you buy it? Here on tap and in howlers (32 oz.) and growlers (64 oz.) to go.

Got food? No, but you can carry-in or order delivery from local joints.

Special Offer: $1 off the first round of beers during your signature visit.

The Beer Buzz: When asked why he started a brewery, Brewer Bill had two reasons: First, he needed work. Second, he had already been homebrewing and people were telling him his brews were good. Opening in Hudsonville puts him within the greater Grand Rapids beer-o-sphere and yet provides some local brew for a community that doesn't have a whole lot going on.

The bright little taproom for this small production brewery is just about a 20-minute drive from downtown Grand Rapids. Blonde wood floors and white walls keep things bright. A bear skin on the wall and a few other taxidermist's odds and ends give it some character, and of course the beer gives you the real reason to come here. Beer pours are divided into 3 pricing categories, Class I to Class III, depending on the complexity and cost of creating it. Growler fills for beers greater than Class I also bump up a notch. All beers and categories are listed on a chalkboard menu behind the bar. There's a dart room by the side door coming in from the little parking lot there.

Free Wi-Fi. Mug club. On Facebook.

Directions: Take I-196 west toward Holland and get off on Exit 69 for Chicago Dr. Merge onto Chicago Dr (M-121) and continue 5.2 miles. Turn left on 36th Ave and the brewery is on the left there.

Stumbling Distance: *Pike 51 Brewery* inside *Hudsonville Winery* is also in town and in this book.

ARCADIA ALES

Founded: 1997 (2013)
Address: 701 East Michigan Avenue • Kalamazoo, MI
Website: www.arcadiaales.com
Annual Production: 30,000 barrels with capacity for 60,000

Staple Beers:
» ANGLERS ALE
» IPA
» HOPMOUTH DOUBLE IPA
» LOCH DOWN SCOTCH ALE
» SKY HIGH RYE PALE ALE

Most Popular Brew: IPA

Tours? Check the website for the schedule.

Samples: Yes.

Where can you buy it? On tap and in growlers. Cans and bottles in Michigan and 7 other states: IL, KS, KY, MO, NJ, OH, and PA.

Got food? Yes.

The Beer Buzz: Based out of Battle Creek, this English-ale inspired brewery has had big success. So much so that they decided to open a second brewery here in Kalamazoo. Ironically, when Tim Suprise first founded Arcadia, their first choice of location was Kalamazoo. When that didn't pan out, they chose Battle Creek. See Arcadia's story in their Battle Creek listing. This 30,000 square-foot facility, situated on the banks of the Kalamazoo River, will provide them with the increased production to keep up with demand and expand their distribution. The pub serves food along with their great beers, and there is even an outdoor beer garden. The riverside location also means that you can paddle up to their canoe/kayak dock.

Directions: Follow Business I-94 all the way into downtown Kalamazoo. That route comes just to the edge of the Kalamazoo River at Michigan Ave and King Highway. Go east here in Michigan Ave, over the bridge, and the brewery is on the left (north) side of the street.

Stumbling Distance: *Bell's Eccentric Café* is just a short walk down Michigan Ave (west) from Arcadia. The rest of the magical Kalamazoo brew zone isn't much farther.

BELL'S ECCENTRIC CAFÉ & BREWERY

Founded: 1985
Brewmaster: Larry Bell, President/Founder
Address: 355 East Kalamazoo Avenue • Kalamazoo, MI
Phone: 269-382-2332
Website: www.bellsbeer.com
Number of Beers: Up to 40 on tap

Staple Beers:
» Amber Ale
» Kalamazoo Stout
» Midwestern Pale Ale
» Oarsman Ale
» Porter
» Third Coast Beer
» Two Hearted Ale

Rotating Beers:
» Black Currant Oarsman
» Blackberry Lemon Oarsman
» Black Note
» Bourbon-Barrel-Aged Varieties
» Chocolate Covered Cherry DCS
» Debs' Red
» Double Cream Stout (DCS)
» Le Batteur
» Le Contrebassiste
» Le Pianiste
» Mad Scientist Ale
» Oberon
» Quinannan Falls Special Lager
» Smoked Lager
» Sparkleberry
» Third Coast Old Ale (TCOA)
» Wedding Ale
» The Wild One
» Toasted Coconut Espresso TCOA
» THE LIST IS ETERNAL; MANY SPECIAL
BREWS ARE ONLY SOLD HERE ONSITE

Tours? Free 45-minute tours on most (double check) Saturdays at 12:30PM, 1:30PM, 2:30PM and 3:30PM, and Sundays at 1:30PM, 2:30PM and 3:30PM. Just sign up on a list in the atrium.

Samples: Yes, sample flights.

Best Time to Go: Is there a bad time? During one of the live music or film events or brewing demos perhaps.

Where can you buy it? Here on site in pints and growlers. In 19 states plus Puerto Rico and D.C. (see the Beer Finder on their website)

Got food? Yes, appetizers such as dips, chips, pretzels, soups and salads, barbecue plates, a few sandwiches, and more, plus a kids' menu. Vegetarian and gluten-free items.

Special Offer: Not participating.

The Beer Buzz: Many may have already heard the stories of a guy named Larry who started brewing in a soup kettle and fermenting in garbage pails. Some humble beginnings for what is now one of the largest craft brewers in America. The massive production facility is down the road in Galesburg/Comstock, and while the soup kettles now only make soup for the attached brewpub's menu, this is the original location. This was the

BELL'S in the U.P.?

Already one of the top craft breweries in the US, Bell's Brewing continues to grow each year. Larry Bell made the announcement in 2013 that they would be opening a production brewery in Escanaba. Situated in the Whitetail Industrial Park, this production brewery is actually a division of the granddaddy of all Michigan brewers, Bell's Brewery. The first brews from here were developed at Bell's original location in Kalamazoo and patrons have been trying them out at Bell's Eccentric Café. Unfortunately for beer fans, Michigan law prohibits them from having another tap room, and there are no plans for this facility to be open to the public. But you can follow along on social media: Facebook.com/UpperhandBrewery and Twitter @UpperHandBeer

first Michigan production brewery to open an on-site pub. This location brews a lot of special beers, some of which may never be seen again. With up to 40 taps, the variety is impressive throughout the year.

The Eccentric Café—with stained glass windows, a fountain in the foyer, a mosaic Michigan on the floor—offers great food along with those great beers, and live music in a separate performance area.

Directions: Business I-94 takes you into downtown Kalamazoo. From the east it eventually becomes the one-way Kalamazoo Ave. Follow this to the railroad tracks at Kalamazoo and Porter St, and it's on the right. From the west side, it becomes the one-way Michigan Ave. Take this all the way to where it meets Kalamazoo, stay in the left lane, and take the U-turn into Kalamazoo Ave. Again it is on the right at Porter St.

Stumbling Distance: Across Kalamazoo Ave, find Water Street and walk two minutes down to *Kalamazoo Beer Exchange* (211 E Water St, 269-532-1188, kalamazoobeerexchange.com). 28 beers on tap plus a cask, and you watch the various draft beer prices go up and down on video screens as people buy (or don't buy) each brew. Like the stock market: buy low. Hope to be there when the market crashes!

BILBO'S PIZZA

Founded: 1976 (brewing since 1996)
Brewers: John Hindman and Jackson Allen
Address: 3307 Stadium Drive • Kalamazoo, MI 49008
Phone: 269-382-5544
Website: www.bilbospizza.com
Annual Production: 120 barrels
Number of Beers: 5–8 on tap

Staple Beers:
» DRAGON RED
» SLEDGEHAMMER
» THUNDERBIRD IPA
» WIZARD WHEAT

Rotating Beers:
» CHERRY OR RASPBERRY WIZARD WHEAT
» HONEY BLONDE
» HONEY PORTER
» PUMPKIN PIE LAGER

Most Popular Brew: Wizard Wheat

Brewmaster's Fave: Thunderbird IPA

Tours? Not really, but if the brewers are there and free, they'll chat.

Samples: Yes, flights of 5 for about $3.

Best Time to Go: Open daily at 11AM (noon on weekends). Wednesday, Saturday, and Sunday are best for pints. Happy hour runs 5–6:30 Monday through Friday and there's a weekly special from 9PM to close.

Where can you buy it? Only here on tap or in growlers to go.

Got food? Yes, voted best pizza in Kalamazoo. Their signature salad dressing is widely known and sold in local grocery stores. The Cheezy Stix come recommended.

Special Offer: Not participating

The Beer Buzz: Located at the edge of town, this is a family-friendly restaurant with its own brews. The bar is huge but booths and tables are abundant as well. An express counter serves the lunch crowd for carry-out.

As you might guess, the name is borrowed from J.R.R. Tolkien's hobbit character, Bilbo Baggins. Restaurant founders John Hindman and Charlie Konett were big fans. Since opening in 1976 Bilbo's has had, at one time or another, all the kids and spouses of the two families working inside; a true family-owned establishment. When the craft brewing craze started to peak in the 90s, they added house beers to the menu. John started brewing. Years later, Jackson, who was working as a manager here, got interested in the brewing side of things. He spent his whole life learning by watching. They switched him from management to brewing for some variety. His first brew went on tap in 2005.

Free Wi-Fi.

Directions: Take US-131 north from I-94 and get off at Exit 36 to go east on Stadium Dr/Business I-94. Drive 1.1 miles and the place is on your right.

Stumbling Distance: Head downtown for the breweries there. Bilbo's has a second location as well at 6202 S Westnedge Ave in Portage (269-323-8855) but it doesn't serve the house beer.

BOATYARD BREWING CO.

Founded: 2013
Address: 432 East Patterson Street • Kalamazoo, MI 49007
Phone: 269-808-3455
Website: www.boatyardbrewing.com

Beers:
» BIMINI BROWN
» BLONDE HORIZON
» CALLEIGH'S IRISH STOUT
» DRIFTWOOD BITTERS
» FAIR WINDS OATMEAL STOUT
» FALLEN SOULS IMPERIAL STOUT
» HALF-CENTURY PORTER
» HOLD FAST PALE ALE
» LAKE EFFECT DOUBLE IPA
» LOST PENINSULA IPA
» MIDNIGHT STAR
» RED AT NIGHT RYE

Where can you buy it? When this opens to the public, here on tap or in growlers to go—for starters.

Special Offer: Not participating.

The Beer Buzz: Dan Gilligan and Brian Steele co-founded this production brewery on Kalamazoo's north side in an old industrial building. Even before they opened their doors they were serving their beer at various beer festivals around Michigan.

No Mug Club, but Yacht Club. On Facebook. and Twitter @BoatyardBrewing

Directions: Take Business US-131 (Park St) north from downtown. Go right on Paterson Street almost 7 blocks and the brewery is on the right, before the railroad tracks.

Stumbling Distance: This brewery is 0.7 mile due north of *Bell's Eccentric Café* and the rest of downtown Kalamazoo's beer scene.

GONZO'S BIGGDOGG BREWING

Founded: 2013
Brewmaster: Greg "Gonzo" Haner
Address: 140 South Westnedge Avenue • Kalamazoo, MI
Phone: 269-382-2739
Website: www.gonzosbiggdoggbrewing.com
Annual Production: 1,600 barrels
Number of Beers: 8 on tap to start

Staple Beers:
» Burning Sun Amber
» Dark Alley Stout
» Dogg Days Golden Ale
» Geyser Brown Ale
» Gonzo's Chocolate Porter
» Hefeweizen
» Pale Ale
» Raspberry Wheat
» Sub-Continental IPA
» VP Ale Vanilla Porter
» Wheat

Brewmaster's Fave: Imperial Stout

Tours? Yes.

Samples: Yes, beer flights.

Best Time to Go: Open Monday–Friday 3pm–1am, Saturday noon–1am, Sunday noon–midnight.

Where can you buy it? On tap and in growlers and kegs to go. Distribution of kegs in southwestern Michigan.

Got food? Yes, a high-end menu in the taproom for a moderate cost.

Special Offer: Not participating.

The Beer Buzz: Gonzo is a well known brewing character here in Kalamazoo. He's been brewing since 1992 and helped get Olde Peninsula Brewing up and running back in the day. A friend got him into homebrewing when he was still working in pharmaceuticals. Gonzo liked it so much, he created his own home brew system. His friend liked that so much, that he wanted Gonzo to build him one too.

Getting serious, Gonzo went to Siebel Institute for brewing and brewpub management certification. He worked at Olde Peninsula thereafter, and then took a job at extract and flavor producer Kalsec, heading up their research brewery. His name is on two of their beer patents. When that project ended, he decided it was high time to start his own brewery.

He found investors and began to gut a former car dealership to house his 15-barrel brewhouse. While there is food in the taproom, the focus here is producing beer for distribution.

Mug Club. Free Wi-Fi.

Directions: Kalamazoo and Michigan Ave function as opposing directions of Business I-94 through downtown. Westnedge Ave (M-331) runs north-south across them on the west end of downtown. The brewery is half a block south of Michigan Ave on the right (west side of the road) on Westnedge.

Stumbling Distance: At the other end of this block is *Rupert's Brew House.*

OLDE PENINSULA BREWPUB & RESTAURANT

Opened: St Patrick's Day, 1996
Brewmaster: Dan Kiplinger
Address: 200 East Michigan Avenue • Kalamazoo, MI 49007
Phone: 269-343-2739
Website: www.oldepenkazoo.com
Annual Production: 650 barrels
Number of Beers: 8–10 on tap, 16 different brews per year

Staple Beers:
» Haymarket Cream Ale
» Midnight Stout
» OP IPA
» Rockin' Raspberry Wheat
» Stout Chocula
» Sunset Red

Rotating Beers:
» B4W Barleywine
» Downtown Brown
» Gingerbread Porter
» Porter
» Pumpkin Ale
» Summer Hefeweizen
» Tornado Ale
» Vanilla Porter
» Single-hop IPAs and Double IPAs from time to time

Most Popular Brew: OP IPA

Brewmaster's Fave: His award-winning Barleywine

Tours? Yes, but reservations required. $10 includes the tour and a guided tasting of all the tap beers. Call 269-389-0800.

Samples: Yes, 5-oz samples for $1.50 each.

Best Time to Go: Open daily at 11AM. Happy hour 3–6PM and after 10PM Monday–Friday.

Where can you buy it? Just here on tap and in growlers to go. Pours come in 5-, 10-, 16-, and 22-oz sizes and also one liter.

Got food? Yes, a full menu with appetizers, soups and salads, sandwiches, grilled pizzas, fish, steaks, and more.

Special Offer: Not participating

The Beer Buzz: This was the first strictly brewpub to open in Kalamazoo, and it did so on St. Patrick's Day in 1996. The big, corner brick building was originally an eatery back in 1874: the Peninsula Restaurant. So you can see where the current name came from. Between its birth and the incarnation of the brewpub it manufactured stoves, rented rooms, bound books, and sold clothes, among other things. A tornado ripped through town in 1980 and the building subsequently got a complete overhaul. It is again serving great food but in the modern era has a 7-barrel brew system to make house beers.

Brewer Dan started brewing in college, and got his first job at Bell's when the now mega-brewer was just getting warmed up. (There were only half a dozen people on staff!) Dan started the KLOB (Kalamazoo Libation Organization of Brewers) back in 1993, a homebrew club that now has over 100 members. He took the reins at Olde Peninsula in 2003, and has won some awards over the years, including a silver for his bourbon-barrel-aged barleywine in 2007 at GABF.

Directions: If you come into Kalamazoo from the east, take Business I-94 and it becomes Kalamazoo Ave downtown. Turn left on Rose St, drive three blocks and turn left on Michigan Ave. The brewery is on the right at the corner of Michigan and Portage. From the west, Business I-94 goes right into downtown and takes a right, becoming Michigan Ave. Follow it to the corner of Michigan and Portage.

Stumbling Distance: For another good beer bar check out *Central City Tap House* (359 S Kalamazoo Mall, 269-492-0100). 20 taps, a cask, loads of bottles, and a full menu.

RUPERT'S BREW HOUSE

Founded: 2013
Chief Brewer: Adam Wisniewski
Address: 773 West Michigan Avenue • Kalamazoo, MI 49007
Phone: 269-337-9911
Website: facebook.com/Ruperts-Brew-House
Annual Production: 800–900 barrels
Number of Beers: 9 on tap (one is nitro); 50 brews per year

Staple Beers:
» BRITTNEY'S CREAM ALE
» DOCTOR STEVE'S IPAILMENT
» DOUBLE HIGHPA
» M-43 PORTER
» MASTIFF DROOL
» MATCHES THE DRAPES AMBER
» NOT SO PEANUT BUTTER PORTER
» SUPER BONUS SOUR

Rotating Beers:
» VARIOUS STYLES THROUGHOUT THE YEAR WITH A FOCUS ON SOURS

Brewmaster's Fave: Brittney's Cream Ale

Tours? Sure, if people are interested.

Samples: Yes, sample flights ("train rides").

Best Time to Go: Open daily until bar closing.

Where can you buy it? Only here on tap and in growlers, plus plans for cans.

Got food? No, but food trucks and local delivery sources.

Special Offer: A free sticker and $1 off your first beer or flight during your signature visit

The Beer Buzz: Owner/brewer Mark Rupert got into homebrewing for the fun of it, but soon saw it is a way to support his family. Prior to the brewery, this location was The Strutt, a popular music venue in K-zoo, and Boogie Records before that. While Mark is bringing the beer here, he also wants the live music focus to remain.

The 1.5-barrel system is a "step up from homebrewing" and can be seen under glass inside the pub. Mark brought in Brewer Adam who has won several national homebrewing awards. They intend to focus on sour ales. Adam also started as a homebrewer and got obsessed with it.

Directions: Business I-94 through downtown Kalamazoo goes right past here. From the west side of downtown where I-94B changes from Stadium Dr to Michigan Ave, the brewery is on the corner of Michigan and Academy St.

Stumbling Distance: This brewery is close to *Western Michigan University* and *Kalamazoo College*. *Up and Under Sports Bar* (711 W Michigan Ave, 269-373-1412, theuandu.com) is close by for game days and has a good craft beer selection. *Gonzo's Biggdogg Brewing* is at the other end of this block.

Kalamazoo House: Bed and Breakfast and Beer!

Often the trick of any good pilsgrimage is finding a designated driver or a tour bus. But wouldn't it be great if you all could just walk from place to place? Michigan's craft beer density is making that a much easier proposition, and a fantastic bed and breakfast in beercentric Kalamazoo has a package for you: the Kalamazoo House Beer Trail.

Situated downtown, this 1878 Queen Anne Victorian home is pub-crawl distance from most of the best beer places in town: Bell's Eccentric Cafe, Olde Peninsula Brewpub, the Beer Exchange, Central City Tap House, Boatyard, Arcadia Brewing Company, Gonzo's Bigg Dogg Brewery, and Rupert's BrewHouse. The special room rate comes with a welcome package that includes a growler, pint glasses, beer-friendly snacks, a bag with a map on it, some credit at the Beer Exchange and more. So a great day/night of K-zoo beer and a fine breakfast waiting for you the next morning. Can't beat this.

(447 W. South St, 269-382-0880, thekalamazoohouse.com)

DARK HORSE BREWING CO.

Founded: 2000
Brewers: Aaron Morse and Bryan Wiggs
Address: 511 South Kalamazoo Avenue •
Marshall, MI 49068
Phone: 269-781-9940
Website: www.darkhorsebrewery.com
Annual Production: 15,000 barrels
Number of Beers: 18 bottled, plus more

Staple Beers:
- Amber Ale
- Boff Brown Ale
- Crooked Tree IPA
- Raspberry Ale
- Reserve Special Black Ale

Rotating Beers:
- 3 Guy Off The Scale Old Ale (Barleywine)
- Double Crooked Tree IPA
- Fore Smoked Stout
- Four Elf Winter Warmer
- Kamita Kölsch
- One Oatmeal Stout
- Perkulator Coffee Doppelbock
- Plead The Fifth Imperial Stout
- Sapient Tripel Ale
- Scotty Karate Scotch Ale
- Thirsty Trout Porter
- Too Cream Stout
- Tres Blueberry Stout
- Plus bourbon-barrel aged versions and one-off sour ales and others

Most Popular Brew: Crooked Tree IPA

Brewmaster's Fave: Aaron: "All depends on the day."

Tours? Yes, on Saturdays and Sundays, about $7, includes a pint glass and samples.

Samples: A sip or two to help you choose.

Best Time to Go: Happy hour is 3–6:09PM. Live music in season in the beer garden.

Where can you buy it? Six-packs and growlers are available on site, plus bottles are sold all over Michigan and in 9 states: IL, IN, MA, MN, NY, OH, PA, VA, and WI.

Got food? Open daily for food at 11AM (noon on Sunday). Soups and chili with beer in them, fresh bread using spent grain, pizzas, calzones, sandwiches on pretzel or ciabatta buns, toasted subs, and desserts. Housemade root beer.

Special Offer: $1 off your first pint on your signature visit—and you can keep the glass.

The Beer Buzz: When you pull into the parking lot you might think "old Western saloon" or even "farm." Across the lot is Dark Horse General Store with a tattoo parlor, a skate shop, and a motorcycle shop. The property was once part of the railroad and had a coal yard. Originally the tap room was a gas station, a pet grooming place and then a sports shop. Now it's a magnificent brewery and pub.

Brewer Aaron was already into beer in high school and started brewing in college. "Instead of spending all our money on beer, we brewed." They started brewing in secret in their dormitory basement and in their bathroom, hiding their brews behind the toilet or under beds. "We made a bunch of bad beer at first." When his parents, who owned a bar, decided to remodel, Aaron suggested they make it a brewpub. They did so in 1997, but it only lasted a year or so. Undeterred, Aaron started brewing in a tiny space in January of 2000. He refurbished the tap room and opened in September the same year. Since then they've been adding space and equipment as they go. They added a solar-powered hot water system, which also heats the tap room. That first year they produced 400 barrels. By 2011, it was 9,200 barrels. By the next year that amount had nearly doubled.

The mug club is huge and $46 gets you a lifetime membership. There's a beer garden in back, a barn with the logo on it, and an outdoor stage for live music. The name Dark Horse is something Aaron's mother pulled out of a book. The other option was Spearfish.

On Facebook as DarkHorseBrewing.

Trivia note: The brewers turned down an opportunity to have Dark Horse beer appear in a Nickelback video because none of them like the band's music.

Directions: From I-94 take Exit 110 and go south on Brewer Street. This becomes Kalamazoo Ave. Pass through the roundabout and the brewery is on the left after the railroad tracks.

Stumbling Distance: Check out *Side Track Ice Cream* on the other side of the train tracks. Need a place to stay? Try *National House Inn Bed and Breakfast* (102 S. Parkview, 269-781-7374, nationalhouseinn.com). *Schuler's Restaurant & Pub* (115 S. Eagle St, 269-781-0600) is a decent place for lunch or dinner including prime rib and London broil. Dark Horse and Bell's are on tap. The building of *The Copper Bar* (113 W. Michigan Ave, 269-781-5400) dates back to 1893 saloon days. Hot dogs, burgers, good beer served in Mason jars, fresh roasted peanuts, shells on the floor. No credit cards!

VILLA BREW PUB & GRILLE (MIDDLE VILLA INN)

Founded: 2006
Brewmaster: Steve Wiersum
Address: 4611 North M-37 Highway • Middleville, MI 49333
Phone: 269-795-3640
Website: www.middle-villa-inn.com
Number of Beers: 4 on tap

Staple Beers:
» THIEVIN' RABBIT CZECH PILSNER

Rotating Beers:
» DOWN AND DIRTY PORTER
» GARDEN DELIGHT LAGER
» TOADHOUSE SCOTTISH ALE

Most Popular Brew: Thievin' Rabbit

Brewmaster's Fave: Thievin' Rabbit

Tours? Maybe by chance or appointment, but there's not much to tour.

Samples: Yes, 4 four-ounce samplers for about $4.

Best Time to Go: Happy hour is 4:30–6PM on weekdays, but beware: they close on Mondays and Wednesdays in summer. Always check the website. Hours change with the seasons. They are busier in the winter, and slower during summer.

Where can you buy it? Only here on tap or in growlers.

Got food? Yes, sandwiches, subs, paninis, salads, appetizers (beer-battered potato wedges!), popcorn, and some dinner entrees such as fish and chips, and beer-battered shrimp. House pizza has its own special beer/fennel seed pizza sauce.

Special Offer: Not participating

The Beer Buzz: Bowling with beer. Gotta admit they go together at least as well as beer and pretzels. This brewpub shares a space inside Middle Villa Inn with a bowling alley that's been around since about 1961. The alleys light up like a disco.

Owner/brewer Steve Wiersum's father bought this place back in 1969, and Steve, in turn, bought it from him. There are 3 banquet halls in the lower level, making this a popular place for wedding receptions.

Any brewer will tell you good beer starts with good water. Middleville has actually received awards from the state of Michigan for the quality of its water.

Free Wi-Fi. ATM onsite.

Directions: M-37 passes right through Middleville and the brewpub is on the west side of the highway as you come into town from the north.

Stumbling Distance: For some good eats and tap beers, find *Sand Bar & Grill* (11368 W M-179, 269-205-2525) nearby *Yankee Springs Recreation Area* near Gun Lake. The white chicken chili gets raves.

PIGEON HILL BREWING CO.

Founded: 2013
Brewmaster: Chad Doane
Address: 500 West Western, Suite 1 • Muskegon, MI 49440
Phone: 231-638-7545
Website: www.pigeonhillbrew.com
Number of Beers: 10 on tap; about 30 styles annually

Staple Beers:
» LMFAO STOUT (OATMEAL STOUT)
» SHIFTING SANDS IPA
» SKEETOWN BROWN ALE
» WALTER BLONDE ALE

Rotating Beers:
» DOUBLE DUNE DOUBLE IPA
» DUCKER RED ALE
» OATMEAL CREAM PIE
» RUSSIAN IMPERIAL STOUT

Most Popular Brew: Too soon to tell.

Brewmaster's Fave: The one in his hand. He has a soft spot for Walter Blonde though.

Tours? Yes.

Samples: Yes.

Best Time to Go: See website for hours and events. Live music on weekends.

Where can you buy it? On tap or to go in growlers. Distribution is planned.

Got food? Some snacks. Food friendly—bring your own.

Special Offer: Receive a hug from the brewer or $1 off your first pint during your signature visit.

The Beer Buzz: Pride and passion are the two elements coming together with this new brewery: Passion for good craft beer and hometown pride. It was the latter that brought the former to what has been a struggling downtown for many years here in Muskegon. The brewery is named after a sand dune that once towered over town until it was removed for industry use in the middle of the last century. Thanks to the partners here, Pigeon

Hill is back but in a different form. (They also note, Pigeon Hill's initials reference the importance of the pH of water in making good beer and other devils in the details of brewing.)

Pigeon Hill's home is the Noble Building, a 1920s auto dealership that lost its luster and got divvied up for office space. The landlord and the brewers put in new garage doors, large windows, and brought back the beautiful original terrazzo floors. The bar and table tops are built from century-old timber recovered from the bottom of Muskegon Lake and milled locally. Many of the light fixtures are also Muskegon in origin: manufacturers Brunswick, SD Warren/SAPPI, and Continental Motors have had homes here.

The atmosphere in the taproom is that of a community gathering space. Relaxed and casual, board games, books, and an old-school Nintendo system are on hand to pass the time. Come on down, and have a chat over a pint.

Directions: From north or south, follow Business US-31 into downtown Muskegon (where it is Shoreline Drive) and turn southeast on 4th St (away from the lake). Go one block and turn right on Western Ave. The brewery is one block down on the right.

Stumbling Distance: Be sure to check out *Unruly Brewing* just a couple minutes down the street as well as *Fetch Brewing* to the north in Whitehall. *Pints & Quarts Pub and Grill* (950 W Norton, 231-830-9889, pintsandquarts.com) has 24 taps in a sports bar environment.

UNRULY BREWING CO.

Opened: End of 2013
Brewmaster: Eric Hoffman
Address: 360 West Western Avenue • Muskegon, MI 49440
Website: www.unrulybrewing.com
Annual Production: 600–700 barrels
Number of Beers: 10 on tap

Staple Beers:
» 1890 (PRE-PROHIBITION CREAM ALE)
» REVEL ROUSER IPA

Rotating Beers:
» BELGIAN STYLES
» BLACK IPA
» PORTER
» PUMPKIN ALE
» SAISONS

Most Popular Brew: Too soon to tell.

Brewmaster's Fave: Revel Rouser IPA

Tours? Yes.

Samples: No.

Best Time to Go: See the website for current hours

Where can you buy it? On tap and in growlers. Distribution in the future.

Got food? Yes, starting in April 2014. (Until then, bring your own.)

Special Offer: A 10% discount off your purchase of Unruly Brewing merchandise during your signature visit.

The Beer Buzz: It wasn't so long ago that Muskegon did not have a single brewery in the area. It was at least a half-hour drive to find one and the homebrewing club lamented this fact. Brewer Eric, a longtime homebrewer, and a few partners decided they could fix that problem. (The guys over at Pigeon Hill, friends of theirs, also had a solution. Great minds think alike.)

It took Eric and Co. just over three years to bring this brewery to fruition. It occupies an 1890 YMCA building, taking up about 2/3 of the main floor and much of the basement. The local symphony converted the upstairs gymnasium into a performance hall. The building spent more than 30 years as an office supply store and for a long time it was attached to the Muskegon shopping mall. When the mall got the wrecking ball, the old YMCA building was luckily spared. Downtown Muskegon had seen better days, but now with two craft brewers within two minutes' walk of each other, downtown Muskegon may be your next beer destination.

Facebook.com/UnrulyBrewing

Directions: From north or south, follow Business US-31 into downtown Muskegon (where it is Shoreline Drive) and turn southeast on 3rd St (away from the lake). Go one block and turn right on Western Ave. The brewery is one block down on the right.

Stumbling Distance: Be sure to check out *Pigeon Hill Brewing* just down the street as well as *Fetch Brewing* to the north in Whitehall.

PAW PAW BREWING CO.

Founded: 2011
Head Brewers: Ryan Sylvester and Trevor Klimek
Address: 929 E. Michigan Avenue • Paw Paw, MI 49079
Phone: 269-415-0145
Website: www.pawpawbrewing.com
Annual Production: 850 barrels
Number of Beers: 10 on tap, plus root beer

Staple Beers:
» Black River Oatmeal Stout
» Paw Paw Wheat
» St. James English Mild Ale
» Two Paws IPA

Rotating Beers:
» Bloody Mary Beer
» Kalamazoo Urban Assault Pale Ale
» Pumpkin Ale
» Vanilla Bean Porter
» 40 Styles Throughout The Year

Most Popular Brew: St. James English Mild Ale

Brewers' Fave: Black River Oatmeal Stout

Tours? Yes, if someone is in the brewhouse.

Samples: Yes, flights of up to ten $1.50 five-ounce beers.

Best Time to Go: Weekdays at 5 to meet the locals, or on Friday–Saturday when it's really hopping.

Where can you buy it? Draft accounts in Southwestern Michigan. Growlers on site.

Got food? Yes, hot and cold paninis, beer cheese with pretzels.

Special Offer: A $1 pint and a keychain during your signature visit.

The Beer Buzz: Owner/partner Fleckenstein says, "We developed this place to be a community location" and the aim is apparent in their flagship English Mild session beer, which folks might have preferred back in the 1860 pub days. "It represents who we are."

Starting up a brewery is no small endeavor as it can take a lot of time and setbacks are common. Fleckenstein considers himself a spiritual guy, and he figured, "If a door shuts, so be it." But as it turned out, all the doors opened: paperwork, a business plan, funding—it all came together like it was fate, and so they started small and with very little debt.

Fleckenstein's sister owns Gracie's Place, an antiques shop across the parking lot. She had this extra building to hold the overflow before they all decided it'd be the best location for the pub. On site they used a SABCO Brew-Magic system and made 2 barrels per day; now this is where the test batches are done and a facility across town takes on the bigger production.

Inside you'll find galvanized metal siding and mugs on the wall made in the basement of Eric Strader down in Indiana. The outdoor patio brings in heaters to extend the season a bit. Free Wi-Fi and an ATM on site.

Directions: From I-94 take Exit 60 and go north on M-40/Kalamazoo St. Take a right (east) on Michigan Ave, drive just over 6 blocks, and watch for the brewery on the left (north) side.

Stumbling Distance: Got some wine drinkers with you? Check out *St. Julian Winery* (716 S. Kalamazoo St, 269-657-5568, stjulian.com) Michigan's oldest and largest. Here's an idea for an outing: paddle the Paw Paw River from here to Benton Harbor where you can visit *The Livery*. Call it a pub float rather than a pub crawl.

Come for *Harvest Fest* in early September when their off-site brewery facility (123 Commercial Ave.) opens to the public and the fest breaks out some free wine. Pick your own blueberries at *Laduc's* (37146 30th St, 269-657-3871, leducblueberries.com).

BRAVO! RESTAURANT AND CAFÉ

Founded: 1987 (beer since 2008)
Brewmaster: Adam Stacey
Address: 5402 Portage Road • Portage, MI 49002
Phone: 269-344-7700
Website: www.bravokalamazoo.com
Annual Production: 60 barrels
Number of Beers: 5 on tap

Staple Beers:
» CHEF'S ALE AMBER

Rotating Beers:
» VARIOUS

Most Popular Brew: Chef's Ale

Brewmaster's Fave: The next one he's brewing

Tours? Sure, if Adam's free and available. But it's pretty small.

Samples: A beer flight of four 4.5 oz. beers for about $6.

Best Time to Go: Open 11:30AM–10PM for food, until 11PM on weekends.

Where can you buy it? Growlers on site.

Got food? Award-winning Italian-American food with a specialization in Tuscany recipes. Wood-fired oven pizzas, steaks, seafood. 3 Diamonds from AAA, 3 Stars from Forbes.

Special Offer: Half-price on Bravo! glassware during signature visit

The Beer Buzz: Brewer Adam has been Chef Adam for more than 20 years at the restaurant. Brothers Shawn and Terry Hagen joined Ann and Don Parfet in opening the restaurant in 1987. The food here has gotten some serious acclaim (see the diamonds and stars in the Got Food comments) and everything is made from scratch. "So why not beer from scratch?" they figured. So they bought Adam a homebrewing kit and soon he was bringing in batches for the staff to try out. In 2008, Adam began making one-barrel batches for the restaurant.

Bravo! offers fine dining in a casual atmosphere so you'll find patrons dressed up nicely at a table next to someone in a t-shirt. The café area is the most casual but there are four dining rooms, some of which are used for banquet events. Menu items are paired with beers or wines from the extensive wine list. If you're just in for the beer, there is a separate bar in back with its own outdoor patio.

Directions: From downtown Kalamazoo on Business I-94/Michigan Ave, take Portage Rd south 0.4 mile and turn right to stay on Portage Rd. Follow it another 3.5 miles south into the adjacent city of Portage and Bravo! is on the right.

Stumbling Distance: Check out the *Air Zoo of Kalamazoo* (6151 Portage Rd, Portage, 269-382-6555, airzoo.org) the aviation history museum and indoor amusement park next to the airport just across the street, or head back downtown for the rest of K-Zoo's beervana.

LATITUDE 42 BREWING CO.

Opened: August 2013
Brewmaster: Scott Freitas
Address: 7842 Portage Road • Portage, MI 49002
Phone: 269-459-4242
Website: www.latitude42brewingco.com
Annual Production: 5,000 barrels
Number of Beers: 16 on tap; 2 casks; 30+ brews per year

Staple Beers:
» LIL' SUNSHINE GOLDEN ALE
» POWERLINE PORTER
» RED BEARD'S INDIA RED ALE
» SPANK DOG PALE ALE

Rotating Beers:
» BEACH CRUISER (UNFILTERED AMERICAN HEFEWEIZEN)
» EL DIABLO (LIL' SUNSHINE WITH CHIPOTLE PEPPERS)
» I.P. EH.
» MIKE'S CAMARO (CALIFORNIA COMMON ALE)
» MILK OF AMNESIA (MILK STOUT)
» OLD CHIN WAG (STRONG ALE)
» SUMPIN' LIGHT

Most Popular Brew: Spank Dog Pale Ale

Brewmaster's Fave: "The one in my hand."

Tours? Not really.

Samples: Yes, $6 for 6 samples.

Best Time to Go: Open daily at 11AM. Happy hour 2–5PM Monday–Friday.

Where can you buy it? Here on tap and in howlers and growlers, six-pack cans, and kegs to go. Across southern Michigan on draft.

Got food? Yes, soups and salads, small plates, burgers and sandwiches, brick-oven pizzas, and a kids' menu.

Special Offer: A free sticker when you get your book signed.

The Beer Buzz: Co-owner Joe Stoddard had been thinking about opening a brewery for five years before this happened. Initially, plans were smaller, maybe just a simple brewpub. He partnered with his brother Todd

Neumann and they brought in Brewer Scott as a consultant. The idea evolved to something much bigger and the brothers made Scott an offer he couldn't refuse. Now it is a production facility with a brewpub attached.

Scott, a Eugene, Oregon native, has been brewing over two decades. He left his head brewer position at Maui Brewing to come be part of Latitude 42. This is a new building, designed specifically for their needs. Scott is blown away by the facility which commits 4,500 of its 11,000 square feet to the brewhouse alone. They have a canning line and room for expansion. During their opening weeks they were going through more than half a dozen barrels a night. "I've done 4 startups and I've never seen anything like this before," said Scott. You can't miss this stainless-steel siding building. They also have outdoor patio and deck seating.

Free WiFi. Facebook.com/Latitude42BrewingCo and Twitter @Latitude42Brew

Directions: From I-94 take Exit 78 for Portage Rd toward Kilgore Rd. Turn south on Portage Rd and continue 2.4 miles and the brewery is on the right.

Stumbling Distance: This is about 15 minutes from downtown Kalamazoo and the breweries there.

Cask-conditioned Ales

Cask comes from the Spanish word for "bark" like tree bark (cáscara). The little wooden barrel holds the beer in the same way bark surrounds a tree trunk I suppose. This is Old School beer storage (think of the original IPAs on their way to India to be drunk right out of the container) and the beer is unfiltered and unpasteurized.

Cask-conditioned ale goes through its secondary fermentation right in the cask or firkin from which it is poured. The yeast is still active and so still conditioning the brew. In many cases, the cask is right behind the bar, tilted on a shelf so the beer is delivered by gravity, without added carbon dioxide. Cask ale will only last a few days if air is going in to replace that draining beer. Some casks have CO2 breathers that allow a bit of gas in but not enough to cause more carbonation. By definition the cask-conditioning can be going on in any tank downstairs as long as it is a secondary fermentation, but the little wooden firkins behind the bar are a rare treat of authenticity.

ROCKFORD BREWING COMPANY

Founded: 2012
Brewmaster: Jeff Sheehan
Address: 12 East Bridge St. • Rockford, MI, 49341
Phone: 616-951-4677
Website: www.rockfordbrewing.com
Annual Production: 1,200 barrels
Number of Beers: 8 on tap plus 2 hard ciders

Staple Beers:
» Carriage House Ale
» Hoplust IPA
» Rogue River Brown
» Sheehan's Irish Stout

Rotating Beers:
» Ain't Jemima (Maple Sap Beer)
» Belgian Multigrain
» Blue Collar Porter
» Cernunnos (Strong Scotch Ale)
» Erbier Strawberry Weiss
» Mocha Porter
» Mocha Stout
» O'brien's Red
» Obsession Session Rye Pale Ale
» Rockford Country (French Farmhouse Ale)
» Sugaree Cyser
» Wheat Nipper
» White Pine Wheat

Most Popular Brew: Carriage House Ale

Brewmaster's Fave: Jeff is usually double-fisted with a Hoplust IPA and Rogue River Brown Ale. These Irish Handcuffs prevent him from holding his other two favorite beers, Carriage House Ale and Sheehan's Irish Stout.

Samples: Yes, $1.50 to $2.50 each, depending on the beer.

Tours? For groups with prior notice, or randomly if Jeff is around and not busy.

Best Time to Go: Open daily at 11am–11pm (9pm on Sundays). Free live music on Thursday nights and an acoustic jam on Sundays.

Where can you buy it? Only here and in growlers, and Carriage House Ale can be found on draft locally.

Got food? Yes, hot and cold subs, various dips (including smoked Great Lakes whitefish), and several simple snacks that go well with beer.

Special Offer: Ask for a free RBC sticker during your signature visit.

The Beer Buzz: Owners Jeff Sheehan, Seth Rivard, and Brien Dews thought it was an incredible coincidence that all three of them had the same idea to open a brewery in Rockford. They were all living in Rockford or had moved to the area before they even knew each other. Each of them found the community to be perfect: good schools, close to Grand Rapids yet great for outdoor activities including, fly-fishing. Brien is the city mayor and had spoken publicly about the need for a brewpub here and that's how Jeff found him. Seth already had planned to go after this niche as well. They decided it was best that they joined forces rather than compete with each other, so they are collaborating on this endeavor.

Jeff studied geology out in Idaho. Really what else was there to do out there? Answer: drink beer. So while the subject matter of rocks was certainly sexy, he was somehow torn away from the field when he took a job working for a local brewery. He moved back to Michigan where he worked at New Holland Brewing for three years before joining this project.

The interior shows a lot of pine wood, tongue and groove work, and a rustic maple bar. Poindexter's, a deli next door, supplies the food through a delivery counter. The upstairs has a Bavarian theme, with long common tables with benches, and views of the Rogue River and dam. An outdoor patio is set alongside the bike trail.

Free Wi-Fi. Facebook.com/RockfordBrewingCompany and Twitter @RockfordBrewing

Directions: From Grand Rapids follow US-131 north about 11 miles and take Exit 97 for 10 Mile Rd. Go east 2.1 miles and turn left on River St. Take the first right on Bridge St and the brewery is on the right.

Stumbling Distance: *Poindexter's Specialty Marketplace* (12 E Bridge St, 616-866-8680, poindextersmarket.com) is a neighboring deli with a Michigan beer cooler, local jams, subs/panini, and much more. The brewery is right on the White Pine Trail, a state trail making for a nice pilsgrimage to the brewery by bicycle.

GREENBUSH BREWING CO.

Founded: 2011
Brewmaster: Scott Sullivan
Address: 5885 Sawyer Road • Sawyer, MI 49125
Phone: 269-405-1076
Website: www.greenbushbrewing.com
Annual Production: 2,200 barrels
Number of Beers: 12 on tap, many more annually

Staple Beers:
» 1825 Belgian Golden Ale
» Anger Black IPA
» Closure
» Distorter Porter
» Dunegräs IPA
» Red Bud Copper Wheat Ale
» Retribution Belgian-Style Ale
» Traktor Kitschy Kream Ale

Rotating Beers:
» 400 Divine Rabbits Agave Nectar Wheat Ale
» Apathy Oatmeal Stout
» Brother Benjamin
» Delusion Imperial Cream Stout (Rye Whiskey Barrel-Aged)
» Doom Slayer (With Maple Sap)
» Isolé Belgian Dubbel
» Jadis Winter White Ale
» Mammoth Winter Weizenbock
» Memento Mori Oktoberfest Ale
» Mr. Hyde Sumatran Cream Stout
» Pain Imperial Milk Stout
» Penitence Rye Stout
» Rage Imperial Black IPA
» Sunspot Hefeweizen
» Ursus Old Winter Ale

Most Popular Brew: Dunegräs, Sunspot, or Anger Black IPA

Brewmaster's Fave: Delusion

Tours? Sure, just stand in the middle of the room and turn around. Larger groups should call ahead, but there is always someone there.

Samples: Taste anything you want. A flight of six 6-oz. beers is about $12.

Best Time to Go: Open daily at noon until 10PM (11PM on Friday–Saturday). Busiest 9–11PM on weekends

Where can you buy it? In house in growlers and 4-packs for high-gravity releases. In stores throughout Michigan, Northern Indiana, and Chicagoland.

Got food? Yes, emphasizing local ingredients and featuring such items as Texas-style brisket, a popular turkey-bacon melt, hummus, soups, and salads. Beer makes its way into the bread pudding and other items.

Special Offer: A free pint glass

The Beer Buzz: Brewer Scott had a previous life as a woodworker. But when he suffered an injury that required 10 weeks of recovery time, he became bored and started homebrewing. His fourth batch, a porter, was well received. "You could totally sell that," he was told. Thus an idea was born and a business plan soon followed. Brewing with a turkey fryer burner, Scott developed 35 recipes and handed out over 9,000 bottles of homebrew. So he already had a fan base before the doors even opened. Business has grown so fast, Greenbush operates an off-site 30-barrel production facility to keep up.

The old brick building, set right on the main drag in Sawyer, was first a Ford dealership and auto shop back in the 1920s, and before becoming a brewery it was a Laundromat and video rental. Inside you'll find corrugated metal on the walls and an open metal-beam ceiling. The bar is long and the many mugs of the mug club ($40 for life) hang above it. The rest of the bar space features tall tables while the brewing area is farther back in the building. Free Wi-Fi on site. On Facebook as GreenbushBrewingCo and Twitter @Greenbush_brew

Directions: From I-94 take Exit 12 and go east on Sawyer Rd less than a quarter mile, just across the railroad tracks, and the brewery is on the left (north) side of the street.

Stumbling Distance: *Journeyman Distillery* (journeymandistillery.com, 109 Generation Dr, Three Oaks, 269-820-2050), which collaborates with the brewery on Delusion, has scheduled tours, a tasting room, and an awesome little menu. *Fitzgerald's* (fitzsawyer.com, 269-426-3489) is just next door, serving highly recommended locally sourced food from an eclectic menu and a list of Michigan craft beers and wines. Nature lovers should not miss the glory of Lake Michigan at *Warren Dunes State Park* under 2 miles to the west.

MICHIGAN BEER CELLAR

Founded: 2010
Head Brewer: Ben Laninga
Address: 500 E Division St. • Sparta, MI 49345
Phone: 616-883-0777
Website: www.michiganbeercellar.com
Annual Production: about 400 barrels
Number of Beers: 15 on tap

Staple Beers:
» BLACK MAGIC RYPA
» BRIT'S BEST
» CELLAR LIGHT
» CELLAR PALE ALE
» HEAD KNOCKER
» IRISH RED
» IRISH STOUT (NITRO)
» MICHIGAN GOLDEN BLONDE
» OATMEAL STOUT
» SUMMER SUNRISE
» TOP SECRET AMERICAN IPA
» UNCLE KRUNKLE'S DUNKELWEIZEN

Rotating Beers:
» DOUBLE BLACK MAGIC IPA
» MOCA JAVA STOUT

Most Popular Brew: Uncle Krunkle's Dunkelweizen

Samples: Yes, 4 six-ounce samplers for about $7, or $1.75–$2 each.

Tours? By chance.

Best Time to Go: Live bands most Saturdays. Happy hour is Tuesday through Friday from 3–6PM, Sunday 6 to close, and Monday all day. Open Monday–Wednesday 3–midnight, Thursday–Saturday 11AM–2AM, Sunday noon–midnight.

Where can you buy it? Only here on tap or in growlers or bottles to go. Nine varieties are distributed around Western Michigan.

Got food? Yes, sandwiches/paninis/wraps, hot dogs, cheese and crackers, and salads.

Special Offer: Not participating.

The Beer Buzz: This brewery was founded in 2010 by Dan Humphrey (father of Nick Humphrey of The Hideout in Grand Rapids). When Dan decided to get out, he posted an ad on Craigslist, which is where Chuck Brown stumbled upon it. Chuck was working for a food-service provider for a university at the time, but his dream was to own a bar. Mission accomplished. He may keep many of the previous owner's recipes, but will bring in his own as well and pump up production a bit. Expect the brews listed here to change a bit.

There's a pool table, a jukebox, and a beer cooler by the door for some carry-out beers. The building is windowless, so it may seem a bit dark in there, or very bright when you come outside during the day. But the interior is nevertheless appealing, with lots of tables, a bit of lounge seating, and some space at the bar. The ceiling has some noise absorption so it doesn't get too loud in here when it's busy. In summer there is a little beer garden out back with metal tables and chairs in a sunny, fenced in cedar-chip area.

The distillery here makes over 60 liquors including habanero vodka, ouzo, brandy, whiskey, and vermouth and they also make their own wines.

Free Wi-Fi. Mug club.

Directions: From Grand Rapids head north on M-37, get off at 13 Mile Rd, and take it east through Sparta. The brewery is on the right side on the east side of town. From US-131 to the west of Sparta, take Exit 101 for 14 Mile Rd. Go west just about 1200 feet and turn left (south) on Edgerton Ave and drive to 13 Mile Rd. Go right (west) about 6 miles and the brewery is on the left just as you enter Sparta.

Stumbling Distance: If you are in the mood for Mexican, try *Downtown Trini's* (148 E Division St, 616-887-2500, downtowntrinis.com) Big Nasty Burrito and more. Closed Sundays though.

OLD BOYS' BREWHOUSE

Founded: 1997
Brewmaster: David Bayes
Address: 971 Savidge Street • Spring Lake, MI 49456
Phone: 616-850-9950
Website: www.oldboysbrewhouse.com
Annual Production: 400 barrels
Number of Beers: 10–12 on tap

Staple Beers:
» CONNOR'S KÖLSCH
» DOGTAIL IPA
» KENNEL KING IMPERIAL IPA
» OLD BOY'S BROWN ALE

Rotating Beers:
» ANNIVERSARY PALE ALE
» BAD RAP APPLE ALE
» BLUEBERRY WIT
» BRAD'S PUMPKIN LAGER
» IRASCIBLE BARREL-AGED WILD ALE
» KISS MY HAGGIS SCOTCH ALE
» MAGNUM BREAK STOUT
» NUTSACK CHOCOLATE/PEANUT STOUT
» ROVER'S WAGGIN RED
» TAIL CHASER PILS

Most Popular Brews: IPAs, but Kölsch in summer

Brewmaster's Fave: Anniversary Pale Ale, Belgians, and Tail Chaser Pils

Samples: Yes, 6 five-ounce beers for about $8.

Tours? Sure, but just call ahead to make an appointment.

Best Time to Go: Open 7 days a week from lunch with shorter hours in winter (check website for sure!). Hoppy Hour is 4–7PM weekdays (all day on Wednesday) and 12–3 on Saturday and Sunday. Live music is often scheduled Wednesday–Saturday. Many specials throughout the week.

Where can you buy it? Right here on tap, or bottles, growlers, 1/6 or half barrels to go.

Got food? Yes, a full bar and menu including burgers, sandwiches, salads, thin-crust pizzas made with brewer's malt. Many dishes use beer in the ingredients, such as a brown ale gravy or beer-battered cod. Many of the ingredients are from local purveyors.

Special Offer: Not participating.

The Beer Buzz: This brewpub is named after man's (and woman's) best friend. Not beer, the original best friend. Old Boy was a much-loved chocolate Labrador whose full name was Brutus "The Snake" Malone. The brewpub is filled with canine memorabilia and you can see the big dog bone from the road as you pass. The building sits along the boat channel which connects Spring Lake out to the Grand River as it flows into Lake Michigan, so it gets plenty of boat traffic stopping in for a cold one and some food. The outside deck overlooks the water, and a boardwalk passes by heading under the M-104 bridge to the south and north to a bike path that circles Spring Lake. Inside is a high-ceiling room busy with dog décor and offering numerous TVs for sports viewing, and a fireplace in a tall stone hearth/wall. There's banquet space here as well.

Brewer David went to high school with the owners and they used to make beer together. When he heard about the new business venture, he asked for a job, which they then offered him. He studied at Siebel in Chicago and put in some time at Great Baraboo Brewing outside Warren, MI. Previously there was a nineteenth century lumber mill on this site, but that was taken out to make room to build the brewery. The three-story tower of beer gets noticed from the highway but the grain tower is only for show. Boaters coming from Spring Lake or Lake Michigan can dock here. The brewery has hopes to expand the seating and storage capacity and add a gazebo in 2013.

Free Wi-Fi. Mug Club.

Directions: From US-31 take Exit 104 to merge into M-104/Savidge St. Drive 0.4 mile east and turn left to reach the frontage road of Savidge St. Turn left again (back the direction you came and drive right into the lot of the brewery.

Stumbling Distance: You're just a few minutes outside of Grand Haven where you can find *Odd Side Ales.*

VANDER MILL CIDER MILL & WINERY

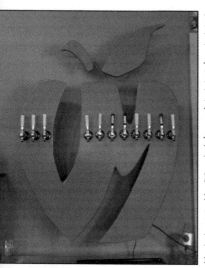

Founded: 2008 (2012 beer)
Brewer: Joel Brower / Paul Vander Heide
Address: 14921 Cleveland Street • Spring Lake, MI 49456
Phone: 616-842-4337
Website: www.vandermill.com
Annual Production: 20 barrels
Number of Beers: 2 on tap (plus 9 ciders)

Staple Beers:
» CHAPMAN'S GOLDEN STRONG ALE (WITH 10% CIDER)

Rotating Beers:
» BIERE DE GAARDE AMBER LAGER

Most Popular Brew: Chapman's Golden Strong Ale

Samples: Yes.

Tours? By appointment is best. Usually on the weekends.

Best Time to Go: Check the website for current hours. Summer open at 11AM. Fall earlier. In winter, they close a couple days a week.

Where can you buy it? Only right here.

Got food? Yes, menus for lunch and dinner with an emphasis on local ingredients, plus some awesome donuts, pies, and ice cream.

Special Offer: A free donut with the signature of your book.

The Beer Buzz: Vander Mill had already made a reputation for itself in hard ciders and wine, but in 2012 they added beer to their list of products. They wanted to be part of the Michigan Brewers Guild and they needed a brewer's license to do that. So why not add some beer? Now they can also take part in the great beer festivals organized by the Guild.

They have 9 ciders on draft all the time, changing with seasons. Cherry, blueberry, raspberry, and other seasonal juices make it into some of the blends. Recently, the winery added a restaurant, which is open for lunch and dinner. You can also get some pretty awesome donuts, pies, and ice cream here.

Free Wi-Fi. Facebook.com/VMCider

Directions: Halfway between I-96 and US-31 on M-104. From US-31 take Exit 104 for Savidge St/M-104. Continue 3.3 miles and Vander Mill is on the left (north) side of the road.

Stumbling Distance: Head back toward US-31 and you can find *Old Boys' Brewhouse* (in this book) just before the bridge on the frontage road on the right (north) side of M-104.

FETCH BREWING CO.

Opening: December 2013
Brewmaster: Dan Hain
Address: 100 West Colby Street • Whitehall, MI 49461
Website: www.fetchbrewing.com
Annual Production: 300 barrels
Number of Beers: 10–12 on tap; 20–30 brews per year

Staple Beers:
» FERAL IPA
» LAZY EYE RYE PA
» PITCHFORK WHEAT
» TREE STUMP COFFEE STOUT

Rotating Beers:
» SEASONALS AND VARIED IPAS AND PALE ALES

Brewmaster's Fave: Tree Stump Coffee Stout

Tours? Yes, any time or by appointment.

Samples: Yes, sample flights.

Best Time to Go: Open daily 11AM–10PM, until midnight on weekends. Watch for happy hour times.

Where can you buy it? Only here on tap and to go in growlers and kegs, with plans to distribute for draft accounts initially.

Got food? Yes, order here and a local restaurant will bring it in.

Special Offer: A $1 off your first pint of Fetch beer during your signature visit.

The Beer Buzz: Whitehall lies on the easterly end of the horn-shaped White Lake, which is in turn separated from Lake Michigan by a short ship channel. The brewery name has nothing to do with throwing a stick for your dog. Rather, it's a nautical term for a length of land or water that wind blows over. Owner/brewer Dan has a background in natural resource management and learned the term in a limnology class, and it has forever stuck with him.

Dan spent more than 20 years homebrewing and had always wanted to eventually go commercial. Neither he nor his wife Jen were completely happy with their jobs, and until very recently there wasn't much in terms of craft brewing in the area. So they took the plunge. Jen's background in finance is that all-important other half to the "open a brewery" equation.

The brewery occupies a 1912 state bank building with vaults, 20-foot ceilings, 18 to 20-inch thick walls, right downtown. Back in the early lumber days of Whitehall this was the first bank and today it is the first brewpub. Dan has plans to brew a wide variety of beers throughout the year as seasons come and go. There are a lot of fruit orchards in the area and he hopes to take advantage of that.

Directions: Just north of Muskegon on US-31, take the Business US-31 exit for Holton Whitehall Rd and head west into downtown Whitehall on Colby St. It's about 1.9 miles on Colby on the right.

Stumbling Distance: Remember *Dog 'n Suds Drive-In* (4454 Dowling St, Montague, 231-894-4991, montague.dog-n-suds.com)? Here's one that dates back to the 1960s and is family owned/operated. Check out the *White River Light Station Museum* (6199 Murray Rd, 231-894-8265, whiteriverlightstation.org) right along the land strip between White Lake and Lake Michigan.

ZONE 2

ARBOR BREWING COMPANY

Founded: 1995
Brewmaster: Mike Moroney
Address: 114 East Washington Street • Ann Arbor, MI 48104
Phone: 734-213-1393
Website: www.arborbrewing.com
Annual Production: 1,200 barrels
Number of Beers: 14 on tap, 30 styles per year

Staple Beers:
» Bollywood Blonde
» Michael Faricy's Irish Stout
» Sacred Cow IPA
» Ypsi Gypsi Pale Ale
» Also, barrel-aged sour ales: Divette, Brune Barrel Aged Brown, And Framboise

Rotating Beers:
» Anahata Chakra Honey Lavender Ale
» Bavarian Bliss Hefeweizen
» Buzz Saw American IPA
» Dark Side Black IPA
» Espresso Love Breakfast Stout
» Festival Saison
» Hop Town Brown
» Jackhammer Old Ale
» No Parking Pilsner
» Oktoberfest Bier
» Phat Abbot Belgian Dubbel
» Phat Abbot Belgian Tripel
» Red Snapper Roasted Pale Ale
» Strawberry Blonde
» Terminator Dopplebock
» Uskratch Maibock
» Wenceslas Winter Fuel

Most Popular Brew: Sacred Cow IPA

Brewmaster's Fave: Buzzsaw American Pale Ale

Tours? By chance or by appointment.

Samples: Yes, about $1 each.

Best Time to Go: Open 7 days a week from lunch to bar close. Happy hour runs all day Monday, weekdays 4–6PM, and Sunday 8PM–midnight.

Where can you buy it? Here on tap and to go in growlers and kegs, plus six-pack bottles and some 750ml bottled varieties. Also, visit their production brewery, Corner Brewery in Ypsilanti.

Got food? Yes, a full menu with appetizers, soups and salads, burgers and sandwiches, and dinner entrees. Check out the pierogi, beer-battered tempeh, and some grass-fed local beef options, plus a kids' menu and many vegetarian options. Latenight menu serves until midnight (11pm on Sunday). Beer-battered fish, including Lake Superior whitefish. Emphasis is on sourcing locally.

Special Offer: Your first beer at Happy Hour prices during your signature visit.

The Beer Buzz: Co-owner Matt Greff studied in Germany when he was in college, which is where he fell in love with beer. This was back before the microbrew renaissance here in the US. When he got back, the mass-market beers wouldn't do, and the German imports were often stale and old. So he found a book and started brewing European styles at home. After putting in some time at a "soul-crushing corporate job," he quit.

He and his wife/business partner Rene, raised some money and opened this brewpub. They were already living in Ann Arbor at the time, but the university town made a smart choice of location anyway: In the 90s, one had to be careful about demographics. Craft beer was still unfamiliar to most and they needed a clientele that was more adventuresome, open-minded, and had disposable income. Additionally, the building they chose to open in had, for the previous 40 years, been home to a series of failed restaurants—an unsettling thought to prospective investors. But as you can see, everything worked out. Matt calls his original customers "Pioneer drinkers of the craft beer scene."

Until recently, Logan Schaedig was head brewer. Logan got his start at Corner Brewery. "I read a beer can. Thought it'd be cool. Turns out it is." Brewer Mike started waiting tables at a local restaurant and volunteered out at Corner Brewery. He eventually got an assistant brewer position with Logan. When Logan left for India to help set up Matt and Rene's Bangalore Arbor Brewing there, Mike stepped up.

The bar room shows exposed brick, a copper-top bar and rail, and surrounding booths and tables. Picnic tables are outside on the sidewalk. The second bar area has darts and shuffleboard.

The brewery is committed to supporting local purveyors and getting regional ingredients whenever possible. ABC and Corner Brewery became Michigan's first solar-powered breweries in 2012. Rooftop panels may cut the establishment's gas usage by half and on-the-grid electricity reliance by up to 20%.

Free Wi-Fi. Mug Club. Facebook.com/arborbrewing and Twitter @ArborBrew

Directions: Take Business I-94 right into downtown from either side of Ann Arbor. Turn south on 4th Ave, drive one block, turn right on Washington St and it's halfway down the block on the left between 4th Ave and Main St.

Stumbling Distance: A superb beer bar in downtown Ann Arbor is *Ashley's* (338 S State St, 734-996-9191, ashleys.com), one of America's best says *Draft Magazine*. Do not miss a visit to *Zingerman's Deli* (422 Detroit St, 734-663-3354, zingermansdeli.com) either.

BIER CAMP

Founded: 2011
Brewmaster: Teo Watson-Albrandt
Address: 1643 S. State Street • Ann Arbor, MI 48104
Phone: 734-995-2437
Website: www.bier-camp.com
Annual Production: 50 barrels
Number of Beers: 2 on tap, always rotating

Beers:
» Brown Ale
» Pale Ale
» Rye PA
» Smoked Porter
» Vienna IPA
» Wheat Ale

Most Popular Brew: Vienna IPA

Brewmaster's Fave: Vienna IPA

Tours? No.

Samples: Yes.

Best Time to Go: Monday–Saturday 11AM–7PM.

Where can you buy it? Only here on site in growlers and half-growlers.

Got food? Pulled pork and smoked brisket sandwiches. Specialty meats.

Special Offer: Not participating.

The Beer Buzz: It's all about the meats here… except when it's about the beer. This popular specialty store added some small batches of house beer in 2013. These are available for take-out only—this is not a bar or brewpub. The specialty meats, including bacon, jerky, sausages, are all done in-house. Food can be eaten in a small lunch-counter deli area or outside on picnic tables in season, but many just come here for take-out. Plans may be in the works for more dining space in the future. These are small batches of beer so they tend to come and go regularly. Watch their Facebook page to see what's on tap and what's on deck.

Facebook.com/Biercamp

The Dry Line

Carrie A. Nation was an infamous hatchet-wielding Prohibitionist known for traveling through the Midwest to preach temperance and often to bust up a saloon or two along the way. There is a photo of Nation being taunted by students at a 1902 rally which is displayed on a historical placard downtown. Drinking and misbehavior had necessitated a police force in 1871.

Division Street, named for the line which divided the land of the two founders of Ann Arbor, became an unofficially agreed upon dividing line: saloons could only open to the west of it, away from where students could get it so easily (though they obviously just had to walk a bit farther). But tavern misbehavior continued until 1903 when the City of Ann Arbor made the Division Street rule a law. Even after Prohibition was reversed in 1933, the Dry Line stayed in effect. But support for temperance dwindled, as did the area east of the Dry Line as the city grew around it, until it was merely the neighborhood around campus. In 1969 a city vote erased all dry lines completely.

Directions: From I-94, take Exit 177 for State St and head north 1.4 miles and the place is on the right. You can also follow State St south from U of Michigan campus to get here.

Stumbling Distance: If you are looking for one of the largest craft beer selections in Ann Arbor (including build your own 6-pack), try *Stadium Market* (1423 E Stadium Blvd, 734-761-9650).

BLUE TRACTOR BBQ & BREWERY

Founded: 2008
Brewmaster: Tim Schmidt
Address: 207 East Washington Street • Ann Arbor, MI 48104
Phone: 734-222-4095
Website: www.bluetractor.net
Annual Production: 630 barrels
Number of Beers: 8 on tap

Staple Beers:
» BEARDED PIG PILSNER
» BUMPER CROP IPA
» PITMASTER PORTER
» SUDWORTH BOCK

Rotating Beers:
» BAD MOON RYEIZEN
» DEMONIC ALE
» OAK-AGED "HANDS OFF MY GOAT!" OATMEAL STOUT
» RUSTY TRACTOR AMERICAN AMBER
» STRAWBERRIES AND CREAM ALE

Most Popular Brew: Pitmaster Porter

Brewmaster's Fave: Anything hoppy

Tours? No.

Samples: Yes, 5–6 for about $6–$7.

Best Time to Go: Open daily from lunch until close. Happy hour offers half off draft beers Monday–Friday 3–6PM and 10PM–1AM.

Where can you buy it? Only here on tap and in growlers and in Mash next door. North Peak and Jolly Pumpkin bottled beers are also sold here.

Got food? Yes, serving lunch and dinner including BBQ ribs and other local meats cooked in a couple of smokers, plus sandwiches, burgers, sliders, salads, and more. Ask about the Cracklin' Chicken cooked on a PBR beer-can.

Special Offer: Not participating.

The Beer Buzz: In keeping with the farm-related name, the interior uses reclaimed barn wood for the walls. Restaurant tables are set back from a bar area that features serving tanks mounted behind it. The bartop has a long frosty strip along it to keep your pint cool. Photos of old tractors hang on the walls, as do a number of awards for the house brews.

Brewer Tim started homebrewing because he "liked the idea of brewing a better beer." He got in at Grizzly Peak as an assistant for a year, took Siebel classes, and then took over at Blue Tractor in 2008.

The brewery is part of the Northern United Brewing Co. along with Grizzly Peak and Jolly Pumpkin Café here in Ann Arbor.

Directions: Take Business I-94 right into downtown from either side of Ann Arbor. Turn south on 5th Ave, drive one block, turn right on Washington St and it's at the end of the block between 4th and 5th Avenues.

Stumbling Distance: *Mash*, right next door, is a bourbon, whisky, and beer bar associated with Blue Tractor and even connected through the basement. Blue Tractor beer is for sale here too. About 3.5 blocks away is *Jolly Pumpkin Café* (311 South Main St, 734-913-2730, jollypumpkin. com/annarbor), no longer brewing, but still serving, the specialized beers of Jolly Pumpkin (see Dexter, MI).

GRIZZLY PEAK BREWING COMPANY

Founded: 1995
Brewmaster: Duncan Williams
Address: 120 West Washington Street • Ann Arbor, MI 48104
Phone: 734-741-7325
Website: www.grizzlypeak.net
Annual Production: 1,650+ barrels (more than any other brewpub in MI)
Number of Beers: 8 on tap

Staple Beers:
» BEAR PAW PORTER
» COUNTY CORK'S IRISH STOUT
» GRIZZLY PEAK PALE ALE
» SHEERWATER IPA
» STEELHEAD RED
» VICTOR'S GOLD

Rotating Beers:
» BITTER TONY'S RYE BITTER
» EL HEFE
» EOB EXTRA PALE ALE
» HUMONGOUS IMPERIAL RED
» LITTLE GIANT LAGER
» OKTOBERFEST
» WHITE CHRISTMAS WHITE ALE
» VARIOUS OTHER SEASONALS, BELGIANS, LAGERS, BARREL-AGED BEERS
   AND MORE

Most Popular Brew: Steelhead Red

Brewmaster's Fave: Sheerwater IPA

Tours? Yes, by appointment. First Tuesday of each month is Brewers' Night in the Den. They present a special beer, hang out, and do tours.

Samples: Yes, 9 for about $12, depends on number of beers.

Best Time to Go: Open daily from lunch until close. Happy hour in both bars runs Monday–Friday 4–6PM. Also in the Den only every night 11PM–2AM.

Where can you buy it? Only here on tap or in growlers, 3-gallon keggies, and ¼ or ½ barrels. They also sell North Peak and Jolly Pumpkin beers in bottles to go.

Got food? Yes, aged steaks, fresh fish, BBQ Ribs, hearth-baked pizzas, sandwiches and burgers.

Special Offer: $1 off your first pint of Grizzly Peak beer during your signature visit.

The Beer Buzz: The largest brewpub in town, and the most productive beer-wise in the state of Michigan, Grizzly Peak occupies a brick building over 100 years old on the corner of Ashley and Washington. The pub has two halves: the half closest to the corner, The Den, is a standalone bar later in the evening when the other half closes down. For decades before the brewpub took it over, this building was home to The Old German Restaurant, and in 2006 the brewpub added The Den. Regulars have their preferred side; a younger crowd dominates the Den later in the evening, though both sides serve the same food and drinks. Sidewalk seating is another option.

Jon Carlson, the man behind Grizzly Peak Brewing, brought together brewers Ron Jeffries (founder of Jolly Pumpkin) and Mike Hall who partnered to create the original line up here. Brewer Duncan got the brewer's itch from his older brother who started drinking Guinness and Bass back in the 80s. Duncan appreciated better beer and picked up homebrewing in the mid-90s. He took a short course at Siebel in Chicago in 2001, got a job at CJ's for 8 months, then signed on as an assistant here from 2001–2003 under Ron. When Ron left to start Jolly Pumpkin at the end of 2003, Duncan took over. He brews on a seven-barrel system brought over from England and you can actually see it from the street through a large-paned window.

TVs pipe in some sports, not just football or basketball, but soccer too. Beers are also served from casks and hand-pulled beer engines.

The brewery is part of the Northern United Brewing Co. along with Blue Tractor and Jolly Pumpkin Café here in Ann Arbor.

Directions: From Business I-94 through downtown Ann Arbor, turn south on 1st Street and go one block to Washington St. Turn left (east) and Grizzly is one block farther on the corner of Ashley and Washington St.

Stumbling Distance: *The Blind Pig* (208 S 1st St, 734-996-8555, blindpigmusic.com) is in a building shared by several businesses. (A blind pig was a place selling illegal alcohol during Prohibition, sort of like a speakeasy.) The Pig itself is a good place for live music and some dancing in a very relaxed club (with an upstairs and downstairs). Have one of 10 Michigan craft beers on tap at *Bill's Beer Garden* (218 S. Ashley St, 734-369-8001, billsbeergarden.com), with outdoor seating all summer, and weekend-only hours in winter.

WOLVERINE STATE BREWING CO.

Founded: 2006
Brewmaster: Oliver Roberts
Address: 2019 West Stadium • Ann Arbor, MI 48103
Phone: 734-369-2990
Website: www.wolverinebeer.com
Annual Production: 1,500 barrels
Number of Beers: 9

Staple Beers:
» AMBER LAGER
» DARK LAGER
» PREMIUM LAGER

Rotating Beers:
» BIG HOUSE BROWN
» CLASSIC AMERICAN PILSNER
» DOUBLE-FISTED DOPPELBOCK
» GULO GULO INDIA PALE LAGER
» GULO NOIR (BLACK VERSION)
» GULO REVILO (RED VERSION)
» PLUS A BARREL-AGED BIG BEER EACH YEAR

Most Popular Brew: Gulo Gulo India Pale Lager

Brewmaster's Fave: Gulo Noir

Tours? By appointment.

Samples: Yes, $1.50 for five-ounce sampler.

Best Time to Go: Open Monday–Thursday 4PM–midnight, Friday–Saturday noon–1AM, and Sunday noon–10PM. Very busy during Wolverine games.

Where can you buy it? On tap here, available in growlers or kegs, and in six-pack bottles in major stores along the I-96 corridor, mostly in the surrounding counties. Four-pack bottles of limited releases. There's a good list of retailers on their website.

Got food? No, but you can bring your own in or order out.

Special Offer: Half off a growler fill during your signature visit.

The Beer Buzz: Watch for the big arrow on the roadside building, showing you the way to the brewery inside an industrial sort of building set back from the road. Just outside the door are some tables and chairs surrounded by a few Tiki torches which create a sort of beer garden/patio.

Brewer Oliver started homebrewing when he was 19 and carried on through college at Western Michigan University where he completed a couple years of undergrad. He transferred to Oregon State to study fermentation science and after four years of college, decided organic chemistry was not for him. He took off and traveled the West. Colorado and Arizona opened up the world of craft beer to him, which hadn't taken off yet in Michigan. He came back to Ann Arbor and ended up taking an assistant brewer gig at Grizzly Peak. One night he was bartending at a local restaurant when Wolverine State Brewing co-founder Trevor Thrall stopped in and ordered a Wolverine. Unfamiliar with the beer, Oliver dug around and found an unopened case in back. The beer was being contract brewed at that time. They got talking, Trevor said they needed a brewer, they made arrangements to meet co-founder Matt Roy at the awesome beer bar Ashley's, and soon after, the deal was sealed.

Wolverine State Brewing is "leading the Lager Revolution in craft beer," says partner (and Beer Wench!) E.T. Crowe. Lagers, of course, take a bit longer to brew. So while they could be banging out 4,000 barrels of ale each year, they chose to make lagers to establish a niche and because it's a challenge. The brewery is 1 mile from the Big House (U of Michigan's football stadium) For the brewers, the wolverine is more than just a university mascot; it is also representative of a ferocious work ethic.

If you want to have a private party or meeting for up to 70 people, rent the Gulo Room with its private bar.

Trivia note: Revilo is Oliver's name backwards.

Directions: This can be easy to miss from the street. From I-94, take Exit 172 and go east on I-94 Business/Jackson Ave. Turn right (south) on Maple Rd which becomes Stadium Blvd, and drive 0.7 mile. Pass Federal Blvd on your right, continue about 200 feet, and look for a sort of narrow alleyway on the right. If you miss it, take the next right before Comerica Bank. The brewery is behind the buildings right on Stadium Blvd.

Stumbling Distance: It's a couple miles away, but before you leave town check out *Bier Camp* (1643 S. State St, 734-995-2437, bier-camp.com) for artisan meats, sandwiches, and, of course, beer.

The Beer Wench

E.T. Crowe is a co-owner and the marketing manager of Wolverine State Brewing Co., but many know her as the Beer Wench. How did this all come about? She has a marketing background and spent some time selling real estate, but her college degree was in English and she is an accomplished writer. Brewery co-founder Trevor Thrall was her neighbor. One day Trevor told her: "I have a proposition for you…" They were looking to take Wolverine State beer beyond just the football season association. They went about interviewing successful and failed brewery owners to find out what they did (or didn't do) right. The nearly unanimous answer was professional marketing. Great beer is one thing; finding your following can be another. Trevor wanted her to take over all the marketing of the brewery and make things happen. But there was a problem: "I knew nothing. I was a wine drinker!" she says. We are not all born beer drinkers, but Crowe took on the mission. They had "beer school" sessions. She and the brewers sat down with sampler glasses and pretzels and started talking and tasting. They even included her in the brewing process, taking her through the world of beer from grain to glass. "I discovered my inner hophead," she admits. "I am the worst kind of advocate: I'm a convert."

She started the Beer Wench blog to chronicle her journey as a woman in beer, and her story—along with her catchy, snarky style—garnered quite a following. "We captured their imaginations using the blog. We spent zero dollars on advertising. Zero! It was all social media." Some might think Twitter and Facebook must be easy, but she knows quite well how much of a work burden it can become. "No way, you are constantly on it. It can be a bit of a ball and chain." But in the end, her efforts paid off. They spent their money where it was important: back in the brewhouse making quality beer. And she used her writing talents and social media savvy to make sure everyone knew about it. Thus, the Beer Wench was born. (Follow her at www.a2beerwench.com)

The Beer Wench is also the best-selling author of romance novels under the name Liz Crowe. Many are set in Ann Arbor, a few even involve breweries.

ROCHESTER MILLS BEER CO. (PRODUCTION BREWERY)

Founded: 2012
Head Brewer: Eric Briggeman
Address: 3275 Lapeer West Road • Auburn Hills, MI 48326
Phone: 248-377-3130
Website: www.beercos.com
Annual Production: up to 100,000 barrels
Number of Beers: 3 for now

Staple Beers:
» CORNERSTONE IPA
» MILKSHAKE STOUT
» ROCHESTER RED

Most Popular Brew: Cornerstone IPA

Brewmaster's Fave: Milkshake Stout year round, Oktoberfest seasonally

Tours? Yes, scheduled tours.

Samples: In the tap room after a tour.

Best Time to Go: Only during scheduled tours.

Where can you buy it? In stores in the surrounding counties for now, but also a bit of product in the tap room for carryout.

Got food? Popcorn in the tasting room.

Special Offer: A highly prized trinket.

The Beer Buzz: When it was time for Rochester Mills Brewing to consider a production facility, the empty lot next to their location in Rochester may have seemed ideal. But the easy access for shipping that the location on Lapeer West Road provided made more sense, and it was only five miles away. Previous to the brewery, the building was occupied by manufacturers of book-binding machinery, then auto seats, and fake rocks for golf courses and landscaping. The building is sectioned off, separating the 50-barrel brewhouse from the cold and dry storage.

Brewer Eric once worked at Big Buck's here in Auburn Hills, but that closed. He took on the head brewer position then at Rochester Mills Brewing in Rochester. When they were ready to open the big production facility, Eric moved over here. They are working hard to keep up with demand before they expand their distribution area.

The tap room walls are covered with breweriana from the private collection of Steve Summers. The short bar has various brewers' coasters under the glass bar top. There are six tap lines here plus some popcorn to munch on. Big windows look out over the grass behind the brewery and a resident groundhog makes an appearance, coming right up to the glass to see what's brewing inside.

Directions: From I-75 take Exit 81 which will lead you onto Lapeer Rd. Follow to the right (south) merging with I-75 Business. Continue south about 0.5 mile and watch for West Lapeer Rd. Turn right (west) and follow it 0.4 mile as it curves north. The brewery is on the left.

Stumbling Distance: Head over to Rochester for a meal at *Rochester Mills's* brewpub and a wider selection of their beers.

GRIFFIN CLAW BREWING CO.

Founded: 2013
Brewmaster: Dan Rogers
Address: 575 S. Eton Street • Birmingham, MI 48009
Phone: 248-712-4050
Website: www.griffinclawbrewingcompany.com
Annual Production: 13,000–15,000 barrels
Number of Beers: 16 on tap

Staple Beers:
» EL ROJO AMBER ALE
» GRAND TRUNK PILSNER
» GRIND LINE PALE ALE
» NORM'S RAGGEDY ASS IPA

Rotating Beers:
» PLATINUM BLONDE LAGER
» SCREAMING PUMPKIN ALE

Most Popular Brew: Norm's Raggedy Ass IPA

Brewmaster's Fave: Grand Trunk Pilsner

Tours? Yes, by appointment.

Samples: Yes, flights of four 5-oz. beers.

Best Time to Go: Closed Mondays. Open at 2PM Tuesday–Friday, Saturday noon to midnight, Sunday noon to 10PM.

Where can you buy it? On site, in 16-oz. cans at local grocery stores, and on tap in local restaurants.

Got food? Yes, open for lunch and dinner with a basic burger/bar food menu that pairs well with the beers.

Special Offer: Griffin Claw Brewing will offer a free beer glass or t-shirt to book owners who come in to have Dan sign their copy of this book. Offer valid while supplies last.

The Beer Buzz: If you are from the area, this new brewery might seem rather familiar. Brewer Dan Rogers already has quite a reputation for his beer and until the opening of Griffin Claw, he was brewing down the street at Big Rock Chophouse.

Dan started out as a chef at the Holy Cow Casino in Las Vegas in the 1990s. He got into brewing and spent seven years at Holy Cow's Brewery (now Big Dog's Brewing Co.). When he came back to his home state of Michigan, he spent five years with now defunct Michigan Brewing Co. and started winning awards. He took the brewmaster job at Big Rock Chophouse, producing four signature beers for the restaurant. Then came the time to step it up. In 2013 they opened this custom-built, state-of-the-art facility. A 12,000-square-foot production brewery means a wider beer audience for Dan as they now distribute. Inside is a tap room, and outside there's a beer garden (as well as a 1937 Chevy beer truck loaded with barrels). Dan's first awards were back in 1998, including a Gold at the World Beer Championships for his Scotch Ale. He gets more each year. He took three medals at World Expo of Beer, including Best in Show for Red Rock Flanders Red Ale in 2009 (and again in 2011). Norm's Raggedy Ass IPA has also seen medals, including a prestigious Gold Medal at the World Beer Cup in 2010–2011, as have many others too numerous to list here.

This neighborhood is known as the Rail District, and Big Rock Chophouse occupies the former Birmingham Grand Trunk and Western Railroad Depot built back in 1931.

Facebook.com/GriffinClawBrewingCompany

Directions: From I-75 heading north out of Detroit, take Exit 65 to go west on 14 Mile Rd. Drive 3.9 miles west on 14 Mile Rd and turn right (north) on Melton Rd. After 0.4 mile, take the 3rd right on Eton St.

Stumbling Distance: *Big Rock Chophouse* (245 S Eton St Birmingham, 248-647-7774, bigrockchophouse.com), Dan's former brewing location, is still a great place for a meal, plus they still serve his beers. They are also home to *Got Rocks Diamond Crown Cigar Lounge,* a cigar bar with loads of whiskeys, wines, and cognacs, as well as the food from Big Rock.

BREWERY BECKER

Planned: December 2013
Brewmaster: Matt Becker
Address: 500 West Main Street • Brighton, MI 48116
Website: www.brewerybecker.com
Annual Production: Up to 1,000 barrels
Number of Beers: 10 on tap, 25 styles annually

Staple Beers:
» NORTH GERMAN WHEAT
» VARGDRICKA (SMOKED JUNIPER MASHED FARMHOUSE ALE)
» VICTORIAN EXPORT STOUT

Most Popular Brew: Too soon to tell!

Brewmaster's Fave: Vargdricka

Tours? Yes, just ask.

Samples: Yes, beer flights.

Best Time to Go: Check website for current hours. Summer opens the beer garden.

Where can you buy it? Here on tap and to go in growlers, kegs, and bottles.

Got food? Limited food, mostly snacks and tapas.

Special Offer: Not participating.

The Beer Buzz: This planned craft brewery will occupy an historic 1871 hotel in downtown Brighton. Brewer Matt has been brewing since 1991. The atmosphere aims to be laid-back and similar to a coffee house. The name remained up in the air at the time of printing. Check the website for news of its opening.

Directions: From I-96 take Exit 147 and follow Spencer Rd west into town. Then turn right on Main St and follow it 0.7 mile. The brewery is on the right.

Stumbling Distance: A great deli and restaurant to check out in town is *The Wooden Spoon* (675 W Grand River Ave, 810-588-4386, woodenspoonmarket.com) They also have some craft beers.

CHELSEA ALEHOUSE BREWERY

Founded: December 2012
Brewmaster: Chris Martinson
Address: 420 North Main, Suite 100 • Chelsea, MI 48118
Phone: 734-475-2337
Website: www.chelseaalehouse.com
Annual Production: 500 barrels
Number of Beers: 10 on tap

Staple Beers:
» Bog Trail Brown Ale
» 402 E Porter
» Haywagon Red
» Hollier 8 Double Black Ale
» Irontown IPA
» Roosevelt Rye PA
» Silo White Ale
» Stove Pipe Stout
» Waterloo Wheat
» Yellowdog IPA

Rotating Beers:
» Morchella Rye Porter
» Winter Wind Oatmeal Stout

Most Popular Brew: Roosevelt Rye Pale Ale or Silo White Ale

Brewmaster's Fave: Bog Trail Brown or Morchella Rye Porter

Tours? Yes, by appointment.

Samples: Yes, a flight of 5 four-ounce samplers is about $6.75.

Best Time to Go: Closed on Mondays. Open 3–11pm Tuesday–Thursday, 11:30am–midnight Friday–Saturday, and noon–8pm Sunday. Check website for seasonal hours.

Where can you buy it? Here on tap and in growlers, and some draft accounts nearby.

Got food? Yes, a variety of salads and sandwiches, snacks, and appetizers.

Special Offer: $1 off your first pint during your signature visit.

Directions: From I-94 take Exit 159 and head north on M-52/Main St for 1.7 miles and the brewery is on the right (by the clocktower).

The Beer Buzz: While Bell's is often credited as being the first microbrewery in Michigan in the modern age, Chelsea was actually the first community to host one: Real Ale Company was a flash in the pan founded in 1982. The city hasn't had a brewery since… until now. Set in a repurposed factory and warehouse building near the historical clock tower right downtown near the railroad tracks, this brewery was founded by owner/brewer Chris Martinson. His background is in biotech but he got his start in craft beer in college. He spent a lot of time homebrewing, mainly keeping his friends well stocked, before getting serious about bringing beer to Chelsea. Three years later, the dream came true.

It's an industrial sort of place but comfortable. The dining space and bar area are separated from each other by a glass wall, reclaimed from another old local building. The bar top is made from old school bleachers.

Board games are on hand and live music provides additional entertainment. Family friendly, but after around 9PM the expectation is for an adult atmosphere.

Free Wi-Fi. Mug Club. Facebook.com/ChelseaAlehouse

Stumbling Distance: Take a free one-hour tour of the *Jiffy Mix Plant* (201 W. North St, 800-727-2460, jiffymix.com) right across the street. *Purple Rose Theatre* (137 Park St, 734-433-7782, purplerosetheatre.org), founded by Chelsea-native Jeff Daniels, is right downtown.

BLACK LOTUS BREWING COMPANY

Founded: 2006
Brewmaster: Mark Harper
Address: 1 East 14 Mile Road • Clawson, MI 48017
Phone: 248-577-1878
Website: www.blacklotusbrewery.com
Number of Beers: 7 to 10 on tap; 30+ seasonals

Staple Beers:
» BLACK BOTTOM OATMEAL STOUT
» DETROIT HIP HOPS APA
» FUNKIN' A APRICOT WHEAT
» PEOPLE MOVER PILSNER
» RED TAO AMBER
» WORLD WIDE WHEAT

Rotating Beers:
» BIRTHDAY BEER (WITH BIRTHDAY CAKE, WHEAT, AND FROSTING)
» CLAW-TOWN VINTAGE BROWN
» COLOMBIAN SKI TEAM COFFEE STOUT
» DARK AND LOVELY BLACK IPA
» DTF TRIPEL
» ESB
» FO CHOCOLATE PORTER
» THE GIFT (ABBEY-STYLE STRONG ALE)
» HONEY HEMP AND OATS
» LOTISTA NEGRA (DARK MEXICAN LAGER)
» MONSTER MASH PUMPKIN ALE
» OKTOBERFEST
» THE SHOCKER IMPERIAL RED
» SWAMI'S PEPPERPALOOZA CREAM ALE
» THAI PEPPER PORTER

Most Popular Brew: Detroit Hip Hops

Tours? Yes, by appointment.

Samples: Yes, 4 four-ounce samplers for about $4.50 plus $1 for each additional.

Best Time to Go: Open daily from noon–1AM (2AM on weekends). Happy hour is 4–6PM Monday–Friday, and again for the last two hours of the night. For lunch check out the Burger and a Pint special. Live music 3–4 nights per week.

Where can you buy it? Only here on tap and to go in growlers.

Got food? Yes, a full menu including sandwiches/wraps, soups and salads, and housemade desserts. Interesting choices include pulled pork, wasabi salmon wraps, beer-battered pickle spears, turkey chili with beer. Michigan wines and meads are also served. There's a kids' menu and a latenight menu after 11PM.

Special Offer: Not participating.

The Beer Buzz: Back in 2006, founders Mark Harper, Michael Allan and his wife Jodi (Mark's sister) were looking for more creative outlets than their careers had to offer. Mark was a psychologist for Detroit Public Schools and Michael did financial planning. A brewpub surely offered some satisfaction for the soul but they were adamant about creating something of high quality and shunned the low quality of the mass produced brews. They managed to strike a balance between making great beer and keeping it affordable for the locals. "Life is too short to drink cheap beer, but not cheaper good beer."

While in college, Brewer Mark took a road trip west and fell in love with the craft beer scene. He came home determined to homebrew. All the recipes were his concepts. Mark is also a musician and plays with the band Zap Toro, which performs here from time to time.

The building, with its big shop windows, used to be a carpet showroom and storage. Copper-topped tables fill the room, and two big projection screens lie in wait for sports on request. Mark personally collected all the fieldstones you see in the concrete bar. Black Lotus brings in a varied mix of families, beer snobs, live music fans, and a good lunch crowd. Adjoining the brewpub is *The Drive In* where you can enjoy over 40 famous courses on 3 golf simulators while drinking Black Lotus beer. There's sidewalk seating in season. Free Wi-Fi. Mug club.

Directions: Take I-75 to Exit 65A or 65B, and get off on 14 Mile Rd. Head west 1.6 miles and the brewery is on the right.

Stumbling Distance: *Off the Wagon Market* (1500 N Crooks Rd, 248-435-4464) is perhaps the closest liquor store in town with a good selection of craft beers, including selections for a build your own six-pack.

KUHNHENN BREWING CO.
PRODUCTION BREWERY

Opened: coming in early 2014
Brewmaster: Bret and Eric Kuhnhenn
Address: 36000 Groesbeck Highway • Clinton Township, MI 48035
Website: www.kbrewery.com
Annual Production: 20,000 barrels
Number of Beers: up to 24 on tap, 50–60 brews per year

Staple Beers:
» AMERICAN IPA
» CLASSIC AMERICAN
» DRIPA (DOUBLE RICE IPA)
» THE FLUFFER (SESSION IPA)
» IMPERIAL CREME BRULE JAVA STOUT
» KUHNHENN FESTBIER
» KUHNIEWEIZEN
» LOONIE KUHNIE PALE ALE
» PENETRATION PORTER
» SIMCOE SILLY

Rotating Beers:
» ALDEBARAN (BELGIAN IPA)
» ANNELIESE AMBER
» BOHEMIAN PILS
» CONUNDRUM (ENGLISH DARK MILD)
» DARK HEATHEN TRIPLE BOCK
» EXPORT STOUT
» 4TH DEMENTIA OLDE ALE
» KUHNIE WIT
» SULLY'S KOLSCH
» WHITE DEVIL (IMPERIAL BELGIAN WIT)
» WINTER WONDER LAGER

Most Popular Brew: Loonie Kuhnie Pale Ale

Brewmaster's Fave: Both brewers say Loonie Kuhnie Pale Ale. It's what started it all for them and so it is near and dear to their hearts.

Tours? Yes, check website and make an appointment for large groups. Otherwise it is quite random.

Samples: Yes, sampler flights.

Best Time to Go: Check the website for current hours.

Where can you buy it? Here on tap and to go in growlers and bottles. All over Michigan, and in Manhattan, Ontario, and even a wee bit in The Netherlands.

Got food? Yes, it will be just a bit more substantial than the Warren menu.

Special Offer: A free piece of logo glassware with the signature of your book.

The Beer Buzz: You can't argue with popularity. Since their beginnings in their father's former hardware store, the Kuhnhenn Brothers have been gaining fans from near and far. Their original brewery in nearby Warren is still brewing, but since the opening of this 36,000 square-foot production brewery in a former home and garden center building, that first location is focusing more on the smaller batches and barrel aging. The 38-barrel brewhouse here is going to have an initial capacity of 20,000 barrels in their first year. The brewers anticipate it will keep going up from there. Like in Warren, this brewery also has a taproom, about 5,000 square feet.

Directions: From I-696 just north of Detroit, take Exit 26 toward M-97. Head north on M-97 about 5.4 miles and the brewery will be on the right. This is about 20 minutes from their original location.

Stumbling Distance: You are a short drive from the original *Kuhnhenn Brewery* in Warren. (It's in the book here).

GREAT BARABOO BREWING COMPANY

Founded: 1995
Head Brewer: Jeremy Alpier
Address: 35905 Utica Road • Clinton Township, MI 48035
Phone: 586-792-7397
Website: www.greatbaraboo.com
Annual Production: 500 barrels
Number of Beers: 5 on tap

Beers:
» BOSTON BLACKSTONE PORTER
» HOPPY HEARTLAND PALE ALE
» IPA
» KINGS PEAK CARABOO WHEAT
» SHARK TOOTH BAY GOLDEN ALE
» SNAKE EYE CANYON RED ALE

Most Popular Brew: Hoppy Heartland Pale Ale

Brewmaster's Fave: IPA

Tours? By appointment.

Samples: Yes, six 5-oz. samples for about $6.

Best Time to Go: Open Monday–Saturday 11AM–2AM, Sunday noon–2AM. Kitchen closes at 1AM (Sunday at midnight). Live music on Fridays, DJs on Sundays, karaoke on Wednesdays.

Where can you buy it? Here on tap or to go in growlers.

Got food? Yes, a full menu of appetizers, soups and salads, burgers, sandwiches, entrees, and even a kids' menu.

Special Offer: Not participating.

The Beer Buzz: On the corner of Moravian and Utica, this long standing restaurant/brewery has a solid reputation for its brews. Inside you'll find a u-shaped bar and a sports bar atmosphere.

You can see the copper brew system in the front corner of the building. The windows of the place are covered, so visits during daylight hours may

still seem like an evening out until you head for the parking lot. There's a covered outdoor patio with plastic tarps to protect you when rain or cold comes calling. Free Wi-Fi. Mug Club.

Directions: From I-94, take Exit 236 for 16 Mile Rd/Metropolitan Parkway. Drive 6 miles west and head south on Utica Rd about 0.4 mile. (You need to make a U-turn to come back and turn right (south) on Utica.)

Stumbling Distance: Check out the three breweries in Warren just south of here.

ATWATER BREWERY

Founded: 1997/2005
Brewmaster: Hazen Schumacher
Address: 237 Joseph Campau Street • Detroit, MI 48207
Phone: 313-877-9205
Website: www.atwaterbeer.com
Annual Production: 12,500 barrels
Number of Beers: 8 plus seasonals and single batch brews

Staple Beers:
» ATWATER D-LIGHT
» ATWATER LAGER (HELLES)
» DECADENT DARK CHOCOLATE ALE
» DETROIT PALE ALE
» DIRTY BLONDE
» GRAND CIRCUS IPA
» PURPLE GANG PILSNER
» VANILLA JAVA PORTER
» VOODOO VATOR DOPPELBOCK

Rotating Beers:
» BLOKTOBER
» BLUEBERRY COBBLER
» CHERRY STOUT
» CONNIPTION FIT DOUBLE IPA
» MAI BOCK
» SHAMAN'S PORTER
» SUMMER TIME ALE
» TEUFEL BOCK (WEIZEN DOPPLEBOCK)
» TRAVERSE CITY CHERRY WHEAT
» UBER URSA IMPERIAL PILS
» VJ BLACK IMPERIAL STOUT
» WINTER BOCK

Most Popular Brew: Dirty Blonde and Vanilla Java Porter

Brewmaster's Fave: Purple Gang Pils or Voodoo Vader

Tours? Scheduled at 7PM each evening except Monday, for a fee.

Samples: Yes, $1 each.

Best Time to Go: Closed on Mondays. Tuesday–Friday 4–11PM, Saturday 2–11PM, Sunday 4–10PM.

Where can you buy it? In growlers and some bottles on site, otherwise in 6-pack bottles throughout Michigan and in 7 states from Wisconsin to North Carolina. Dirty Blonde, Grand Circus, and Atwater Lager are also sold in 12-pack cans.

Got food? No.

Special Offer: Not participating.

The Beer Buzz: This reputable downtown Detroit brewery occupies a 1919 brick building that was originally home to an auto parts manufacturer here in the Rivertown Warehouse District. In 1996 it was renovated to become the fast growing Atwater Block Brewery. The original brew system was set up by a German brewery consultant and a team from Hoefner Brewing Company. They brewed a few batches and left it in the hands of Atwater's new brewer Hazen Schumacher. But the business partners didn't get along and the place closed. It reopened briefly as Stoney Creek Brewery, before new owners Mike Rieth and Howard Hampton bought it and re-opened the brewery as Atwater in 2005. Initially there was a restaurant inside, but they dropped that to focus on what was important: beer. They also deleted the "Block" from their previous name, Atwater Block Brewery. In 2012 Atwater doubled capacity with an internal expansion.

Brewer Hazen got his start homebrewing in Kalamazoo. One day he was invited to a birthday party of craft beer pioneer Larry Bell. He brought homebrew as a gift and soon had himself a job at Bell's Brewery where he spent a couple years before Atwater nabbed him. He leans toward lagers though you can see some ales in the line-up. The Bier Stube is a casual place to hang out for a pint or pick up a growler.

Directions: From the end of Woodward Avenue (MI-1) in downtown Detroit, turn left (east) on Jefferson Avenue. Go 1.5 miles and turn right (south) on Joseph Campau Avenue and the brewery is two blocks down on the right at the corner of Wight Street.

Stumbling Distance: Just down the street, eat at *Andrews on the Corner* (201 Joseph Campau St, 313-259-8325, andrewsonthecorner.com), which serves great fresh food including lake perch, steaks, and much more. They run shuttles to pro sporting events. The brewery is also just two blocks from the *Detroit Riverwalk* along the St Clair River.

BATCH BREWING CO.

Opened: January 2014
Head Brewer: Stephen Roginson
Address: 1444 East Michigan Avenue • Detroit, MI 48216
Website: www.BatchBrewingCompany.com
Annual Production: up to 500 barrels
Number of Beers: 8 on tap

Staple Beers:
» AMERICAN GOLDEN ALE
» BROWN CHICKEN BROWN ALE
» SON OF A BATCH IPA

Rotating Beers:
» THE ETHERIALE BELGIAN STRONG ALE
» WHEATED KOLSCH
» ...AND MANY MORE

Tours? Yes, but it pretty much can be done from your spot at the bar.

Samples: Yes.

Best Time to Go: Watch the website for changes in hours. Open Wednesday–Sunday 4PM–midnight.

Where can you buy it? Only here on tap and to go in growlers.

Got food? No, but the local food truck community will be helping out. Also, they are food-friendly: bring your own.

Special Offer: A free sticker during your signature visit.

The Beer Buzz: This is Detroit's very first nanobrewery. Brewer/owner Stephen Roginson's idea made him the 2013 winner of the Hatch Detroit Business Incubator Contest, a competition that encourages the development of brick and mortar businesses in Detroit and awards money for great startup ideas.

Brewer Stephen started in homebrewing back in the mid-90s. He moved from the suburbs into Detroit proper back in 2010. He is very active in the community and wants to contribute to Detroit's gradual reinvention of itself. One of his ideas is to promote the Motor City as more of a Beer City. In addition to its own aspirations to make great beer, Batch Brewing will also operate as a brewery incubator, to help a couple of startups each year create business plans and get some beers to market before settling into brick and mortar locations of their own. Also, the taproom features a "Feelgood Tap." Each month a percentage of the sales of that particular brew will go to a different local charity.

In addition to the 1,200 square foot taproom, there is a patio out front and a large second-story beer garden. Located in Corktown, Detroit's oldest neighborhood, the brewery occupies a century-old building that got its start as a bar. When Prohibition forced it to become an auto dealership, the bar moved into the basement and became a speakeasy. The original wood bar still exists and they hope to one day refinish it and open a tasting room where the speakeasy was. Right next door is the footprint of the old Tiger Stadium. Can you imagine Ty Cobb perhaps bellying up to that bar back in the day?

Facebook.com/BatchBrewingCompany

Directions: From Woodward Avenue right into downtown Detroit, turn right (west) on Michigan Ave. Drive 1 mile west and the brewery is on the right.

Stumbling Distance: For seriously awesome barbecue, go to *Slows Bar BQ* (2138 Michigan Ave, 313-962-9828, slowsbarbq.com). Next door to that is *The Sugar House* (313-962-0123, sugarhousedetroit.com) serving craft cocktails and craft beers. *Saint CeCe's* (1426 Bagley Ave, 313-962-2121, stceces.com) has great farm-to-table food. *McShane's Irish Pub* (313-961-1960, mcshanespub.com) right next door to Batch, looks like a sports bar but has one of the greatest whiskey selections in town.

COURTESY OF BATCH BREWING

DETROIT BEER CO.

Founded: 2003
Brewmaster: Nate Rykse
Address: 1529 Broadway Street • Detroit, MI 48226
Phone: 313-962-1529
Website: www.detroitbeerco.com
Annual Production: 800 barrels
Number of Beers: 6–9 on tap, 20+ styles per year

Staple Beers:
» Broadway Light
» The Detroit Dwarf Alt
» Grand River Red
» Local 1529 IPA
» People Mover Porter

Rotating Beers:
» Belgian Dubbel
» Cass Ave. Amber Ale
» Doppelbock
» Etoile Noire
» Grand Slam Belgian Tripel
» Hefeweizen
» Hop Rod Red
» Imperial Stout
» Milkshake Stout
» New Kids On The Bock
» Oktoberfest
» Pumpkin Porter
» Steam Tunnel Stout
» Sumatra Coffee Stout
» Tetris Baltic Porter
» Triple Crown Pilsner
» Willie's Kilt Scotch Ale
» Yukon Cornelius' Holiday Ale

Most Popular Brew: Local 1529 IPA

Brewmaster's Fave: Detroit Dwarf Alt

Tours? Yes, by appointment.

Samples: Yes, 5 on a platter shaped like a baseball bat.

Best Time to Go: Open daily at 11AM (noon on Sunday). Happy hour run Monday–Friday from 4–6PM.

Where can you buy it? Only here on tap and in growlers.

Got food? Yes, mostly American fare including appetizers, salads, brick-oven pizzas, pastas, several entrees and sandwiches, plus a kids' menu.

Special Offer: Not participating.

The Beer Buzz: If you are in Detroit for football or baseball, this is the closest brewpub to either Comerica Park and Ford Field. Housed in the refurbished Hartz Building, a 1902 medical supply company, they first started pouring beer in September 2003. The bar is up front with serving tanks standing right behind it. Some large historic photos decorate the walls. Several large TVs pipe in sports in case you didn't get Tigers or Lions tickets. More seating is in back and upstairs, and there are spaces that can be reserved for special events.

Originally from Grand Haven, Michigan, Nate got his degree in biology and then attended UC-Davis for brewing studies. After completing the program he began his professional brewing career in Alaska, working at a couple breweries before returning to Michigan in 2011. He took a job as an assistant brewer here and at sister Royal Oak Brewery, shuttling back and forth between the two. When previous brewer Kevin Rodger left, Nate stepped up to head brewer at this location.

Free WiFi. On Facebook and Twitter @DetroitBrewing

Directions: Heading south on Woodward Avenue into downtown, turn left onto Witherell Street and then take the first right onto Broadway Street.

Stumbling Distance: *Grand Trunk Pub* is spectacular (612 Woodward Ave, 313-961-3043, grandtrunkpub.com). Catch a Tigers ballgame over at *Comerica Park* (2100 Woodward Ave, tigers.com). For some seriously awesome barbecue, you must head a bit west to *Slows Bar BQ* (2138 Michigan Ave, 313-962-9828, slowsbarbq.com).

MOTOR CITY BREWING WORKS

Founded: 1994
Address: 470 West Canfield Street • Detroit, MI 48201
Phone: 313-832-2700
Website: www.motorcitybeer.com
Annual Production: 2,500 barrels
Number of Beers: 7 on tap

Staple Beers:
» Ghettoblaster (English-Style Mild)
» Honey Porter
» Motor City Pale Ale
» Motown Bohemian Lager
» Nut Brown Ale

Rotating Beers:
» 120W-60 Ibu IPA
» 90W-40 Ibu Double Apa
» Corktown Stout
» Greenfield Village Farm House Ale
» Greenfield Village Menlo Light Beer
» Greenfield Village Steam Station Beer
» Motor City Ale
» Old Gear Oil (Barrel-Aged American Sour Brown Ale)
» Oktoberfest
» Pumpkin Ale
» Summer Brew
» ...plus many one-barrel test batches

Most Popular Brew: Ghettoblaster

Tours? Yes, but by prior appointment only.

Samples: Yes, 5 five-ounce samplers (plus one seasonal sampler) for $10.

Best Time to Go: Open daily from lunch to midnight (1AM Friday–Saturday) with the kitchen open until nearly closing time.

Where can you buy it? Here on tap and in growlers and the occasional 22-oz. bottles, and in 6-pack bottles in the Detroit-Ann Arbor area and a bit of the U.P.

Got food? Yes, brick-oven pizzas and chili, salads, cheese plates, artichoke and hot crab dips.

Special Offer: Not participating.

The Beer Buzz: You may have heard of Detroit Mackinaw Brewing, but that's a thing of the past. This was the place but now it's Motor City. Situated at the back of a parking lot not far from Wayne University, the property consists of a production-style facility to the left abutting a tap house on the right. Inside is a concrete bar and old diner tables. Tilework along the walls was done by a local artist and a skylight over the bar keeps the interior bright. A rooftop terrace overlooks the bar below through some windows, and the front of building opens up for fresh air. Right out the back door is Detroit's first Green Alleyway Project.

Founded by John Linnardos and co-owned by Dan Scarcella the brewery also makes their own wines, a hard cider, and some sodas sweetened with Michigan beet sugar.

The Greenfield series of beers come in Groslch-style bottles. The brew system is made from repurposed dairy equipment. In 2012 the brewers added a new bottling line. Watch the website or Facebook for special small-batch releases. Despite the large Canfield parking lot, only 6 spots are the brewery's. Otherwise there are meters on the street or a $5 parking fee in the lot. It is policed carefully.

Directions: From I-75 through downtown Detroit, take M-10 north for 1.7 miles, and get of on Exit 3. Turn right (east) on Forest Ave and then the second right (south) on 3rd St. Go 0.1 mile and turn left (east) on Canfield. The brewery is at the backside of the parking lot on the left on the corner of 2nd and Canfield.

Stumbling Distance: Right across the parking lot and Canfield Street is *Traffic Jam and Snug*, an eclectic brewpub, restaurant, and cheesemaker.

TRAFFIC JAM & SNUG

Founded: 1992 (1965)
Head Brewer: Chris Reilly
Address: 511 West Canfield Street • Detroit, MI 48201
Phone: 313-831-9470
Website: www.trafficjamdetroit.com
Annual Production: 300 barrels
Number of Beers: 5 on tap

Staple Beers:
» IPA
» PILSNER

Rotating Beers:
» BELGIAN WIT
» COFFEE STOUT
» GRAND CRU
» HEFEWEIZEN
» IMPERIAL WIT
» MAIBOCK
» OATMEAL STOUT
» OKTOBERFEST

Most Popular Brew: Pilsner

Brewmaster's Fave: Grand Cru

Tours? By appointment.

Samples: Yes, sampler flights of 3, 4 or 5 eight-ounce beers for about $7.50, $10 and $12.50 ($2.50 each).

Best Time to Go: Open daily at 11AM. Hoppy hour is 3–7PM weekdays.

Where can you buy it? Only here on tap and in growlers or kegs to go.

Got food? Yes, a full eclectic menu including meatloaf, crab cakes, Ethiopian dishes, deep-fried smelt, beer-battered fish and chips, a lentil burger, soups and salads, cheese platter, deep-fried pickle spears, house ice cream, and many desserts. Onsite bakery and creamery.

Special Offer: $1 off your first pint of house beer during your signature visit.

The Beer Buzz: Walk in and it's like being in some sort of museum. This restaurant was founded in 1965 and over the years has garnered an eccentric but positive reputation. Not only is the food varied and eclectic, but cheese and baked goods are being made in-house as is, of course, beer. This is Michigan's very first brewpub, founded in 1992, after the long legal struggle to make that sort of thing possible.

Brewer Chris was doing some construction work for Scott Lowell, the owner, when a brewing job opened up here. An avid homebrewer, he jumped at the opportunity. He worked with Greg Burke (Woodward Avenue Brewers) as a shadow here for one year before taking the reins himself. At that time the cheese making was done by Scott. One day Chris finished off a batch of cheese for Scott who was busy at the time. And so it goes. Since 2001 he's been doing both duties, and even developed a bleu Asiago cheese.

Originally this was a dive bar known as Dog House Bar, but then became Traffic Jam and added Paolo's Pizzeria and the bar for ice cream and a bakery. In the 1970s it all came together—literally. Now it is one big complex of rooms filled with odds and ends, curiosities and antiques. Check out the fountain outside, made with sinks and a bathtub. The brewery is connected to Detroit's underground steam system, so all the boils are produced with community steam. Because dairy equipment operates in a similar fashion to a brew system, Chris is actually using his system for both purposes.

Directions: From I-75 through downtown Detroit, take M-10 north for 1.7 miles, and get of on Exit 3. Turn right (east) on Forest Ave and then the second right (south) on 3rd St. Go 0.1 mile and turn left (east) on Canfield. The brewery is on the right on the corner of 2nd and Canfield.

Stumbling Distance: Right across the street is *Motor City Brewing*.

JOLLY PUMPKIN ARTISAN ALES

Founded: 2004
Brewmaster & General Mischief-maker: Ron Jeffries
Address: 2319 Bishop Circle • Dexter, MI 48130
Phone: 734-426-4962
Website: www.jollypumpkin.com
Annual Production: 7,700 barrels (about 3,000 is JP)
Number of Beers: 14+ beers

Staple Beers:
» BAM BIERE (FARMHOUSE ALE AGED IN OAK)
» BAM NOIRE
» CALABAZA BLANCA (BELGIAN BIERE BLANCHE)
» LA ROJA
» ORO DE CALABAZA
» WEIZEN BAM BIERE

Rotating Beers:
» BIERE DE MARS (MARCH)
» FUEGO DE OTOÑO (OCTOBER)
» LA PARCELA (WITH PUMPKIN, SEPTEMBER)
» LUCIERNAGA (GRAND CRU, JUNE)
» MADRUGADA OSCURA (BELGIAN-INSPIRED STOUT, FEBRUARY)
» MARACAIBO ESPECIAL (NOVEMBER)
» NOEL DE CALABAZA (DECEMBER)

Most Popular Brew: Bam Biere and La Roja

Brewmaster's Fave: Bam Biere and Wanderer, a session IPA

Tours? In planning. Check the website for scheduled times.

Samples: Yes.

Best Time to Go: Tap room is in process. Check the website for hours.

Where can you buy it? In 750ml bottles throughout Michigan and much of the continental USA. On tap and in growlers at Jolly Pumpkin Café in Ann Arbor and on Old Mission Peninsula outside Traverse City.

Got food? No.

Special Offer: A free sticker, bumper sticker or some other such highly prized trinket with the signature of this book.

The Beer Buzz: Most beer fans know Jolly Pumpkin as a maker of sour ales. This is a different kind of funky brewing. Open fermentation using 10-barrel dairy tanks. A tricky business as with all the "contaminants" used to make these sour ales, the potential for infections to spread between batches is always possible. JP is boldly going where some brewers hesitate. Everything gets aged in barrels from a few weeks to several years. All beers get secondary fermentation with wild yeast in oak barrels.

Brewer Ron is an icon in the brewing industry. He and Mike Hall got Grizzly Peak up and running before Ron branched out to create Jolly Pumpkin. JP started here in Dexter in a location over on Broad Street. The brewery grew, taking over other suite spaces in the original building until the entire 10,000 square feet were theirs. In February 2013, JP moved to this new location in what was a long abandoned building. They now have 60,000 square feet to work in. The brewery is divided in two: Jolly Pumpkin on one side, and then through a clean room (must keep the JP "contaminants" contained) to the other side where North Peak products are brewed for distribution. (See North Peak in Traverse City).

Oro de Calabaza was once declared the best Belgian-style golden ale in the world by *The New York Times*, while La Roja made *GQ Magazine's* list of the Top 50 Beers in the World.

Bottling at Jolly Pumpkin had been entirely by hand in the beginning—a gravity wine filler and hand-rolled labels. With the new digs they now have a machine that helps a bit. Barrels come from a variety of places. Firestone Walker sends them theirs. They get barrels from brewers who *don't* want their beer to be sour. Old wine and bourbon barrels for beer that have lost their bourbon flavors. Everything is oak.

Jolly Pumpkin is part of the Northern United Brewing entity.

Directions: From I-94, take Exit 167 and turn north on Baker Rd. Drive 1.9 miles, turn right on Dan Hoey Rd. Continue 0.4 mile, turn right on Bishop Circle. Where that splits, go left on Bishop Circle East and the brewery is 0.2 mile on the right.

Stumbling Distance: *Terry B's Restaurant* (7954 Ann Arbor St, 734-426-3727, terrybs.com) is situated in an 1850s farmhouse and offers fine dining with a *Wine Spectator*-honored wine list and a nice selection of Michigan craft beers.

HARPER'S RESTAURANT & BREWPUB

Founded: 1996
Brewmaster: Scott Isham
Address: 131 Albert Avenue • East Lansing, MI 48823
Phone: 517-333-4040
Website: www.harpersbrewpub.com
Number of Beers: 6 on tap

Beers:
» BELGIAN WIT
» BLACKSTRAP PORTER
» GROVE ST. PALE ALE
» HARPER'S ALE ENGLISH MILD
» RASPBERRY WHEAT
» SPARTAN WHEAT

Most Popular Brew: Spartan Wheat

Tours? Sure, if someone is around and free.

Samples: Yes, sample flights.

Best Time to Go: Happy hour is daily from 4–7PM.

Where can you buy it? Only on tap here or in growlers and kegs to go.

Got food? Yes, a full bar/restaurant menu of appetizers, soups and salads, sandwiches, pizzas, pasta and burgers.

Special Offer: Not participating.

The Beer Buzz: Located very close to Michigan State University, this brewpub and restaurant is also a popular college hangout. Students come for dancing in the evenings.

Directions: From US-127, get off at Exit 78. Go east on M-43/Saginaw St. After 0.2 mile take the slight right on Grand River Ave and continue 1.1 miles. Turn left on Abbot Rd and take the next right on Albert Ave. The brewery is on the left and there is a parking lot across the street.

Stumbling Distance: You can't come to East Lansing and not visit *HopCat* (300 Grove St, 517-816-4300, hopcatel.com), the 2nd location of the Grand Rapids beer bar, this one with 100 craft beers on tap. Looking for fresh cheese curds, ice cream? Try the *MSU Dairy Store* (1140 S. Anthony Hall, 517-355-8466, dairystore.msu.edu).

FENTON WINERY & BREWERY

Founded: 2008 (brewery 2009)
Brewmaster: Matt Sherrow
Address: 1545 North Leroy Street • Fenton, MI 48430
Phone: 810-373-4194
Website: www.fentonwinery.com/The_Brewery.html
Annual Production: barrels
Number of Beers: 12 on tap, 25+ styles per year

Staple Beers:
» BEACH HEAD BELGIAN TRIPEL
» EMINENT DOUBLE IPA
» IGNESCENT AMBER
» GLUTEN FOR PUNISHMENT CREAM ALE (GLUTEN-FREE)
» HEAD-ON COLLISION BLACK IPA
» MIDNIGHT WHEAT PORTER
» OASIS WHEAT
» SCOTTISH WEE HEAVY
» STAGGERING BULL IMPERIAL NUT BROWN ALE
» UNBRIDLED IPA

Rotating Beers:
» BLUEBERRY BLONDE
» DOUBLE CHOCOLATE OATMEAL STOUT
» HONEY AMBER
» OKTOBERFEST
» PETITE SAISON
» ST. GIN'S IRISH STOUT
» SMOKED PORTER
» WIDOWMAKER RUSSIAN IMPERIAL STOUT

Most Popular Brew: Oasis Wheat and Ignescent Amber

Brewmaster's Fave: Head on Collision BIPA and the heavier beers

Tours? Yes, and watch for scheduled wine-making classes.

Samples: Yes, $1 each for a 2.5-ounce pour (more some special limited brews) (Wines are 4 samples for $6.99).

Best Time to Go: Open Monday–Thursday 3–10PM, Friday–Saturday 1PM–12AM, and Sunday 1–6PM. Friday and Saturday nights are busiest and live music and beer events are often scheduled.

Where can you buy it? Here on tap and in growlers. Bottles of beer for sale (must actually be drunk here).

Got food? Yes, sandwiches, snacks, desserts, artisan cheese and meat selections, fresh fruit.

Special Offer: Not participating.

The Beer Buzz: Husband and wife team Matt and Ginny Sherrow operate this ever-expanding winery and brewery. Matt left the corporate world in 2007 and they opened the winery soon after that. Matt picked up a homebrew kit and found he liked brewing beer. He tried it out on some regulars and the response was good enough to encourage them to add the brewery a year after they opened.

They added the lounge in 2011, which is a nice community gathering place with sofa and lounge chairs, a TV, and even a fake fireplace. Local art on the walls is for sale. A small bar offers the tastings, but you can buy full glasses as well and hang out with friends. All the tables have boxes of Trivial Pursuit cards on them.

The winery offers 20 varieties; the fruit wines sell best. The ice wine and house port have won awards. Along with the beers there are 3 wines and 3 sodas on tap. Throw in the board games and it's a pretty family-friendly place as well. An event space is also available. Free Wi-Fi. Mug Club.

Directions: From US-23 take Exit 80 and turn north on Torrey Rd. Turn right (east) on Long Lake Rd, drive 1 mile, and turn left (north) on Leroy St. The winery is on the left.

Stumbling Distance: The winery/brewery also has homebrewing supplies and an expanded brewhouse at their location at 1370 Long Lake Road in Fenton. They are planning a tap room there as well.

WOODWARD AVENUE BREWERS

Founded: May 1997
Brewmaster: Greg Burke
Address: 22646 Woodward Avenue • Ferndale, MI 48220-1810
Phone: 248-546-3696
Website: www.thewabsite.com
Annual Production: 650 barrels
Number of Beers: 8 plus 2 guest taps

Staple Beers:
» Custom Blonde
» Detroit Maiden IPA
» Hefty Weizen
» Raspberry Blonde

Rotating Beers:
» Biere Brunet
» Bout Stout Russian Imperial Stout
» Custom Porter
» Gluten-Less Maximus IPA
» Green Bullet IPA
» Le Rouge French Amber
» Pumpkin Ale
» Steam Beer
» Vanilla Porter

Most Popular Brew: Custom Blonde or Detroit Maiden IPA

Brewmaster's Fave: Detroit Maiden IPA

Tours? No.

Samples: Yes, a taste or two but not flights or the like.

Best Time to Go: Open daily at 11AM (noon on weekends). Weekly neighborhood party on Mondays with ½ off food after 4PM. Happy hour Tuesday–Friday 3–7PM. Cheap pints on Sundays. The pool hall has live music 10 times per month.

Where can you buy it? Here on tap or to go in growlers, and next door in the pool hall.

Got food? Yes, but no burgers and no deep fryer. Sandwiches and salads, some Mexican fare, jalapeno-lime hummus, honey-porter bread.

Special Offer: Half off a pint of their beer during your signature visit.

The Beer Buzz: Welcome to what the neighbors call the WAB. Chris Johnston, one of the owners, used to tour in a band, and one of the things he liked was visiting all the breweries along the way. His brother Grant went to brewing school and joined Chris and his wife Krista, as well as a childhood friend Brian Reedy, to create this place. Grant was the original brewer. Back in 2006 Greg walked in for a beer the same day a brewer was leaving for school. The Michigan Beer Guild's slogan "The Great Beer State" came from these guys.

The two-story building has an upstairs and downstairs bar as well as some sidewalk seating in summer. Michigan license plates are nailed to the walls. In pleasant weather the bar opens a garage door creating a 20-table outdoor patio. A pool hall, The Loving Touch, is attached and has a bar as well. It used to be a massage parlor (what you think). There is a cool sort of lounge area under a skylight in back.

Brewer Greg is a University of Michigan graduate who did the American Brewers' Guild Craft Brewer apprentice program back in 1994. He got his start at Grizzly Peak in Ann Arbor and worked at several other breweries including Motor City, Redwood Lodge, Traffic Jam & Snug and Atwater. Free Wi-Fi. ATM onsite.

Directions: From the west on I-696 take Exit 16 and go right (south) 1.3 miles on Woodward Ave. The brewery is on the left. From Detroit take I-75 Exit 58 and go west on Seven Mile Rd to Woodward Ave. Then go right (north) about 2 miles and the brewery is on Woodward and Troy.

Stumbling Distance: *One Eyed-Betty's* (175 West Troy Street, 248-808-6633, oneeyedbettys. com) is serious about craft beer and serves great food, 47 on tap, 100+ in bottles, lots of whisky. Open for hangover breakfast on weekends.

REDWOOD BREWING CO. (THE REDWOOD STEAKHOUSE BREWERY & GRILL)

Founded: 1996
Brewmaster: Steve "Konrad" Connor
Address: 5304 Gateway Center Drive • Flint, MI, 48507
Phone: 810-233-8000
Website: www.redwoodbrewingco.com
Annual Production: 900+ barrels
Number of Beers: 10 on tap, often a cask or two as well, plus a guest tap

Staple Beers:
» Brown Porter
» American IPA
» Cream Stout
» Kölsch
» Munich Helles
» Pale Ale
» Redwood Light

Rotating Beers:
» Alt
» American Imperial Stout
» Anniversary Ale (Barleywine)
» Dust My Brown Ale
» English Winter Ale
» Hairy Little Sista (Session Hoppy Lager)
» Jim's Hefe
» Kick Start My Arse (Hazelnut Coffee Cream Stout)
» Love You Long Time (Session IPA)
» Märzen
» Munich Dunkel
» Oktoberfest
» as well as cask selections

Most Popular Brew: Cream Stout

Brewmaster's Fave: Helles, Jim's Hefe, and American IPA

Tours? Groups should make an appointment ahead of time.

Samples: Yes, $1.25 to $2 each.

Best Time to Go: Open daily for lunch and dinner. Check out live music in the Sequoia Lounge on Friday–Saturday, as well as on Wednesday nights in fall and winter. Happy hour runs weekdays 3–7PM with low beer prices.

Where can you buy it? Only here, on tap or in growlers.

Got food? Yes, a full steakhouse menu that includes wild game, mesquite grill items, a wood-fired oven for pizzas, seafood and a raw bar, and much more. Upscale food, casual atmosphere.

Special Offer: Up to two $1 pints of happy hour beers during signature visit (Kölsch, Light, Helles, Pale Ale or Porter).

The Beer Buzz: This huge wood-lodge affair is pretty easy to spot from the interstate. And while it may seem like a steakhouse (because it is), it won Best Small Brewpub in 2008 at the Great American Beer Festival. Stout fans are going to especially like this place as Brewer Konrad has silver medals from the Great American Beer Festival for both his Cream Stout and Hazelnut Coffee Cream Stout.

Konrad spent 15 years as a computer programmer and took up homebrewing on the side. His passion for beer grew, and he started going on what I

like to call pils-grimages (travels to go see where the beer is made). He has since traveled to 44 states and 16 countries in search of good beer, and to this day, all his trips revolve around it. His programming job got shipped to India twice in three years. After the second time he stopped in at Redwood Brewing, where he was a mug club member, and was offered a part-time brewing assistant job by then assistant brewer Dave Shaw (now in Frankenmuth at Sullivan's Black Forest Brew Haus). He took it, of course, and when Dave left, Konrad stepped up. Then when head brewer Bill Wamby moved on to Rochester Mills Brewing, Konrad took the reins.

The gleaming copper brew system stands behind a long bar to the left as you walk in. Above the bar, banners dedicated to the various beer awards hang from the rafters. The dining room is quite large and there's even an outside patio. While this is considered fine dining, the atmosphere is nevertheless casual. There is a martini bar and a very good wine list. Free Wi-Fi. Mug club.

Directions: From M-23 take Exit 90 and go east on Hill Rd to the first left, Gateway Center. Redwood is on the left behind The Spa at Gateway Centre, but you'll need to do a U-turn to come back and turn right (west) to get there. From I-75 from the south take I-475/U.A.W. Freeway and get off on Hill Rd at Exit 2. Go left (west) to get to Gateway Center.

Stumbling Distance: *The Red Baron* (2495 S Center Rd, Burton, 810-744-1310) a barbecue joint in nearby Burton always has at least 30 Michigan beers on tap.

FRANKENMUTH BREWERY

Founded: 1862
Brewpastor: Jeff Coon
Address: 425 South Main Street • Frankenmuth, MI 48734
Phone: 989-262-8300
Website: www.frankenmuthbrewery.com
Annual Production: 8,000+ barrels
Number of Beers: 8 on tap

Staple Beers:
» Batch 69 American IPA
» Classic American Blonde
» Hefeweizen Ale
» Munich-Style Dunkel Lager
» Pilsener Lager
» Red Sky Irish-Style Ale

Rotating Beers:
» English IPA
» Harvest Ale
» Oktoberfest Lager
» Imperial Stout Lager
» Schwarzbier
» Tornado Black IPA
» Twisted Helles Lager
» Winter Bock Lager

Most Popular Brew: Pilsener and Dunkel, but Oktoberfest in season.

Brewmaster's Fave: It varies, but Oktoberfest is his favorite style to brew.

Tours? Yes, when someone is available. Better chances on weekends.

Samples: Yes, 4 ounces of anything on tap for $1.50 each.

Best Time to Go: Happy hour runs 6–8PM. Wednesday offers $5 growler refills.

Where can you buy it? Growlers here and throughout Michigan, Indiana, Florida, Ohio, Pennsylvania, and Wisconsin.

Got food? Yes, a full menu of burgers, sandwiches, wraps, soups and salads, appetizers, pizzas, and entrees including steaks and seafood. Brats, among other things, are local, and beer is incorporated into some of the recipes.

Special Offer: Get a free Frankenmuth Brewery sticker during your signature visit.

The Beer Buzz: In a town settled by German immigrants, it's no surprise the brewing tradition started early. The first commercial brewery dates to 1857. The Frankenmuth Brewery has been around since 1862. The Geyer Brothers owned it for a time. The brewery suffered a fire and even an F3 tornado in 1996 (leaving the original solid copper lauter tun you can see outside). It reopened as a brewpub in 2003 but closed again in 2006 for financial reasons, then reopened again three years later. In 2009 new owners took over and whipped things into shape. The only thing left from the 19th century is a brew cellar.

This is a big place: space for 432 diners plus 250 more on the patios outside overlooking the Cass River. Its banquet services are popular for weddings—note the copper brew kettle turned into a gazebo.

That's no typo on 'Brewpastor' above. Brewer Jeff is an ordained minister and gets hired to do weddings in the brewery. Jeff started homebrewing on a turkey burner—outdoors—because his wife kicked him out of the kitchen due to the smell. (She let him back in when he was done.) Jeff learned from a neighbor who, conveniently, was a German immigrant.

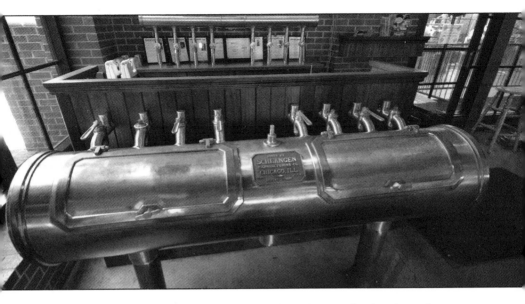

He's helped out by production brewer Jordan Fagan who has been brewing with him for years. As is common in the German tradition, most of the beers here are lagers. The brewery has silver medals for its Pilsener and Red Sky Ale from the World Expo of Beer.

Due to the convoluted brewing laws in Michigan, the downstairs bar has to buy their own beer from the brewery upstairs. They have to pay a distributor for that trip down the steps. They are also licensed to make wine. Free Wi-Fi.

Tip: Try to come during a monthly performance of musical/dance group Da Frankenmuda Fratz'n: dancing, singing, accordion playing, banging benches, and ringing bells. The locally founded group performs across the state and even gets invited to Germany. Lots of fun.

Directions: From Exit 144 on I-75 head east on Dixie Highway 2.8 miles. Turn left on Junction Rd (becomes Genessee St) and drive 4.8 miles, then turn right on Main St. The brewery is 0.3 mile on your left.

Stumbling Distance: Don't miss the *Lager Mill Beer Store & Brewing Museum* (701 Mill St, 989-652-3377), with over 400 craft beers, brewing and wine making supplies, and more. The small museum holds some breweriana, antiques, and some historical information about Frankenmuth's brewing history. Family-owned and operated since 1949, *Kern's Sausages* (110 W. Jefferson, 989-652-2684, kernssausage.com) offers 34 varieties of housemade Bavarian-style sausages.

SULLIVAN'S BLACK FOREST BREW HAUS & GRILL

Founded: May 2003
Brewmaster: David Shaw
Address: 281 Heinlein Strasse • Frankenmuth, MI, 48734
Phone: 800-890-6877 or 989-652-6060
Website: www.blackforestbrewhaus.net
Annual Production: 300–460 barrels
Number of Beers: 10 on tap and 2 guest taps

Staple Beers:
» GRATEFUL RED
» LOST SAILOR IPA
» PIRATE'S PORTER
» SULLY'S STOUT
» WOODY'S GOLD

Rotating Beers:
» SHORT POLACK MAIBOCK
» SLOW ROGGEN
» WALLY'S WEIZENBOCK

Most Popular Brew: Woody's Gold or Lost Sailor IPA

Tours? If you call ahead, maybe. It's a small facility.

Samples: 10 four-ounce samplers for about $12.

Best Time to Go: It's slow and laid back during the day, busy at night. Closed on Mondays. Also, there's no lunch Tuesday–Thursday and Sundays from January to April.

Where can you buy it? Right here only, or take it out in growlers.

Got food? Yes, they do wedding receptions here, but there is also a full menu with pizzas, prime rib, seafood, fish and chips, burgers and sandwiches, and salads. Cheddar ale soup! They also do catering.

Special Offer: $2 off one pint during your signature visit.

The Beer Buzz: Lutheran missionaries from the Province of Franconia in the Kingdom of Bavaria settled Frankenmuth ("Courage of the Franconians") on the Cass River in 1845. The German heritage here is strong and you can see the town embraces it fully. This banquet hall and brewpub took its name from famous wooded mountains along the Danube in southwestern Germany. Since 1996, a couple other brewing projects tried to make a go of it at this location, and it was vacant a few years before Tim and Tom Sullivan took over the property in 2003. The building has a certain European character to it with a central stone tower.

Brewer David started homebrewing when he was 21 and put in 8 years at Redwood Brewing as an assistant. He started as Sullivans' 3rd brewer and has been here since 2006. "I love the town. The people are nice." His Lost Sailor IPA won a gold medal, and his Pirate's Porter won Bronze at the Great American Beer Festival in 2009.

Weddings and banquets are popular here, but it is just as good for some casual dining and, of course, serious beer drinking. There are booths and tables near the bar, and an outdoor patio is open in season. A couple of TVs are above the bar.

Free Wi-Fi. Mug club. Facebook.com/sullivansblackforest

Directions: Heading north into Frankenmuth at the very southern end of town on M-83 take a right (east) on Weiss St which curves a bit to become a north-south street. The brewpub is on the right a block later at Heinlein Strasse.

Stumbling Distance: *Frankenmuth Valley Chocolate Haus* is next door. Think beer and chocolate pairings. Or maybe *Frankenmuth Cheese Haus* (561 S Main St, 989-652-6727, frankenmuthcheesehaus.com) is more your style.

THE BARN TAVERN

Founded: 2011 (as brewery)
Brewmaster: Cody Rubio
Address: 207 S. Bridge Street • Grand Ledge, MI 48837
Phone: 517-622-8686
Website: Facebook.com/pages/The-Barn-Tavern/170514551966
Annual Production: 300 barrels
Number of Beers: 4 on tap

Staple Beers:
» IPA
» Pale Ale

Rotating Beers: Staple Beers:
» Ledge Climber (Blonde Ale With Local Honey)
» Porter
» Varies, but two at a time

Most Popular Brew: IPA

Brewmaster's Fave: IPA

Tours? Not really much to see.

Samples: Yes.

Best Time to Go: Happy hour runs 1–6PM Monday through Friday. Dollar tacos on Tuesdays, burger special on Wednesdays. A DJ spins tunes on Saturdays; trivia night is on Thursdays.

Where can you buy it? Only here on tap in pints or 26 oz. pours. Growlers only if they are not running out of a batch.

Got food? Small pizzas, burgers, sandwiches, and appetizers including pretzels and beer-battered onion rings.

Special Offer: Not participating.

The Beer Buzz: Let your eyes adjust first if you walk in on a sunny day. There's a lot to look at in here, some of it historical. A wagon hangs from the ceiling—the big wooden kind, not a kid's Radio Flyer. This bar has been around quite a long time, and if you look at some of the old black and white photos you can see it was once a cigar shop and a pharmacy. The old-school bar still remains. Expansion knocked out a wall into a next door bakery years ago. The idea to add a brewery came when the smoking ban was about to take effect.

Jack Budd was the original brewer; he passed the reins to Cody. Cody started homebrewing in college. In chemistry class all his professors were talking about it. He is a local fellow and had been a regular at the bar. This being a small town, beer prices are rather cheap. Other beers, both mass market and craft, are available.

There's an ATM and Wi-Fi on site, plus a pool table, shuffleboard, a jukebox, and some Slim Jims. In season, you can drink out back on the patio.

Directions: Highway M-40 passes through the south side of Grand Ledge, connecting to M-100 which goes right through town south to north to south first on Jefferson St, then turning right (northeast) on Bridge St. The brewery is on the right side of Bridge St right before the bridge if you're heading north.

Stumbling Distance: You might want to go see The Ledges at Riverwalk just a short walk from here (probably best before you drink). Catch bluegills at Fitzgerald Park Dam.

HOMETOWN CELLARS WINERY AND BREWERY

Founded: 2006 (brewery 2009)
Brewmaster: Aaron Hale
Address: 108 East Center Street • Ithaca, MI 48847
Phone: 989-875-6010
Website: www.hometowncellars.com
Annual Production: 65 barrels
Number of Beers: 8 on tap

Staple Beers:
» IPA
» Oatmeal Stout
» Pilsner

Rotating Beers:
» Barleywine
» Cherry Wheat
» Coffee Stout
» English Mild
» Hoppy Old Ale
» Irish Red
» Various Pale Ales

Most Popular Brew: IPA or Oatmeal Stout

Brewmaster's Fave: Hoppy Old Ale

Tours? No, it's just a one-barrel system.

Samples: Yes, 4 five-ounce samplers for about $5.

Best Time to Go: Open Tuesday–Wednesday 11AM–7PM, Thursday 11AM–10PM, Friday 1PM–11PM, Saturday 12PM–11PM. Closed Sunday and Monday. Fridays host karaoke nights.

Where can you buy it? Only here and in growlers to go.

Got food? A bit of pre-packaged cheeses and meat sticks, otherwise you can carry-in or order delivery.

Special Offer: A free pint glass!

The Beer Buzz: Hometown Cellars opened as boutique wine shop and winery and then added the beer a few years after that. Owners/brothers Ken and Tom Hale started out making wines and beers at home, and when they started getting more and more friends and family visiting on bottling day, they decided to go pro. Ken and his son Aaron produce 30 varieties of wine. The winery had been successful for its first three years, but the need to serve beer was nevertheless obvious. With a small winery license, the establishment couldn't stock beer, but there was no reason they couldn't brew it themselves. Ken's son Tony, a graduate of Western Michigan University, loved Bell's Brewing when he was in Kalamazoo, and when he returned here to his hometown of Ithaca, he took on the beer-brewing duties. Hometown Cellars also produces meads made with honey from Carson City. Aaron also produces the mead/cider hybrid known as cysers using cider from Uncle John's Cider Mill in St. John's.

For 100 years Beebe Furniture was here, but that was divided into a sort of mini-mall with a handful of shops. The original building was lost to a fire in 1986 and then rebuilt. The front room of the shop has a large-screen TV and a handful of tables. Steps lead up to a sort of mezzanine area that can be reserved for private events. Parking is out front on the street. Free Wi-Fi.

Directions: From US-127 outside Ithaca, take Exit 117 and follow US-127 Business. Stay on this; it becomes Center Street and the winery/brewery is on the left.

Stumbling Distance: *Hearthstone Oven* next door (126 S Pine River St, 989-875-6836) is operated by a Mennonite family and serves sandwiches, casseroles, baked goods, and a good meatloaf sandwich.

51 NORTH BREWING COMPANY

Opened: January 2013
Brewmaster: Adam Beratta
Address: 51 N. Broadway St. • Lake Orion, MI 48362
Phone: 248-690-7367
Website: www.51northbrewing.com
Number of Beers: 10 beers on tap

Staple Beers:
» Dog Way IPA
» Lake Orion Light
» Spencer Island Rye Pale Ale
» Velvet Moose Chocolate Oatmeal Stout
» Tangerine Wheat
» Wind Walker Northern English Brown Ale

Rotating Beers:
» Belgian Dubbel
» Carmale
» Jalapeno Ale
» Oktoberfest
» Pumpkin Ale
» Vanilla Porter

Samples: Yes, a flight of six 6-oz. pours for about $11.

Tours? Yes, any time.

Best Time to Go: Open at 11AM daily. Watch for live music and open mic night.

Where can you buy it? Here on tap and in growlers to go.

Got food? Yes, appetizers, soups and salads, and sandwiches, plus a kids' menu.

Special Offer: $2 off your first pint during your signature visit.

The Beer Buzz: This is a good place to stop to fill 'er up, and always has been. In fact, back in 1932 it opened as a gas station. When owners Don and Mary Ginhart were looking for a home for their planned brewpub, Lake Orion looked like a fine choice. This historic building was occupied by the town's downtown development authority. When the Ginhart's decided this location would be perfect, the authority stepped aside. Now that's a commitment to development.

Don has been around good beer for a very long time. Back in college, he started homebrewing with friends, including Jim Pericles, who would go on to be brewmaster at Boston Beer Co. When Don found a brew-on-premises option in Detroit, he found himself elbow to elbow with Pat Scanlon, a prominent Michigan brewer (Rochester Mills, Royal Oak, Detroit Beer Co.). Years later he used the BOP equipment of the Kuhnhenn brothers over in Warren and ended up working in the brew supply shop for a while. Finally, homebrewing partners Paul Makowski, Kelly Tyrrell, and Matt Charbonneau helped him to decide to move forward with the brewery. Mary runs the food side of things and manages to work beer into many recipes.

Brewer Adam's beer has won awards, including a World Expo of Beer Gold for Paint Creek Wheat. He got his start helping out at Redwood Lodge in Flint and then made a name for himself at Great Baraboo Brewing before moving here.

Mug Club. Free Wi-Fi.

Directions: Heading north from Auburn Hills about 6.7 miles on M-24, turn right onto Broadway St. Continue 0.2 mile and the brewpub is on the left.

Stumbling Distance: *Rochester Mills Beer Co.* is about 10 miles southeast on Orion Rd from Lake Orion.

EAGLEMONK PUB & BREWERY

Founded: 2012
Brewmaster: Dan Buonodono
Address: 4906 West Mount Hope Highway • Lansing, MI 48917
Phone: 517-708-7350
Website: www.eaglemonkbrewing.com
Annual Production: 350 barrels
Number of Beers: 6–9 on tap; 20+ styles per year

Staple Beers:
» DELTA PORTER
» IRISH RED
» MARCY STREET STOUT
» RED EYE RYE
» PLUS ONE OF HIS FOUR IPAS IS TYPICALLY ON

Rotating Beers:
» BELGIAN WIT
» BRUDER KOLSCH
» CZECH PILSENER
» EAGLEMONK IPA
» EASY BLONDE ALE
» INSTIGATOR DOPPELBOCK
» MICHIGAN WHITE
» RAVEN BLACK IPA

Most Popular Brew: Red Eye Rye (or Raven Black IPA when it's on).

Brewmaster's Fave: Red Eye Rye

Tours? Yes.

Samples: Yes, $9 for 5 0z glasses.

Best Time to Go: Closed Mondays. Open 3–10PM Tuesday–Thursday, noon–11PM Friday & Saturday, noon–8PM Sunday.

Where can you buy it? Here on tap and to go in growlers, howlers, or kegs.

Got food? Yes, housemade pizzas, panini, and salads.

Special Offer: $1 off your first pint during your signature visit.

The Beer Buzz: Brewer Dan actually comes from the family of a winemaker. His grandfather was well known in the area. One day over 30 years ago, Dan stopped in at his local wine supply shop, and the shopkeeper asked him: Ever try making beer? And so it began. He homebrewed for many years while working in IT for the State of Michigan. When he took an early retirement, he and his wife Sonia realized they now had an opportunity to pursue a dream they had had for years: open a brewpub. Dan looking for something north of Lansing, but couldn't find a good location. A property in Lansing kept popping up in searches, and one day, just for kicks, he pulled into the parking lot. He fell in love with the place. Curiously, it is about a mile from where his father was born. This 1937 building was originally a butcher shop and for many years a party store (Michiganese for "liquor store"). It was empty and waiting when Dan found it. Still, it would take him and his brother 51 weeks to completely gut and renovate the place to its current beery state. The brewery name combines the symbols of America and the iconic brewer.

Directions: From I-496 across Lansing, take Exit 3 for Waverly Rd heading south about 0.4 mile. Turn right (southwest) on Lansing Rd. After 0.5 mile turn right on Mt Hope Hwy. It is 0.5 mile on the right.

Stumbling Distance: See also *Midtown Beer Co.* here in Lansing and the beer options in East Lansing (especially *HopCat*).

MIDTOWN BEER COMPANY (MBC LANSING)

Founded: 2013
Brewmaster: Brandon Cook
Address: 402 South Washington • Lansing, MI 48933
Phone: 517-977-1349
Website: www.midtownbeerco.com
Annual Production: <100 barrels
Number of Beers: 14 on tap; 1–2 of them house beers

Tours? No.

Samples: Yes.

Best Time to Go: Open daily. Monday–Thursday 11AM–11PM, Friday–Saturday 11AM–12AM, Sunday 12PM–9PM. Happy hour 3–7PM weekdays.

Where can you buy it? Here on site only.

Got food? Yes, a full menu including soups, salads, nachos, sweet potato fries and some really good burgers.

Special Offer: Not participating.

The Beer Buzz: Some were shocked when Michigan Beer Co. went beer belly up in the summer of 2012. Bankruptcy for the Webberville brewery, however, did not mean the end of MBC here in Lansing. While Michigan Beer Co. Lansing was a direct seller of the defunct brewery's products, it remained a separate business entity. Happily, with the same initials and a slight change on the name, Midtown Beer Co. has carried on. Now the former tap room is excelling as a dining location while featuring a variety of Michigan craft beers and other products. They brew small batches of their own beer onsite. General manager and chef Marc Wolbert sources locally as much as possible, and they've developed a good reputation for their burgers, among other things. Brewer Brandon makes a small batch of beer weekly (a few gallons).

MBC is warm and well-lit with hardwood floors and high ceilings. A large TV pipes in sports. Watch for live music.

Directions: From I-496 right through Lansing, get off on Exit 7A and go north on Grand Ave to Lenawee. Turn left, drive one block and turn right (north) on Washington. MBC is on the left. If coming to Lansing from the west, use Exit 6, turn left (north) on Washington.

Stumbling Distance: For some more great local food, head to The Soup Spoon Café (1419 E Michigan Ave, 517-316-2377, soupspooncafe.com). First Friday of every month is a featured firkin. See also *EagleMonk Pub & Brewery* here in Lansing and the beer options in East Lansing (especially *HopCat*).

LEXINGTON BREWING CO. (OLD TOWN HALL WINERY)

Founded: April 2013
Brewmaster: Steve Velloff
Address: 5475 N. Main • Lexington, MI 48450
Phone: 810-359-5012
Website: www.oldtownhallwinery.com
Annual Production: 800 barrels
Number of Beers: 5 on tap

Beers:
» BANANA-RAMA GERMAN WHEAT
» CHOCOLATE HAZELNUT PORTER
» CREME ALE
» HOP TO IT BABY IPA
» PILSNER
» RASPBERRY RYE
» STOUT
» TROPICANA ALE

Tours? Yes, by chance when the brewer is here. They do farm tours over at the vineyard and hop farm.

Samples: Yes, sample flights.

Best Time to Go: Friday nights in the summer. Open Memorial Day to Labor Day seven days a week. Check the website or call for hours, especially in winter when opening days might only be Friday–Sunday. Live music on weekends.

Where can you buy it? Here on tap and to go in growlers.

Got food? A bit. Expect brats and a few other beery foods, small sandwiches, some hard ciders, and of course wine.

Special Offer: Not participating.

The Beer Buzz: Connie Currie and Steve Velloff were software executives in Chicago when they decided to become "refugees from corporate America." They completed the wine-making certification program at UC-Davis (which required a prerequisite 2.5 years of chemistry and biology!) and came to Michigan in 2005 to plant a 20-acre vineyard near the shores of Lake Huron. Thus was Blue Water Winery and Vineyards born, selling its first wines in 2009. In addition to the vineyard they operate Old Town Hall Winery in a historical building in Lexington. The first floor was once a fire hall, the second an opera house, and the third a Mason hall. It's on the Michigan Historical Registry. In 2012 they began work on converting the back third of the winery into a microbrewery under glass. The previous owners had slapped a cinderblock addition off the back of the building which Connie and Steve have turned into a sort of German-style beer hall with picnic tables and a stage for live acts on the weekends.

One of those live acts is likely Stella and the Hot Kielbasas; Connie plays clarinet and button accordion. Also out at the vineyard is a hop farm, the bounty of which will end up in their winter beers. Watch for grape and hop harvest parties as fall approaches. Check out their website for a link to their appearance on Under the Radar Michigan on Detroit Public Television.

Directions: Just 80 miles from Detroit. Take M-25 right into downtown Lexington and it becomes Main St. The winery/brewery is on the east side of Main St.

Stumbling Distance: Check out *Blue Water Winery and Vineyards* (7131 Holverson Rd, Carsonville, 810-622-0328, bluewaterwinery.com) as well. Plan your visit around an area event (LexingtonMichigan.org). There are plenty of B&Bs in the area.

FORT STREET BREWERY

Founded: 2005
Brewmaster: Doug Beedy
Address: 1660 Fort Street • Lincoln Park, MI 48146
Phone: 313-389-9620
Website: www.fortstreetbeer.com
Annual Production: 425 barrels
Number of Beers: 7 on tap, 2 staples and 60+ styles year round

Staple Beers:
» DOUG'S TURBO SARSAPARILLA
» LINCOLN LAGER

Rotating Beers:
» BEERNORMOUS (IMPERIAL STOUT)
» CORKTOWN RED
» DOWNRIVER RED (ALTBIER)
» MICHIGAN MONKS (BELGIAN IPA)
» SNOWPLOWED (WITH OATS, RYE AND JUNIPER)
» SUMMER SUNSATION (SAISON STYLE)
» SUPERMASSIVE BLACK HOLE OF DELICIOUSNESS (RYE STOUT WITH MICHIGAN TART CHERRIES)
» TRIPEL CROWN
» UP NORTH LAGER (PILSNER AND RYE)
» PLUS WEEKLY CASK-CONDITIONED ALES

Most Popular Brew: Changes with the seasonal rotations.

Brewmaster's Fave: He tends to like the farmhouse/Belgian styles best.

Tours? By appointment.

Samples: Yes, $1 for a five-ounce pour.

Best Time to Go: Open daily from lunch until late. At 11AM most days, but noon on Saturday, 1PM on Sunday. Happy hour runs Monday–Friday 3–6PM, Saturday noon–6PM. Check the website calendar for awesome specials on beer and food.

Where can you buy it? Here on tap or in growlers or kegs to take away.

Got food? Yes, pizzas, sandwiches, appetizers, and salads. Highlights include beer cheese soup, pierogis, brats, Scotch eggs, hot pretzels, chicken, and cod, with a lot of beer battering going on as well.

Special Offer: Not participating

The Beer Buzz: On a street corner in Lincoln Park, is this large open beer hall with dark wood floors, sports banners hanging from the high ceiling. Big windows let in a lot of light, and TVs can be seen in all directions, including a projection screen set up at one end of the house. Serving tanks stand behind the long bar, and the brewhouse is behind glass in the back.

Brewer Doug studied at Siebel in Chicago and then got a lot of experience brewing throughout Michigan and Ohio. Before Fort Street had even opened, he was the man for the job. Their website keeps a running tally of how many beers they've tapped.

Every Thursday Doug brings out a cask-conditioned ale, so the number of styles in a year can be quite large. To get an idea of what beers have come before, see the beer release posters along the hall to the restrooms. Other adventures await with a menu of beer cocktails such as Lager Rita made with Lincoln and some tequila. Corktown Red is named after Detroit's nickname given to the city by its Irish immigrant population. Free Wi-Fi. FSB Fan Club (like mug club without the mugs). Facebook.com/fortstreetbrewery

Directions: From I-75 heading west from downtown Detroit, take Exit 43 onto Schaefer Highway toward Fort St. Turn right (south) on Fort St and continue 2 miles; the brewery is on the right at the corner of Fort and Warwick.

Stumbling Distance: *Henry Ford Museum* (20900 Oakwood Blvd, Dearborn, 800-835-5237, thehenryford.org) is about 7 miles northeast of here or 15 minutes driving. You can hardly visit Detroit and not give a little attention to its famed car industry. The Henry Ford Museum is way more than just about Mr. Ford. Kennedy's limo, Lincoln's theatre chair, the Rosa Parks bus are all there, and there are even factory tours.

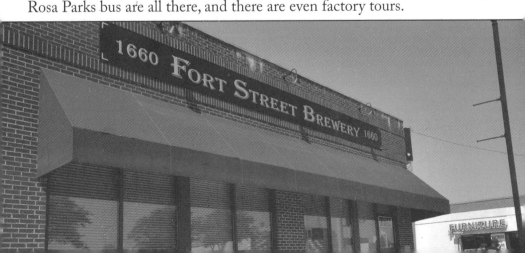

BAD BREWING COMPANY

Founded: 2012
Brewmaster: Brian Rasdale
Address: 440 South Jefferson Street • Mason, MI 48854
Phone: 517-676-7664
Website: www.badbrewing.com
Annual Production: 200 barrels
Number of Beers: 10–14 on tap, 10–15 styles per year

Staple Beers:
» Ash Street Amber
» Brothel Brown
» Kracken IPA
» No Stout About It
» Wicked Wit

Rotating Beers:
» Mud In Your Rye (Jet Black And Hoppy)
» Sunrise Citra Pale Ale
» Super D West Coast Style IPA (West Coast-Style IPA)
» many more brews, but usually around 4 IPAs on at a time

Most Popular Brew: Brothel Brown and Kracken IPA.

Brewmaster's Fave: Super D

Tours? Yes, if Brian's in and available.

Samples: Yes, about $4.25 for a flight of four 3.5 oz glasses.

Best Time to Go: Open daily, Monday–Thursday from 3PM, Friday–Sunday from noon. Closes at 10PM, except Friday–Saturday at midnight. Busy weekend nights.

Where can you buy it? Here on tap and to go in growlers, a very few draft accounts.

Got food? Not really, just some packaged snacks, but you can carry in your own food.

Special Offer: $1 off your first pint during your signature visit.

The Beer Buzz: Built in 1879, this brick building is rumored to have been a brothel at one point back in the day (thus the brown ale's name), but that's not what makes this "BAD." The name is a bit of an old joke among friends, standing for Brian After Dark, a sort of tongue-in-cheek expression for 'uh oh, it's after dark, Brian's been drinking again.'

Brian homebrewed for more than ten years before he started the brewery. When he got laid off from his previous job, he—with the prompting of his girlfriend—decided to make the jump to commercial brewing. He had always thought about the idea and took the chance. "I don't want to be 60 years old some day and saying I made really good beer—I could have done that."

Brian offers a constant rotation of beers. With the small batches—he has a 2.5-barrel system—he has the freedom to play around a lot. "If I want to try something crazy, I can do it." He keeps a few standards on tap and mixes the rest up. Many patrons come back on a weekly basis for their favorite beers and to see what's new. The space shows wood floors and exposed brick, and has the comfy feel of a small corner pub.

Mug Club. On Facebook.

Directions: About 20 minutes south of Lansing and half hour north of Jackson. Take US-127 and use Exit 64 for Kipp Rd. Go east about 0.3 mile and turn left (north) on Jefferson St and drive 0.8 mile. The brewery is on the left.

Stumbling Distance: One option for food to carry in would be The Vault Deli (368 S Jefferson St, 517-676-2696, thevaultdeli.com), a stellar made-to-order sandwich shop. Mason is also known for its many antique dealers. Also, don't miss the historic courthouse. Mason was originally built to be the capital of Michigan, before Lansing ended up with the job.

ORIGINAL GRAVITY BREWING CO.

Founded: June 2008
Brewmaster: Brad Sancho
Address: 440 County Street • Milan, MI 48160
Phone: 734-439-7490
Website: www.ogbrewing.com
Annual Production: 800 barrels
Number of Beers: 6–8 on tap

Staple Beers:
» County Street Amber
» Primordial Porter
» Southpaw IPA
» 2-Wheeler Witbier

Rotating Beers:
» Belgian Training Wheels (Golden Ale)
» Bellywasher Scotch Ale
» Chrome Truk Nutz Belgian Style IPA
» Dunkelweizen
» Evil Overlord Dark Belgian Ale
» 440 Pepper Smoker (Smoked-Malt Amber With Jalapeno)
» Fresh Hop Dark Ale
» Funky Enough IPA
» High Five Imperial IPA
» Lumpy (Oatmeal Stout On Nitro)
» Mason Brewer's Best (English Mild)
» Old Skool Altbier
» Root Down (Ginger Beer With 4% ABV)
» Sean Of The Red
» Southside Brown Ale
» Train Jumper Black IPA

Most Popular Brew: Southpaw IPA

Brewmaster's Fave: County Street Amber

Tours? Yes, if Brad is not too busy. Best to set up an appointment.

Samples: Yes, $1.75 for each 3 oz. sample.

Best Time to Go: Open 3–11PM weekdays, 11:30AM–11PM Saturday, noon–6PM Sunday. Happy hour all day Monday, and 3–6PM Tuesday–Friday.

Where can you buy it? Here on tap and to go in growlers, a few area draft accounts.

Got food? Yes, a few sandwiches and snacks.

Special Offer: A free Original Gravity sticker.

The Beer Buzz: Brewer/owner Brad started homebrewing back in 2002. When he grew disillusioned with his work as a mechanical engineer in the automotive industry, he thought, why not open a brewery? While he lives in Ypsilanti, he found nearby Milan (MY-lan) a better location as it didn't already have a brewery and he preferred its small-town charm. He can bike to work.

The brewery occupies a simple brick building—a former auto parts store—just before the railroad tracks in Milan. Inside it feels like a real tap room: the floors are concrete, the decoration is minimal, and the brewhouse is right there in the open over a half wall separating the brewing from the drinking. Chairs and tables (some with lamps made out of growlers) are spread throughout, and you get your beers (and food) from the counter, deli style. A chalkboard shows you what's on tap today. The beer menu changes rapidly as Brad moves a lot of small batches (10 gallons) through here. He has no plans to get big or conquer the world: what he has here is family friendly and "the intimate sort of brewery that I'm passionate about."

Brew Crew (sort of like Mug Club). Free Wi-Fi.

Directions: South of Ann Arbor about 20 minutes, take US-23 to Milan and take Exit 27. Head south into town on Dexter St (Carpenter St). Turn left (east) on County St and the brewery is on the right just before the train tracks. Coming from the south take Exit 25, turn left taking Main St to Dexter and head (right) north a block to County St.

Stumbling Distance: *Roy's Barbeque and Hamburgers* (25 Wabash St, 734-439-1737) does delicious, affordable food with a small-town, unpretentious atmosphere. In season, watch for the *Original Gravity Farmer's Market* on Wednesdays.

LIBERTY STREET BREWING CO.

Founded: December 2008
Brewmaster: Joe Walters
Address: 149 West Liberty Street • Plymouth, MI 48170
Phone: 734-207-9600
Website: www.libertystreetbeer.com
Annual Production: 400 barrels
Number of Beers: 12 on tap, up to 30 annually

Staple Beers:
» The American IPA
» Liberty Belle Blonde Ale
» Liberty One Porter
» Red Glare Amber Ale
» Starkweather Stout
» Steamy Window California Common

Rotating Beers:
» C Monster
» Clementine Lemon Thyme
» 42nd Parallel
» Punkin Pie Ale
» Pub House Brown
» Siamese Dream

Most Popular Brew: The American IPA

Brewmaster's Fave: Steamy Windows

Tours? Yes. By appointment is best, but randomly sometimes works out.

Samples: Yes, a five-ounce pour for $1.50, or 4 pours for $5.50.

Best Time to Go: Open from 3PM weekdays, from 11AM on Saturday, noon on Sunday. Happy hour is Monday–Friday 3–7PM. Sunday–Wednesday are discounted growlers fills.

Where can you buy it? Here on tap and in growlers, around Lower Peninsula Michigan in 6-pack bottles.

Got food? Yes, chips and salsa, popcorn, hummus, small pizzas, hot pretzels.

Special Offer: $1 off your first pint during your signature visit.

The Beer Buzz: This painted brick place feels a bit classy for a brewpub, what with the artwork (including bronze statues), the fancy woodwork around the bar, the black-tile bar top, and stained glass above the front door. And hey, it is classy, but don't feel you need to wear a jacket or anything; patrons may be playing board games. The woodwork is from the building's previous role as a martini bar. The building dates back to 1890, and it lasted as a meat market until into the 1940s before becoming an antiques shop until 2004. The upstairs room seats 75 but opens only for some monthly live music or private parties. A terrace in back, enclosed by a brick wall, has two picnic tables for outdoor drinking.

Brewer/owner Joe was drawn to the science part of homebrewing. He saw it on TV, did a Google search, and didn't sleep for two days. And then he dived right in. "Everyone tells you how great your beer is; you want more people to tell you how great your beer is." Soon he was homebrewing more hours than working, so it only made sense to make the brewing his work. "I'm fortunate enough that my wife let me put us into the poorhouse." We hope that is hyperbole. His porter has won awards. In 2011 he added a winery in the basement as well. To keep up with demand he gets 100 extra barrels brewed at Liquid Manufacturing in Brighton which is also where the bottling is done. He hopes to open his own production brewery in the near future.

See the little "bullet" hole in the front window? Local legend has it that as a kid, a previous owner riding by on his bicycle took a shot at his brother with his BB gun. (The Daisy BB Gun factory used to be in Plymouth.) Fellas, look for Peenut the Nut Inspector in the latrine.

Directions: Coming from Detroit on I-96, take Exit 173A toward Newburgh Rd and stay on it as it merges into Schoolcraft, and then onto Wilcox Rd. Turn left on Mill St and 0.2 mile later turn right on Liberty St and the brewery is on the left. If coming from the west on I-96, take I-275 south, Exit 28 for Ann Arbor Rd, go right (west) and take a right (north) on Lilley Rd which becomes Mill St. It's 1.4 miles to Liberty St; turn right.

Stumbling Distance: Downtown Plymouth has nice sidewalk cafes. The *Box Bar & Grill* (777 W Ann Arbor Trail, 734-459-7390) is OK for food, but their beer list is in the hundreds. *Hermann's Olde Town Grille*, formerly Lower Town Grille, (195 W Liberty, 734-451-1213, hermannsotg.com) gives bar food a good name and has some Michigan craft beers on tap and in bottles. *CJ's Brewing* (14900 Beck Rd, 734-453-4455, cjsbrewery.com) has a second location in Plymouth, but the beer is brewed offsite.

QUAY STREET BREWING COMPANY

Founded: 1996
Brewmaster: Joslynn Dowd
Address: 330 Quay Street • Port Huron, MI 48060
Phone: 810-982-4100
Website: www.quaybrewing.com
Annual Production: 600 barrels
Number of Beers: 8 on tap (2 seasonals)

Staple Beers:
» BLACK RIVER STOUT
» BLUE WATER PALE ALE
» MICHIGAN CREAM ALE
» NUTTING BETTER BROWN ALE
» QUAY STREET WHEAT
» RASPBERRY WHEAT

Rotating Beers:
» APRICOT HEFEWEIZEN
» GOLD
» IPA
» MAIBOCK
» ORGANIC ESB
» PILSNER
» PORTER
» RED
» SCOTCH ALE

Most Popular Brew: Michigan Cream Ale

Brewmaster's Fave: Depends on the season, but prefers hoppier beers.

Tours? By appointment.

Samples: Yes, $1 for each five-ounce sampler.

Best Time to Go: Open daily. Happy hour is later in the evening, around 8PM, depending on the season (less often in summer).

Where can you buy it? Only here on tap and in growlers, 5-gallon keggies, and kegs to go.

Got food? Yes, a full menu plus a separate pub fare menu. Hummus, duck tenders, peel and eat shrimp, baked brie, wild mushroom risotto, steaks, chicken entrees, soups and salads, seafood, wild lake trout, perch, and whitefish. Housemade root beer.

Special Offer: Not participating at this time.

The Beer Buzz: Situated in downtown Port Huron right on the Black River, this building has been a cosmetology school and even an unemployment office. The split-level dining area overlooks the river, which flows just a short distance from here to empty into the St. Clair River. The main bar is in a separate area up front with an old wood bar and dark wood accents among the small collection of booths. Large windows behind the back bar look out to the river and to the industrial skyline of Canada across the water. You can also see the nearby nanobrewery/winery Vinomondo from here.

Dennis and Jeanne Doyle purchased the brewpub in 2013. Dennis himself is a homebrewer who decided to leave corporate life. They intend to keep the same great food menu and build up a larger selection of beers. In fact, they're hoping to triple the beers on tap by the end of 2014 and focus more on hoppier beers. The chef and Joslynn will collaborate on some menu items and specialty brews.

Joslynn started as a homebrewer. When she took a job waitressing at the restaurant, she started assisting the brewer Greg Eagen, whom she calls a "wonderful mentor." She also trained at the Siebel Institute in Chicago. When Greg left to go into teaching, she stepped into the position.

The cooking oil gets recycled to biodiesel. The stories of the beer names are on the menu. Free Wi-Fi. ATM on site.

Directions: Coming into Port Huron on I-94/I-69, take Exit 271 for Business I-69. After about a mile it merges onto Oak St. Continue 2.7 miles, turn left (north) on Military St, cross the bridge, and turn right on Quay St. The brewpub is on the right.

Stumbling Distance: *Fuel Woodfire Grill* (213 Huron Ave, 810-479-4933, fuelwoodfiregrill.com) offers a great BBQ experience and a rotating list of craft beers. *Wolverine Market* or "Wolvo's" (713 Huron Ave, 810-982-0966) is the place to go for carry-out craft beer.

ROCHESTER MILLS BEER CO.

Founded: June, 1998
Head Brewmaster: Forrest Knapp
Address: 400 Water Street • Rochester, MI 48307
Phone: 248-650-5080
Website: www.beercos.com
Annual Production: 1,500 barrels
Number of Beers: 10 on tap, plus 2–4 seasonals; 22+ styles per year

Staple Beers:

» BRICKSHOT ESB
» CORNERSTONE IPA
» LAZY DAZE LAGER
» LAZY DAZE LIGHT
» MILKSHAKE STOUT
» PAINT CREEK PORTER
» PLEZURES PALE ALE
» ROCHESTER RED
» SACRILICIOUS STOUT
» WATER STREET WHEAT
» WIT'S ORGANIC

Rotating Beers:

» DOUBLE IPA
» MAIBOCK
» MILLS PILS CZECH PILSNER
» OKTOBERFEST
» MANY MORE: A BOCK IN SPRING, A BROWN IN FALL

Most Popular Brew: Cornerstone IPA

Brewmaster's Fave: "That's like picking a favorite child!" His favorite child is either Mills Pils or Paint Creek Porter, but don't tell the children.

Tours? Yes, by appointment.

Samples: Yes, 5 four-ounce samplers for about $8.50.

Best Time to Go: Open 11:30AM daily (noon on Sunday). Happy hour is 4–7PM weekdays. On Tuesdays and Thursdays get cheap growler refills. Live music on Friday and Saturday night (no cover). Free pool Sunday–Thursday.

Where can you buy it? Here on tap and to go in growlers or six-pack cans (canned and brewed in their Auburn Hills facility). Draft accounts and cans throughout Michigan.

Got food? Yes, appetizers, salads, sandwiches, pizzas, pastas and other entrees. Highlights include beer cheese soup, lobster mac and cheese, and jambalaya. Kids' menu also.

Special Offer: Half off the price of a sampler flight during your signature visit.

The Beer Buzz: Once the site of Western Knitting Mills, an 1844 woolen mill on Paint Creek and Clinton River, the 1896 brick building which stands here today produced socks, gloves, and mittens—including gloves for World War I soldiers—before closing in 1939. The spacious brewpub keeps the original diagonal wood floors and open-beam ceilings. Enjoy the outdoor patio in season.

Brewer Forrest "lucked into it" as he says. He got his start at Big Buck's now defunct brewpub in Auburn Hills working for brewer Eric Briggeman. "He needed an assistant; I needed a job." He continued to help out Eric when they both came to work for Rochester Mills. When the production facility opened out in Auburn Hills, Eric took on that task and Forrest assumed the head brewer position here. Mike Plesz, one of the owners, started Royal Oak Brewing and Detroit Brewing. Breweriana throughout the brewpub and brewery comes from the private collection of Stan Summers.

Seasonal beers change from year to year. The Martini Lounge can be reserved for private events. Free Wi-Fi. Mug Club. ATM onsite. Also, a Bike Club membership food and beer discounts, weekly rides, and other perks. The brewery hosts one of the largest Oktoberfest celebrations in Michigan, after Frankenmuth's, in late September/early October.

Directions: From M-59 just south of Rochester, take Exit 46 for M-150/Rochester Rd and head north 3.4 miles. Turn right (east) on 3rd St and then take the third left (north) on Water St. The brewery is on your right.

Stumbling Distance: Looking for a traditional Michigan Coney Dog? Try *Lipuma's* (621 N Main St, 248-652-9862). Don't miss *Clubhouse BFD* (2265 Crooks Rd, 248-289-6093, chbfd.com) one of the Top 100 Beer Bars in the USA according to *Draft Magazine*. Don't miss *Rochester Mills* larger brewery out in Auburn Hills for tours.

BASTONE BREWERY

Founded: 2004
Head Brewer: Rockne Van Meter
Address: 419 South Main Street • Royal Oak, MI 48067
Phone: 248-544-6250
Website: www.bastone.net
Annual Production: 860 barrels
Number of Beers: 8 on tap, 6 staples and 2 rotating

Staple Beers:
» Dubbel Vision
» Main Street Pilsner
» Monutmental Blonde
» Nectar De Dieux Triple
» Royal IPA
» Witface

Rotating Beers:
» Hefeweizen
» Helles
» Imperial IPA
» Milk Stout
» Oktoberfest
» Pilsner
» Rauchbier
» Saison Noir

Most Popular Brew: Royal IPA

Tours? Yes, by appointment.

Samples: Yes, 6 four-ounce samplers for about $7 (7 for $8, 8 for $9).

Best Time to Go: Happy hour daily 3–6PM.

Where can you buy it? Here on tap and to go in growlers. North Peak beers are sold here in 6-pack bottles.

Got food? Yes, an unusual collection of hors d'oeuvres including soups, salads, Belgian frites, fresh mussels, artichoke fritters, plus sandwiches (lobster club, portabella mushroom), thin-crust pizzas on granite slabs, large/small desserts, and a couple dozen wines. Kids eat free on Sundays.

Special Offer: Not participating.

The Beer Buzz: Another partner in the North Peak brewing entity, Bastone is a Belgian-style bar in an Art Deco building in downtown Royal Oak. Many of the beers here have won awards, and you can see proof on the wall. The main restaurant shows exposed brick walls and open ductwork, a bar top of tin, a floor of old-school mosaic tiles, and wood ceilings. Sit outside on the sidewalk in season. While there are a couple of TVs at the bar for some sports potential, the atmosphere is more of a classy restaurant than a brewpub (though it is still a casual place, in the end). Boards hanging above the bar show the current beers on tap.

Free Wi-Fi. No mug club, but Beer Club. Facebook.com/BastoneBrewery

Directions: From I-696 south of Royal Oak take Exit 16 toward Woodward Ave. Turn north on Main St and go 0.8 mile to the brewery; it will be on your right at the corner of 5th St.

Stumbling Distance: In the basement is the 70s-decor nightclub *Craft* (craftbar.net) which, as the name implies, focuses on craft beers and cocktails and features live music on some weeknights and DJs on the weekends. *Monk Beer Abbey* (monkbeerbar.com) opened here within the complex in 2013 and features Bastone's beer as well as a nice long list of Belgian brews, and *Vinotecca* is also under the same roof. *Jolly Pumpkin Café* (218 S Main St) is in the planning process and will offer food and the beers of the mother brewery just up the street.

LILY'S SEAFOOD GRILL & BREWERY

Founded: 1999
Brewmaster: Scott Morton
Address: 410 South Washington Avenue • Royal Oak, MI 48067
Phone: 248-591-5459
Website: www.lilysseafood.com
Annual Production: 550 barrels
Number of Beers: 7 on tap

Staple Beers:
» A. Strange Stout
» Propeller Island Pilsner
» Reggie's French River Red
» Sven And Ollies IPA
» Whitefish Bay Wheat

Rotating Beers:
» Big Bonnie Blonde
» Fairbanks Point Framboise
» Oktoberfest

Most Popular Brew: Sven and Ollies IPA

Brewmaster's Fave: Reggie's French River Red

Tours? By appointment.

Samples: Yes, seven 2.5-ounce samplers for about $5.50.

Best Time to Go: Open daily for lunch and dinner. Happy hour is 2PM–2AM on Monday, 2–6PM on Tuesday–Friday, and 11AM–6PM on Saturday.

Where can you buy it? Only here on tap and in growlers to go.

Got food? Yes, a fantastic line up of seafood. From 10PM–close there is a late-night menu. Kids' menu and house root beer are also available. Weekend brunches are popular.

Special Offer: $5 off a taster flight during your signature visit.

The Beer Buzz: Lily's is named for the owners' grandmother, and one of the beers is named for their grandfather Alexander Strange. It's a real family business here, and while they are all Michiganders, the idea came by way of Florida. Brewer Scott grew up in Michigan but lived for a time in Florida where he helped his older brother Bill open a raw bar in Jacksonville Beach. Twenty-two years later he was married with four kids and had opened 3 raw bars. Two of them, Ragtime Tavern in Atlantic Beach and A1A Ale Works in St. Augustine, had also become brewpubs. (They still exist but are under new ownership.) But the schools weren't too good there and he missed the four seasons, so he moved back to Michigan and started Lily's with his brothers Tom and Bob and their father Jack.

Located in what was once an S.S. Kresge store (a company that became Kmart in 1977), the restaurant/brewery got a makeover from the owners to give it some atmosphere, including some aquariums spread throughout, seafood sculptures with reclaimed metal, and family photos (including one of Lily herself) and local art on the walls. The copper brew system is visible through windows. The wine list is extensive and Scott's wife Susan, who manages the restaurant, is a sommelier. They sell special carrying bags that hold two growlers or 5 bottles of wine.

There's outdoor patio seating in summer. Mug club membership is for life. ATM onsite. Free Wi-Fi.

Directions: From I-696 south of Royal Oak take Exit 16 toward Woodward Ave. Turn north on Woodward Ave and soon after take a slight right on Washington Ave and go 0.7 mile to the brewery; it will be on your left.

Stumbling Distance: Allergic to seafood? Cross the street for some good Italian-style pizza at *Antica Pizzeria Fellini* (248-547-2751).

MILLKING IT PRODUCTIONS (MIP)

Founded: May 1, 2010
Brewmaster: Scott King
Address: 4847 Delemere Avenue • Royal Oak, MI 48073
Phone: 248-462-1338
Website: www.millkingit.com
Annual Production: 2,000 barrels
Number of Beers: 3 in cans, up to 4 seasonals on draft

Staple Beers:
» AXL PALE ALE
» BRIK IRISH RED
» SNO WHITE ALE

Rotating Beers:
» DESL STOUT
» JET BLACK IPA

Most Popular Brew: Brik Irish Red on draft, Axl Pale Ale in cans.

Brewmaster's Fave: Axl Pale Ale

Tours? Yes, by appointment or just drop in during the business day.

Samples: Yes, during a tour.

Best Time to Go: During the business day.

Where can you buy it? In Meijer supermarkets and other chains throughout Michigan; more common in the Detroit Metro area. Draft accounts in the neighborhood.

Got food? No.

Special Offer: A deep discount on a six-pack of their beer during your signature visit.

The Beer Buzz: This production brewery operates in a nondescript industrial building which people seem to stumble across despite its off-the-beaten-path location (and lack of signage). Business is booming and everything they make or are about to make is already sold. MIP joins a growing number of brewers moving to 16-oz. cans rather than bottles.

Brewer Scott got his start homebrewing in high school. He and a friend also used to make wine in their lockers. He studied English and Philosophy at U of Michigan and headed out west for a graduate program. In Seattle he helped out some brewers and put in some keg-washing time before heading to Boulder, CO. But the brewing industry started getting crowded and in 1993 he decided to move to Michigan. He put in some time at Bell's, Frankenmuth, and Detroit Mackinaw Brewing before he opened King Brewing in Pontiac in 1994. That brewery closed in 2009, and Scott took his talents to this growing beer mecca of Royal Oak.

Scott's mission is craft brew kept simple. He prefers to make good, accessible session beers and focus on just a few styles. Though MIP is available throughout Michigan, the brewers like to keep their beer close and know where it is going. For now there are the 3 flagship beers being canned, plus up to 4 seasonals which go out for draft accounts with no immediate plans for canning. Kristy Smith, the president/keg cleaner/taxpayer, is also the tour guide.

Directions: From I-75 take Exit 65 for 14 Mile Rd heading west. Go 3.5 miles and turn right (north) on Delemere Rd. The brewery is the second building on the left.

Stumbling Distance: When you're done here, head over to the collection of brewers nearby in downtown Royal Oak.

ROYAL OAK BREWERY

Founded: 1995
Brewmaster: Tim Selewski
Address: 215 East 4th Street • Royal Oak, MI 48067
Phone: 248-544-1141
Website: www.royaloakbrewery.com
Annual Production: 1,100 barrels
Number of Beers: 5–8 plus 2 guest taps

Staple Beers:
» NORTHERN LIGHT
» PAPPY'S PORCH SIPPIN' PORTER
» ROYAL PRIDE IPA

Rotating Beers:
» ALT
» COFFEE AND CREAM STOUT
» DOUBLE IPA
» GREAT WHITE IPA
» IMPERIAL STOUT
» MARGARITA WIT
» 90 SHILLINGS SCOTCH ALE
» OKTOBERFEST
» RASPBERRY WHEAT
» ROYAL OAK RED
» SNOWDRIFT WINTER ALE
» STEAM BEER
» SUICIDE BLONDE (TRIPLE FERMENTATION FOR 14% ABV)
» WIT
» A CASK ALE EVERY FRIDAY

Most Popular Brew: Royal Pride IPA

Brewmaster's Fave: Oktoberfest or 90 Shillings Scotch Ale

Tours? Yes, by appointment with one week notice for up to 20.

Samples: Yes, 5 five-ounce samplers for about $6.50, plus $1.50 for each extra.

Best Time to Go: Open daily for lunch until midnight (2AM Friday–Saturday). Happy hour is 3–6PM Monday–Friday. A bit of live music on the deck in summer, occasionally in winter as well. Watch Facebook for upcoming events. Busiest in November–December due to numerous private holiday parties.

Where can you buy it? Only here on tap or in growlers or kegs to go.

Got food? Yes, a full menu and bar, with pastas, brick-oven pizzas, sandwiches, soups and salads. Beer cheese soup, beer-battered fish and chips, mac and cheese with andouille sausage, shepherd's pie, muffaletta, Korean tacos, and giant soft pretzels.

Special Offer: Not participating.

The Beer Buzz: A long established beer landmark here in downtown Royal Oak, this brewpub is a sister company to Detroit Beer not so far down the road. Royal Oak was a sort of sleepy edge-of-Detroit community back in the late 1990s, and became a surprise cosmopolitan place almost overnight it seems. The brewpub opened just before that transformation happened. The building was once an antiques store and exposed brick runs along one wall. There is abundant table seating plus a good number of spots at the bar. The copper brew system was custom built to fit in the narrow space behind the bar. While not a sports bar per se, there are plenty of TVs throughout if you want to see a game. Chill in the bier garden, an outdoor deck in back with ceiling fans and a bar.

To keep with the times, Royal Oak Brewery redid their line up in 2012, keeping the three staples, but then developing a constant rotation of specialty beers to keep return customers exploring. A complete remodel in early 2013 updated the interiors, replacing the old wood bar with concrete and modernizing a bit.

Brewer Tim began homebrewing in the early 90s, took the plunge in 1997 to attend Siebel in Chicago for a Certificate in Brewing, and landed here one month later.

Free Wi-Fi. Mug club.

Directions: From I-696 south of Royal Oak take Exit 16 toward Main St/Woodward Ave. Turn right (north) on Main St and continue 0.8 mile and turn right (east) on 4th St and the brewery will be on your left.

Stumbling Distance: *Lily's Seafood* and *Bastone* are short walks from here, making this a nice hat-trick for a brewpub crawl.

SHERWOOD BREWING CO.

Founded: August 31, 2006
Head Brewer: Corey Paul
Address: 45689 Hayes Road • Shelby Township, MI 48315
Phone: 586-532-9669
Website: www.sherwoodbrewing.com
Number of Beers: 4–6 on tap

Staple Beers:
» Buxom Blondde Ale
» Cork County Red Ale
» Green River Wheat IPA
» Mistress Jade's Hemp Ale
» Verry Cherry Trippel
» Wildflower Saison
» Wintertwined Wheat Wine

Tours? By appointment.

Samples: Yes, including beer flights.

Best Time to Go: Open daily at 11:30AM (noon on Sunday). Live music on the weekends.

Where can you buy it? Only here on tap and to go in growlers. Also 6-gallon and ½ barrels available.

Got food? Yes, for lunch and dinner. Appetizers include a few less common items such as poutine, hot pretzels, and potato pancakes. Soups and salads, burgers and sandwiches, pizzas, and fish and chips.

Special Offer: Not participating.

The Beer Buzz: Situated in a strip mall on the west side of Hayes Road, this roomy tap room has tables down the center and booths along the wall to the right. The brewhouse is behind a green graffiti wall on the left. The high industrial ceilings are painted orange, and a beer bottle collection runs along the top of the walls around the room. Half-barrels rest on a toboggan. Owner Ray Sherwood is himself a brewer but Corey handles the production these days.

Easy parking in the large lot out front. Free Wi-Fi. MugLess Club. Facebook.com/SherwoodBrewing

Directions: From I-94 north of Detroit, take Exit 240 onto M-59/ William P Rosso Hwy toward Utica. Drive 6.8 miles and turn right (north) on Hayes Rd. The brewery is on the left (west) side of the street beyond a large parking lot in a strip mall.

WITCH'S HAT BREWING CO.

Founded: December 26, 2011
Head Brewer: Ryan Cottongim
Address: 22235 Pontiac Trail • South Lyon, MI 48178
Phone: 248-486-2595
Website: www.witchshatbrewing.com
Annual Production: 360 barrels
Number of Beers: 7–12 on tap including meads

Staple Beers:
» Big Doedish Double IPA
» Edward's Portly Brown
» Hyppie Girl Blonde
» Three Körd Kölsch
» Train Hopper IPA

Rotating Beers:
» B-Cubed Pilsner
» Bear-Ass Wheat
» Fear Of The Dark Black
  Barleywine
» Holy Confusion Barleywine
» The Kipper Scotch Ale
» Night Fury Imperial Stout
» 1908 Smoked American Wheat
» Oktoberfest
» Rumble Under The Red Light
» Simcoe Session IPA
» Tuscan Coffee Stout
» Witch Hunt Stout

Most Popular Brew: Train Hopper IPA

Brewmaster's Fave: Train Hopper IPA, Edward's Portly Brown and Big Doedish DIPA

Tours? Yes, randomly if you're lucky or by appointment.

Samples: Yes, 5 five-ounce samplers for about $7.50.

Best Time to Go: Open daily at 2PM and on until 9PM on Sundays and Mondays, 11PM Tuesday–Thursday, and midnight on Friday–Saturday.

Where can you buy it? Here on tap and to go in growlers or 32-oz. "growlettes" (plus Doedish and occasional others in limited onsite 22-oz. bombers), or on tap in a number of establishments around Southeast Michigan (see the website for a list).

Got food? Yes, but just a few sandwiches, cheeses and meats from IGA plus all-you-can-eat popcorn for $2. But it's food friendly: order in or bring you're own. They make their own root beer and cream soda.

Special Offer: A free Witch's Hat pint glass with during signature visit.

The Beer Buzz: Witch's Hat depot was an actual train station, but it burned down in 1908 and was later rebuilt and moved to the middle of town in McHattie Park. Owners Ryan and Erin Cottongim were actually married at the park in 2007. Their brewery of the same name is set in a strip mall at the edge of town. It's a cozy place, almost like a coffee-shop vibe, with a gas fireplace, local art for sale on the walls, some board games, and a couple of TVs. The table tops show Erin's bottle cap collection.

The brew system stands behind the bar along the wall to the right. This is a far cry from what got the couple started in the brewing habit. In 2004 they stumbled upon a used Mr. Beer homebrew kit at a garage sale and Ryan started brewing, quickly moving beyond anything a Mr. Beer could produce. This place has been a dream of theirs ever since. When both he and Erin got laid off from their jobs, they decided to take the plunge. They are both South Lyon natives and grew up loving the place, so the location was a no-brainer. Erin makes the mead.

Try a Steam Engine, which is a blend of 1908 and Train Hopper. Edward's Portly Brown is named after the owners' Springer Spaniel and 5% of all sales are donated to the Humane Society of Huron Valley, a great no-kill local animal shelter. The mug club mugs are exceptionally cool hand-blown glass from the Dearborn Glass Academy.

Free Wi-Fi. Mug Club.

Directions: From I-96 north of South Lyon, take Exit 153 and go south on Kent Lake Rd. At Silver Lake Rd turn left (east) and take the next right (south) on Pontiac Trail which becomes Lafayette as you head through town. Cross 9 Mile Rd and the brewery is in the strip mall beyond the parking lot on to the right (west).

Stumbling Distance: Looking for some other beers to go? Check out *Country Acres Market* (12596 10 Mile Rd, 248-437-4910) for a fantastic beer selection.

COPPER CANYON BREWERY

Founded: 1997
Head Brewer: Todd Parker
Address: 27522 Northwestern Highway • Southfield, MI 48034
Phone: 248-223-1700
Website: www.coppercanyonbrewery.com
Annual Production: 400 barrels
Number of Beers: 7 on tap plus root beer

Staple Beers:
» Copper Canyon Alt
» Devil's Peak IPA
» Munich Helles
» Northwest Gold

Rotating Beers:
» Buffalo Jump Coffee Stout
» Killer Canyon Porter
» Miri Maibock
» Summer Zest
» plus two handpulls—an IPA and a dark beer

Most Popular Brew: Devil's Peak IPA

Brewmaster's Fave: "Depends on my mood. Would you pick your favorite kid?"

Tours? Only by appointment.

Samples: Yes, samplers of six beers plus a root beer for about $8.

Best Time to Go: Happy hour is daily from 3–7PM. Growler refills are cheaper on Sundays and Wednesdays.

Where can you buy it? Only here on tap (pints and 25-oz. pours) plus growlers to go. Some bottles on rare occasions.

Got food? Yes, previously this was a steakhouse but now has a broader menu including burgers, sandwiches, soups, salads, brick-oven pizzas, beer-battered fish, and even a Coney dog.

Special Offer: Not participating.

The Beer Buzz: Located down a frontage road, Copper Canyon is easily spotted with its somewhat wood-lodge exterior and a grain silo out front.

The name Copper Canyon comes from the copper-clad brew system, and to match, the building has copper front doors and trim. Inside is an amber-lighted spacious dining space with a fireplace at one end. The bar maintains a humidor and a smoking room, with its own bar and TV, just for cigar smokers. A beer garden space is outside.

Brewer Todd has a Masters in marine biology, but he decided to give brewing a shot. He has brewed professionally for over 14 years and as a homebrewer for over 24. He started working in California, then Wisconsin at Pioneer Brewing, then Michigan. He's put in time at Rochester Brewing and Royal Oak Brewery. He gives Beerposiums the first Saturday of every month. A small fee gets you in for some tasting and talking.

Free Wi-Fi. Mug Club.

Directions: If you take I-696 to Southfield, you will merge onto M-10 here. From the east take Exit 10 onto M-10, take the fork right toward Lahser Rd, turn left on 11 Mile Road and continue on Northwestern Hwy. Brewery is on the right about 1 mile from that fork. From the west take Exit 8 onto M-10, drive 1 mile, take Exit 18A onto US-24/Telegraph Rd. Go 0.8 mile, turn right on Northwestern Hwy and it is half a mile more on your left.

Stumbling Distance: *New Seoul Garden* (27566 Northwestern Hwy, 248-827-1600, newseoulgarden.com) is right across the parking lot with some very good Korean BBQ.

SUE'S COFFEE HOUSE

Founded: July 2006
Brewmaster: Pat Hool
Address: 201 North Riverside Avenue • St. Clair, MI 48079
Phone: 810-326-1212
Website: www.suescoffeehouse.com
Number of Beers: 4 on tap

Possible Beers:
» ENGLISH ALE
» IPA
» OKTOBERFEST
» STOUT
» SUMMER LAGER

Tours? By appointment.

Samples: No.

Best Time to Go: Open daily at 7AM (8AM on Sunday, no alcohol until noon).

Where can you buy it? Here on tap and to go in growlers (but not for premium beers).

Got food? Yes, great sandwiches, salads, soups and some sweets, plus the usual Italian-style coffee house drinks. Burgers on special nights (Thursday–Saturday at time of printing).

Special Offer: Not participating.

The Beer Buzz: If you think this is a nice coffee shop with great food facing the St. Clair River... well, you're right. But it is also a little brewery and cigar lounge. Beyond the dining room and barista station through a stone arch is a tasting room which opens out into the outdoor mall area behind the establishment. You'll see a sign for the Man Cave as well. Husband and wife team Sue and Pat Hool operate this little gem in St Clair. She was looking for something to do when her kids grew up and moved away, and she had always dreamed of owning a coffee shop. Pat likes to make beer and has a humidor on site. They also serve wine by the glass, carafe and bottle. I think we all win here.

Anita's Catering does cooking demos here from time to time (Anita works here and makes much of this amazing food). This is a nice community gathering spot as well as a great stop on any road trip up along the St. Clair River. You can watch the big boats pass very close to shore here.

Free Wi-Fi. On Facebook.

Directions: M-29 becomes Riverside Ave and passes right through town along the St. Clair River. The coffee house is part of Riverside Plaza opposite the river.

Stumbling Distance: *Marine City Fish Co.* (240 S Water St, Marine City, 810-765-5477, marinecityfishcompany.com) is a good place for dinner—homemade pasta, fresh local fish—and serves a lot of Michigan beers and wines.

GRANITE CITY FOOD & BREWERY

Founded: 2006
Brewmaster: Cory O'Neel in Iowa
Address: 699 West Big Beaver Road • Troy, MI 48084
Phone: 248-519-1040
Website: www.gcfb.net
Annual Production: 700 barrels
Number of Beers: 4

Staple Beers:
» Broad Axe Stout
» Brother Benedict's Bock
» Duke Of Wellington IPA
» Northern Light Lager

Most Popular Brew: Northern Light

Samples: A tray of eight 3-oz. samples for about $4.95.

Best Time to Go: Open daily: Monday–Thursday 11AM–1AM, Friday–Saturday 11AM–2AM, Sunday 9AM–10PM. Happy hour runs weekdays 3–6PM, Saturday–Sunday noon–5PM, and every night 9PM–close.

Where can you buy it? Growlers on site (or any of the other 27 Granite City locations)!

Got food? Yes, flatbread pizzas, soups and salads, seafood, pasta, burgers, steaks and monthly specials. There are also a gluten-free and kids' menus.

Special Offer: Not participating.

The Beer Buzz: First founded in 1999 in St. Cloud, Minnesota, this brewpub franchise has expanded throughout the Midwest. They have a very unusual brewing process which they call Fermentus Interruptus™. The wort is actually prepared in their central brewing facility—a 25-barrel brewhouse in Ellsworth, Iowa—and then shipped to this location where it is fermented. The name comes from the 19th-century industry that built St. Cloud: quarrying granite.

The restaurant is a stand-alone building just off the interstate. Plenty of parking.

Directions: From I-75 take Exit 69 for Big Beaver Rd. Go west and the brewery is on the south side of the road. You need to make a U-turn to come back to it.

Stumbling Distance: *Shield's* (1476 W Maple Rd, 248-637-3131, shieldspizza.com) isn't a bad place for a square pizza and a beer. Plus there are many more breweries in the surrounding communities: Birmingham, Royal Oak, Ferndale, Southfield, etc.

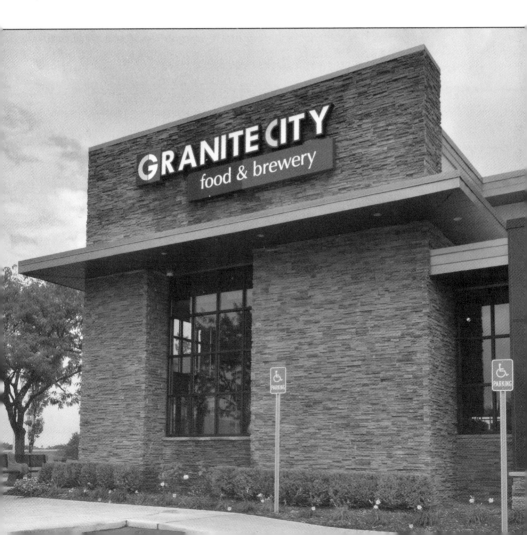

DRAGONMEAD MICROBREWERY

Founded: May 1997
Head Brewer: Erik Harms, with Spencer Channell and Brad Etheridge
Address: 14600 East 11 Mile Road • Warren, MI 48089
Phone: 586-776-9428
Website: www.dragonmead.com
Annual Production: 2,600 barrels
Number of Beers: 47 on tap at time of printing; 72 styles and rising, aiming for 139 styles on tap

Staple Beers:
» CROWN JEWELS IPA
» DARK KNIGHT BLACK IPA
» ERIK THE RED (IRISH-STYLE ALE)
» FINAL ABSOLUTION BELGIAN TRIPPEL
» SIR WILLIAM'S ESB
» UNDER THE KILT WEE HEAVY (SCOTCH-STYLE ALE)

Rotating Beers:
» WAY TOO MANY TO LIST HERE. SEVERAL BEERS ON NITRO TAPS AND TWO HAND PULLS. SEE THE COMPLETE LIST ON THEIR WEBSITE.

Most Popular Brew: Final Absolution

Brewmaster's Fave: Erik the Red

Tours? Yes, but the 45-minute tour is by prior appointment.

Samples: Yes, 5 five-ounce samplers for about $11

Best Time to Go: Open Monday–Wednesday 3–11PM, Thursday 11AM–11PM, Friday–Saturday 11AM–midnight, Sunday 1–8PM. Watch for live music on weekends and check out firkin Mondays.

Where can you buy it? On tap and to go in growlers. Regionally throughout the Lower Peninsula. Five varieties are available in 12-oz. bottles.

Got food? Yes, burgers, cheese and crackers, poppers, chicken tenders, fries, dragon wings, pretzels, some pizza and more. Otherwise, it's food friendly: you can carry in your own, and they have menus from other establishments for ordering delivery.

Special Offer: A bottle label & coaster package during the signature visit.

The Beer Buzz: Walk in and see the suit of armor, the dragon wrapped around a tower on the tap handle, and the mosaic behind the bar. My first thought was *Dungeons & Dragons*. In fact, two of the three founders, Larry Channell, Earl Sherbarth, and Bill Wrobel, were huge D&D fans and much of what you see in the pub comes from Larry's private collection. Bill made the stained glass. All three of them have put in time with the auto industry. Larry was working at Chrysler when Bill came as a co-op student "a long time ago." Earl is Bill's father-in-law. They started making wassail and meads before moving on to beer. Bill bought Earl a homebrew kit and they made an English ale. They liked it and kept going. When they went to work on their brewery plan, it was just for distribution at first. But when they added the tap room in 1998, it became apparent fans wanted to pop in and sit at a bar. Note the cut where the last bar expansion took place.

Until 2013 this was known as "The Biggest Nanobrewery in the World," meaning brewing batches under 4 barrels per batch. There may be a crazy number of beers here, especially when you count the number of styles in a year, but batches were typically very small, usually 93 gallons. A popular brew might last two weeks or less in the pub. The goal of the brewers is to brew one of every known style, and they are aiming at the 139 officially recognized styles. In order to accomplish this, they did an internal expansion in 2013 to multiply their capacity sevenfold. Their next pub expansion will include 75 taps.

They aren't looking to just make a lot of high-gravity brews but rather keep true to those styles. And not just any old recipe will do, either: in order to count a style as done, their brew needs to make it to a medal round in world-wide competition or be used to train beer judges (such as Final Absolution has been). Ingredients for each beer are shipped in from the land of origin of that particular style. Numerous medals for the beers hang from the walls. Plus RateBeer put them in the top 50 brewers in the world, and they were dubbed Detroit's Best Brewpub in 2012.

Free Wi-Fi. There is a passport club so members can keep track of where they've been in the brewery's long list of beers.

Directions: From I-696 take Exit 26 for Groesbeck. If you are on the north side of the interstate (ie. coming from the east on I-696), you need to cross over to the south side of the interstate (on Bunert Rd) and take that service drive (eastbound 11 Mile Rd) just past Bunert Rd to find the brewery on the right.

Stumbling Distance: Good for some ordering in: *Lazybones Smokehouse* (27475 Groesbeck Hwy, Roseville, 586-775-7427) for some barbecue and *King's Pizza* (16273 E 11 Mile Rd, Roseville, 586-772-5330).

FALLING DOWN BEER COMPANY

Founded: March 29, 2013
Brewmaster: Mark Larson
Address: 2270 East 10 Mile Road • Warren, MI 48091
Phone: 586-799-2739
Website: www.fallingdownbeer.com
Annual Production: 500–700 barrels
Number of Beers: up to 16 on tap; a new beer each week

Staple Beers:
» ANGRY BEAVER DOUBLE BROWN
» BLOOD ORANGE IPA
» CHERRY BLONDE
» NINJA CHICKEN PALE ALE

Rotating Beers:
» CAMPFIRE BROWN
» ELDERBERRY WHEAT
» ENGLISH MILD
» IRISH OLD ALE
» MUSCOVADO STOUT
» SUMMER IPA
» SUMMER WHEAT

Most Popular Brew: Ninja Chicken Pale Ale

Brewmaster's Fave: Muscovado Stout

Tours? Yes, anytime you come in and Mark is there.

Samples: Yes, 4 six-ounce samplers for about $7 (excluding limited batches).

Best Time to Go: Hours vary, check the website. Closed Mondays. Live music on many Thursdays and Saturdays.

Where can you buy it? On tap and in growlers. Some keg distribution in the area, cans in the works for 2014.

Got food? Yes, burgers and sandwiches, and some deep-fried things.

Special Offer: Not participating.

The Beer Buzz: Owners Mark Larson and George Lang both started as homebrewers. Being a homebrewer makes you popular, and it wasn't long before they realized they were making all this beer and not drinking hardly any of it themselves. Solution? Start a brewery. The startup took two years to get going in a former family diner, opening in March of 2013. By August they already were remodeling to make more room for some live music.

The name Falling Down is an inside joke among friends. One time while Mark was out drinking with buddies, he got up to use the restroom after his first beer and fell right off his barstool. They teased him that he was "falling down drunk" after just one beer.

The styles come and go here as Mark loves to try new things and switch them up. On a personal level he prefers the dark English-style ales. His Muscovado Stout is a winter seasonal and takes its name from a type of unrefined brown sugar.

Directions: From downtown Detroit take I-75 to I-696 and go east. Take Exit 19 for Couzens Ave/10 Mile Rd. Turn left on 10 Mile Rd and the brewery is 0.6 mile on the right.

Stumbling Distance: Be sure to check out the other two breweries in Warren.

Courtesy of Falling Down Beer Company

KUHNHENN BREWING CO.

Founded: 2000
Brewmasters: Bret and Eric Kuhnhenn
Address: 5919 Chicago Road • Warren, MI 48092
Phone: 586-979-8361
Website: www.kbrewery.com
Annual Production: 1,000 barrels
Number of Beers: up to 24 on tap, 50–60 brews per year

Staple Beers:
» AMERICAN IPA
» CLASSIC AMERICAN
» DRIPA (DOUBLE RICE IPA)
» THE FLUFFER (SESSION IPA)
» IMPERIAL CREME BRULE JAVA STOUT
» KUHNHENN FESTBIER
» KUHNIEWEIZEN
» LOONIE KUHNIE PALE ALE
» PENETRATION PORTER
» SIMCOE SILLY

Rotating Beers:
» ALDEBARAN (BELGIAN IPA)
» ANNELIESE AMBER
» BOHEMIAN PILS
» CONUNDRUM (ENGLISH DARK MILD)
» DARK HEATHEN TRIPLE BOCK
» EXPORT STOUT
» 4TH DEMENTIA OLDE ALE
» KUHNIE WIT
» SULLY'S KOLSCH
» WHITE DEVIL (IMPERIAL BELGIAN WIT)
» WINTER WONDER LAGER
» PLUS BOURBON-BARREL AGED VARIETIES

Most Popular Brew: Loonie Kuhnie Pale Ale

Brewmaster's Fave: Both brewers say Loonie Kuhnie Pale Ale. It's what started it all for them and so it is near and dear to their hearts.

Tours? Yes, but call and make an appointment otherwise it is quite random.

Samples: Yes, five pre-selected samplers for about $9, or choose your own 5 for about $13.

Best Time to Go: Monday–Thursday 11AM–midnight, Friday–Saturday 11AM–2AM. Call for Sunday hours.

Where can you buy it? Here on tap and to go in growlers and bottles. All over Michigan, and in Manhattan, Ontario, and even a wee bit in The Netherlands.

Got food? Free popcorn, plus 8-inch pizzas, stuffed jalapenos, pretzels, cheese and cracker boards with sausages

Special Offer: A free piece of logo glassware with the signature of your book.

The Beer Buzz: This 1929 building was originally a blacksmith's. Eric Sr. (the brewing brothers, Eric Jr. and Bret's father) bought the building back in 1972, and the family ran it as a Lutz Hardware. Bret and Eric sold homebrewing supplies out of the store as well. When a Big-Box hardware store forced them out of business, they divided the building and opened the microbrewery and a brew-on-premises operation in one side while a sporting goods store occupied the other. Eventually they needed to expand and they knocked out the central wall and took over the whole space. Brewing on premises was no longer feasible for space reasons so they discontinued that in 2010. To keep up with the incredibly growing demand, Kuhnhenn Brewing opened a production facility in nearby Clinton Township. This will also be open to the public, and its much larger capacity will allow this location to focus more on smaller specialty batches and barrel aging.

The taproom still has the old wood floor and exposed brick, but there's a big square bar with a brass rail in the middle of the space. Medals for their beers hang from the lights above the bar. Big windows look out onto the street and let in a lot of light. The brewery occupies the back of the building, and the serving tanks in back use collapsible bladders inside, which is common in Germany but not in the US for some reason. The current tap list is on a large chalkboard. Real ales are served on occasion as well. They also make root beer, wines, and meads, including metheglins, which are meads flavored with herbs or spices. According to RateBeer.com this was the 10th best brewer in the world.

Free WiFi

Directions: From I-696 east of I-75 and just north of Detroit, get off on Mound Rd (Exit 22) heading north into Warren. Continue 3 miles and turn right on Chicago Rd. The brewery is immediately on the left.

Stumbling Distance: A local square pizza that gets raves here in Warren is *Buddy's* (8100 Old 13 Mile Rd, 586-574-9200, buddyspizza.com).

SPORTS BREWPUB

Founded: 1996
Brewmaster: John Grwzya
Address: 166 Maple Street • Wyandotte, MI 48192
Phone: 734-285-5060
Website: www.sportsbp.com
Number of Beers: 10

Staple Beers:
» IPA
» IRISH RED
» MARK'S WEINER DOG STOUT
» NAKED BLONDE
» RASPBERRY WHEAT
» SOLACE WHEAT

Rotating Beers:
» CHERRY ALE
» HOPPIN' HONEY IPA
» OKTOBERFEST
» SUMMER SQUEEZE (LIKE A SHANDY)

Most Popular Brew: Naked Blonde

Brewmaster's Fave: IPA

Tours? No.

Samples: Yes, $1–2 for a 4-ounce pour.

Best Time to Go: Open Monday–Wednesday 11AM–11PM, Thursdays 11AM–midnight, Friday–Saturday 11AM–2AM, and Sunday noon–10PM. Happy hour is 3–5PM weekdays.

Where can you buy it? Only here on tap (10- and 22-oz. pours) and in growlers and keggies.

Got food? Yes, free popcorn. A full menu with 75 kinds of sandwiches, burgers, and wraps, plus soups and salads, warm pretzels basted in wheat beer, hand-tossed pizza with wheat-beer and herb pizza sauce. Deep-fried ravioli, fried pierogi, lake perch, a beer-battered option for fresh walleye on Fridays, and beer battered pickles. Fish dinners every day during Lent.

Special Offer: Not participating.

The Beer Buzz: While this little place may be a surprise in Wyandotte, beer historians know better. The first brewer here was the Marx Brewery back in 1863. In 1896 it was briefly known as the Wyandotte Brewery, and then it merged with Eureka Brewing in 1910. During Prohibition they made ice and malt extract (you can brew with that, you know) and were punished for it but otherwise off the hook. Despite surviving Prohibition, they closed their doors in 1936.

The name says it all: walk in and the walls are coated with sports memorabilia and photos and 25 TVs showing the games. Absent that, this could be an old-fashioned diner: retro tables and booths, glass block in the walls, neon lights, a jukebox, and the counter seating one would expect. The brewhouse is in the front corner visible from outside through the window. There is also outdoor seating with a large awning protecting it from sun or rain.

Free Wi-Fi. Beer Club.

Directions: Take I-75 southwest of Detroit to Exit 42 for Outer Drive. You need to turn right and make a U-turn to head east/southeast on Outer Dr one mile. Turn right on Jefferson Ave and stay on it for 3.3 miles even as it becomes Biddle Ave. Then turn right on Maple St and the brewpub is on the right.

Stumbling Distance: Don't miss one of the best beer bars around, right here in town: *The Oak Café* (1167 Oak St, 734-283-8380, theoakcafe.com) with 40 brews on tap and knowledgeable staff.

CORNER BREWERY (ARBOR BREWING CO.)

Founded: 2006
Brewmaster: John Ritenour
Address: 720 Norris Street • Ypsilanti, MI 48198
Phone: 734-480-2739
Website: www.cornerbrewery.com
Annual Production: 4,500 barrels
Number of Beers: 10 on tap, 25 styles through the year

Staple Beers:
» BOLLYWOOD BLONDE
» BUZZ SAW AMERICAN IPA
» SACRED COW IPA
» YPSI GYPSY APA

Rotating Beers:
» DEMETRIUS AGED PALE ALE
» FIGJAM QUADRUPEL
» FLAMBOYANT WILD RED
» FRAMBOOZLED
» GREEN GIANT ORGANIC IMPERIAL PILSNER
» MACKINAC FUDGE STOUT
» MR DELICIOUS DOUBLE IPA
» RYECLOPS IMPERIAL RYE
» SODIBO
» VIOLIN MONSTER AUTUMN ALE

Most Popular Brew: Buzzsaw American IPA

Brewmaster's Fave: Green Giant Organic Imperial Pilsner

Tours? By chance or by appointment.

Samples: Yes, about $1 each.

Best Time to Go: Afternoons in the beer garden. Open daily 2PM Monday–Thursday, noon Friday–Sunday. Happy hour 4–6PM, Monday–Friday.

Thanks from the bottom of our barrels
to the following individuals who invested their
time and money to help build the
Corner Brewery.

Where can you buy it? Here on tap or in growlers, plus six-packs, 750ml bottles, and kegs to go. Glasses are 10 oz., ½ liter, (and full liters until 7PM).

Got food? Yes, sandwiches, brats, burgers, warm pretzels, stone-baked pizzas.

Special Offer: Your first beer at Happy Hour prices during your signature visit.

The Beer Buzz: Michigan law prohibits distribution from a brewpub (with a brewpub license). However, Matt and Rene Greff, owners of the highly successful brewpub Arbor Brewing Co. in Ann Arbor, wanted to make more beers and give them to the wider world. By now residents of Ypsilanti, they found a manufacturing office building that had been vacant for more than a decade. The single-story industrial building with concrete floors and plenty of parking proved to be ideal. It was built in 1922 and is now part of an historic district, so the remodeling had to be done carefully. Like its sister brewery, Corner Brewery is solar-powered, saving nearly half of the gas they once used and perhaps as much as a fifth of the electricity they had pulled off the grid. ABC was the first solar-powered brewery in Michigan.

The taproom is roomy and bright with a lot of outside light and features a long L-shaped bar with windows behind it looking out into the beer garden. The rest of the room offers a collection of mismatched tables and chairs, and some booths.

Brewer John had a psych degree from University of Michigan. He volunteered at Corner, decided he preferred brews to loose screws, and headed off to Siebel Institute for brewer training. He returned and worked his way up to head brewer. The folks at Corner are crazy so the university degree still applies. Watch for his Party Shark hat which he makes people wear when they are having a bad day.

Watch for the six to eight beer release parties throughout the year hosted by the owners Matt and Rene.

Free Wi-Fi. Mug Club. ATM on site. Facebook.com/CornerBrewery and Twitter @CornerBrew

Directions: From I-94 take Exit 183 for Ypsilanti and turn north on Huron St. Follow this about 1.5 miles and turn right (east) on Forest Ave. Go 0.2 mile and turn left on Norris St and the brewery is right there. From Ann Arbor it is shorter mileage but about the same travel time (20 minutes) to just take Washtenaw straight out to Huron St and turn left (north) to get to Forest Ave.

Stumbling Distance: Lots of history here in Ypsi: *Michigan Firehouse Museum* (110 W Cross St, 734-547-0663, michiganfirehousemuseum. org) and *Ypsilanti Automotive Heritage Museum* (100 E Cross St, 734-482-5200, ypsiautoheritage.org). *Sidetrack Bar & Grill* (56 E Cross St, 734-483-1490, sidetrackbarandgrill.com) is known for great burgers and beer tastings. Owner Dave French also serves his own Frog Island Beer here (contract brewed offsite). Ypsilanti is home to one of the biggest Elvis fests (mielvisfest.org), typically held in July.

ZONE 3

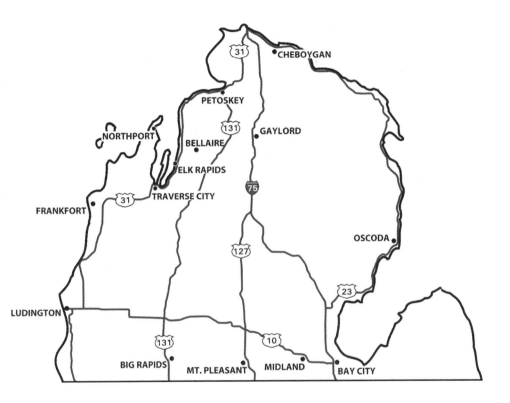

FLETCHER STREET BREWING CO.

Founded: 2003
Address: 124 West Fletcher Street • Alpena, MI 49707
Phone: 989-340-0931
Website: www.alpenabeer.com
Number of Beers: 11 on tap plus sarsaparilla

Staple Beers:
» Cool City Kolsch
» IPA
» Lumber Lager Red
» Papermaker Pilsner
» Sink Hole Stout
» Tactical Black IPA
» Thunder Bay Bock
» Windiate Weizenbock

Tours? By appointment.

Samples: Yes, beer flights.

Best Time to Go: Closed Sunday and Monday. Live entertainment on Saturdays.

Where can you buy it? Here on tap and to go in growlers.

Got food? Yes.

Special Offer: Not participating.

The Beer Buzz: Once the site of a paper factory, this building has been fashioned into a great microbrewery. High ceilings and lots of space as one might expect from an industrial-type building. Beer garden space outside. Views of the Thunder Bay River are notable.

Directions: Come into Alpena on US-23 or M-32 and follow either into downtown. Either intersects 2nd Ave. Take that northeast and it crosses the bridge over the river. The first left is Fletcher St and the brewery is on the left.

B.A.R.T.S. BREWERY

Founded: 2006
Brewmaster: Marty Rapnicki
Address: 804 East Midland Street • Bay City, MI 48708
Phone: 989-891-0100
Website: www.bartsbaycity.com
Annual Production: 450 barrels
Number of Beers: 11 on tap

Staple Beers:
» Hefe Weizen
» IPA
» Light
» Oatmeal Stout
» Red Ale
» Toughman Dopplebock

Rotating Beers:
» 357 Ale
» Baltic Porter
» English Pale Ale
» Kölsch With Rye
» Oktoberfest
» Rappsody Ale
» ...and other Seasonals

Most Popular Brew: IPA

Brewmaster's Fave: Oktoberfest

Tours? Yes, free but by appointment.

Samples: Yes, get all 11 on tap in sampler glasses for about $13.

Best Time to Go: Watch for winter hour changes. Cheaper growler fills on Tuesdays. Stables is open daily at 5PM (4PM on Thursday and Saturday) and features live music, DJs and more.

Where can you buy it? Only here on tap or in growlers to go.

Got food? Yes, a full menu including steaks, fish & chips, burgers and sandwiches, appetizers and salads, and wood-fired oven pizzas. Beer finds its way into a few of the recipes.

Special Offer: Get $1 off your first pint during your signature visit.

The Beer Buzz: B.A.R.T.S. is an acronym for everything that's going on in this one building: Banquets, Art's Grilled Pizza, Restaurant, Tap Room, and Stables. While Stables is a martini and cigar bar in the back of the building with live music, the building did indeed once have stables within. In the late 1800s, during the heyday of the logging industry, this was a mill with horses in the basement.

This is a spacious establishment with old hardwood floors and a pressed tin ceiling. Seating is in booths and at a few tables, and the wood bar is long with a few small TVs mounted about the room. The brewing system is visible from the outside through the front windows and through windows along the booths inside. The banquet halls, often used for hosting weddings, are on the second floor. Hours for the pub vary with the seasons, but Stables is always open and serves the brewery's beer. Brewer Marty started as a homebrewer but put in professional time at a lot of other places before arriving here.

Directions: From I-75 take Exit 162 and head east on Business I-75/M-25 into Bay City. Turn left (north) on Euclid Ave, drive 4 blocks, and turn right (east) on Midland St. After 0.6 mile when Midland starts to bend left, be sure to make the right turn to stay on Midland. Drive past 5 blocks and the brewery is on the right.

Stumbling Distance: If you are in the mood for some German food and good beer—local and German—check out *Stein Haus* (1108 N Water St, 989-891-2337, steinhausbaycity.com).

Beer School At BARTS

Rex Halfpenny, the man behind the excellent free quarterly publication *The Michigan Beer Guide*, comes here once a month (3rd Tuesday at time of printing) to host Beer Studies 501. He talks about a particular style of beer and presents samples of said style along with some food to go with it. Very enlightening, very delicious. Reservations are required and the price is just around $20.

TRI-CITY BREWING COMPANY

Founded: 2007
Brewmaster: Paul Popa
Address: 3020 North Water Street • Bay City, MI 48708
Phone: 989-894-4950
Website: www.tricitybrewing.com
Annual Production: 555 barrels
Number of Beers: 12 on tap

Staple Beers:
» CHARITY ISLAND IPA
» FORTUNATO (BELGIAN-STYLE TRAPPIST ALE)
» GIANT SLAYER RUSSIAN IMPERIAL STOUT
» HELL'S HALF MILE (HELLES LAGER)

Rotating Beers:
» BLACK IPA
» BROWNHOIST NUT BROWN ALE
» DRAGON SLAYER (GIANT SLAYER IN BOURBON
   BARRELS)
» DRY DOCK IRISH STOUT
» HEFEWEIZEN
» MON TRESOR LAVENDER-INFUSED BELGIAN
   TRIPEL
» LUMBERJACK PALE ALE
» OKTOBERFEST
» PHELAN IRISH RED
» PHOENIX GOLDEN ALE
» REGIMENTAL RESERVE (WEE HEAVY IN BOURBON BARRELS)
» TORCHON BELGIAN PALE ALE
» WEE HEAVY SCOTCH ALE

Most Popular Brew: Hell's Half Mile

Brewmaster's Fave: "I like 'em all. It depends on the season."

Tours? Sure, if someone's there and available.

Samples: Yes, 4 four-ounce samplers for about $4.

Best Time to Go: Wednesdays and Thursdays 4–10, Fridays 4–11PM and Saturdays noon–11PM. Wednesday nights offer live acoustic music.

Where can you buy it? Here on tap and in growlers or six-packs, and bottles in stores throughout Michigan.

Got food? Just some free popcorn, but carry-in is OK and menus are on hand to order out.

Special Offer: Get the Mug Club price on a pint and/or growler fill during your signature visit.

The Beer Buzz: Brewer Paul and fellow founder Kevin Peil work at Dow together. Both are chemists with a passion for beer, and like most homebrewers, they used to talk about opening up a brewery. Then it went beyond just talk.

Now they operate this popular local brewery in an old warehouse building, the kind with the barrel roof. Inside is a roomy, friendly tap room with tables and a tile-topped central bar. A second room connects for more space. Live music is on from time to time or maybe just some spinning vinyl. Three TVs bring in the news or sports. Through the door in back is the much larger production area complete with a bottling line.

The brewery uses some local ingredients (beet sugar for Belgian brews, Michigan lavender) and sends its spent grain to local farmers. The brewery name is for the Tri Cities: Midland, Bay City and Saginaw. Some of the beer names are also nods to local names and places. Phoenix was an old area brewery name, Charity Island is home to a local lighthouse, Brownhoist was a crane company back in the day, and Hell's Half Mile was a part of Water Street down by the river in Bay City. The Great Lakes Loons, a minor league baseball team over in Midland, exclusively offers Loon Summer Ale at the stadium (their golden ale).

Loon's Summer Ale, Hell's Half Mile and Hefeweizen all won awards at the 2012 US Beer Tasting Championship. Free Wi-Fi.

Directions: From I-75 take Exit 162 and head east on Business I-75/M-25 into Bay City. Turn left (north) on Euclid Ave, drive 4 blocks, and turn right (east) on Midland St. After 0.6 mile when Midland starts to bend left, stay on it as it becomes Vermont St, crosses the Liberty Bridge, and then becomes Woodside Ave. Take a left (north) on Johnson St for 0.3 mile, and go right (east) a couple blocks later on Water St. The brewery is just down another block on your right.

Stumbling Distance: *Hooligan's Food & Spirits* (989-894-2938) next door across the parking lot has great beer too, as well as pizza, wings, sandwiches and the like.

SHORT'S BREWING CO. (PUB)

Founded: December 2002
Head Beer Farmers: Joe Short and Tony Hansen
Pub Brewers: Ryan Hale and Luke Whitley
Address: 121 North Bridge Street • Bellaire, MI 49615
Phone: 231-533-6622
Website: www.shortsbrewing.com
Annual Production: 2,000 barrels
Number of Beers: 20 on tap, 10–12 regulars, 6–8 R&D beers, smallest batch is 200 gallons. Beers you can't get anywhere else and perhaps never again.

Staple Beers:
» BELLAIRE BROWN
» CHOCOLATE WHEAT
» HUMA LUPA LICIOUS (AMERICAN IPA)
» LOCAL'S LIGHT
» MAGICIAN DARK RED LONDON ALE
» PANDEMONIUM PALE ALE
» PONTIUS ROAD PILSNER (WITH FLAKE MAIZE)
» THE SOFT PARADE FRUIT (INFUSED RYE ALE WITH RASPBERRY, BLACKBERRY, BLUEBERRY, AND STRAWBERRY JUICE—NO EXTRACTS)
» VILLAGE RESERVE COMMON ALE

Rotating Beers: (way too many to list here—see their website!)
» AGAVE PEACH WHEAT
» BLACK CHAI CREAM ALE
» RICHARD IN THE DIRT BELGIAN TRIPEL
» S'MORE STOUT

Most Popular Brew: Can change from week to week as concept beers come and go and something new and crazy catches everyone's attention.

Ryan's Fave: Anything with Belgian yeast. Evil Urges Belgian Dark Strong Ale, Pangalactic Gargleblaster Double Belgian IPA (with Galaxy hops a reference to Hitchhiker's Guide to the Galaxy).

Tours? By appointment only. Generally Sunday afternoons, $10/person, and with two weeks advance request. Use the form on their website or email tours@shortsbrewing.com.

Samples: Yes, flights of 5 five-oz. samplers around $9

Best Time to Go: Open daily at 11AM. Really crowded in summer, early afternoons are good. Fall or Spring. Heck, even winter. Live music is common.

Where can you buy it? Growlers, 6-packs of some of the exclusive beers. (Also statewide from the brewery in Elk Rapids.)

Got food? Yes, soups and salads, appetizers, sandwiches, pizzas, and daily specials and a kids' menu.

Special Offer: Not participating.

The Beer Buzz: When I first set foot in this brewpub, Brewmaster Joe Short was providing tasters to a group of travel journalists. Set in the former Bellaire Hardware Store, which was also a boat repair shop in the logging days, the modest brewpub had plans to make a separate production facility. Not two years later, the Elk Rapids facility opened and soon after that, even that location had to multiply its production. Now that little brewpub is part of an operation that is one of the top producers of beer in Michigan.

Renovations to the old brick building began in 2003 and finished a year and a half later. A 1970s cinder-block addition to the building is now an expanded seating area with a stage for live music. Performers are in here 3 days a week in summer and Friday–Saturday in winter. They pass the hat for an honor-system cover charge. Joe and Tony Hansen, head of brewing productions, develop most of the recipes, which can get a bit unusual—Joe's Carrot Cake Beer, for example—but creativity is encouraged throughout the staff.

Joe got his start as a homebrewer back in college in Kalamazoo. He dropped out to pursue that passion. He started working at the now defunct Traverse Brewing Co., spent time at also defunct Michigan Brewing Co. and then became head brewer at Jackson Brewing Co. (Zig's Kettle and Brew) at the age of 22. He lasted two years before the urge to do his own thing overwhelmed him. A Rapid City native, Joe looked for a place to set up shop and found this vacant hardware store. Pub Brewer Ryan Hale came here from Arbor Brewing, but Joe still gets in on the equipment over here from time to time. Tony comes up with a lot of the recipes. Before Ryan there wasn't much in terms of Belgian style beers (Joe loves hoppy stuff), but Ryan pushed for it. His Belgian IPA went over very well. In 2012 they added a second bar at the pub so folks can get their beers faster, and then they brought in Luke so they could increase production each week. Specialty bottle releases from the production facility go on tap here too.

Directions: M-88, which runs between US-131 and US-31, passes right through downtown Bellaire. Short's is near the corner of Bridge and Broad Streets, right on M-88.

Stumbling Distance: Check out *Bellaire Smokehouse* (508 N Bridge St, 231-533-5069, bellairesmokehouse.com) for smoked and fresh meats and seafoods. The smoked whitefish is awesome. Call first for seasonal hours; they are not open year-round. They also carry lots of craft beers in bottles. For a place to stay, there are several B&Bs and camping, but *Shanty Creek Resorts* (5780 Shanty Creek Rd, 800-678-4111, shantycreek.com) is the biggie, with golfing in summer, skiing in winter, and a free shuttle into Bellaire.

BIG RAPIDS BREWING CO. (BLUE COW CAFÉ)

Founded: 2008
Head Brewer: Charles Freiberg
Address: 119 North Michigan Avenue • Big Rapids, MI 49307
Phone: 231-796-0100
Website: www.bluecowcafe.com
Annual Production: 50 barrels
Number of Beers: 4 on tap

Beers:
» IPA
» Fruit-infused seasonal beers
» Stouts
» Strong Ale
» Wheat Ales

Most Popular Brew: Strong Ale

Brewmaster's Fave: IPA

Tours? No.

Samples: Yes, 4 four-ounce samplers for about $8.

Best Time to Go: Monday 11AM–9PM, Tuesday–Friday 11AM–late, Saturday 9AM–late, Sunday 9AM–9PM. The café's brunch shouldn't be missed.

Where can you buy it? Only here at the bar and in growlers to go.

Got food? Yes, a French-influenced menu focusing on local farm-to-table ingredients. Breads, salads, soups, crepes, sandwiches, and entrees ranging from Michigan pork chops, Filet Mignon, and Lake Superior whitefish to Thai curry, blue mussels, and salmon. Marvelous egg dishes and other breakfasts during brunch hours.

Special Offer: Half price on a single appetizer during your signature visit.

The Beer Buzz: Situated in the historic downtown of Big Rapids, Blue Cow Café is already well known by many locals and travelers for its great food. Ingredients are locally sourced whenever possible, and the menu may be tweaked according to the seasonal items. Owner Connie Freiburg explains why they brew beer: "We are making everything from scratch.

Why are we buying beer when we can make it? If there's a way to make it ourselves, we'll do it." In fact, they acquire local hops for a fall wet-hopped beer. Charles was not previously a homebrewer but learned for the purpose of brewing at the café. The local homebrewers' club frequently chooses a style, and then members brew separately and meet up to compare the results. Suggestions for recipe changes come from the beer club. "It's been an evolution," says Connie. While the particular beers may vary from time to time, they try to keep an IPA, a stout or a strong ale, something on the lighter side, and some sort of seasonal fruit beer (a tart cherry stout, for example) on tap.

The café is casual and cozy, with a fireplace in winter and a patio on the walk out front in summer. Local art on the walls is for sale. They serve Great Lakes Coffee, from a micro-roaster in Detroit. The shop area in front also sells a nice selection of bottled wines and other Michigan beers in six-packs. There is a full bar on the right as you walk in; the dining room is to the left, with tables covered with white linens and looking rather classy. A room in back can be reserved for special events. Free Wi-Fi.

Directions: From US-131/M-20 to the west of Big Rapids, take Exit 139, heading east into town on Perry Ave. Turn left to stay in US-131/M-20 headed north, then turn right on Maple St (still M-20). Take the next left (north) on Michigan Ave and the place is right there on the left.

Stumbling Distance: In summer, a farmers' market is held on Tuesdays and Fridays at City Hall downtown. Big Rapids is the Tubing Capital of Michigan, so try *Saw Mill Tube & Canoe Livery* (231-796-6408, sawmillmi.com) if you want to get on the Muskegon River for the day. Snowmobilers can enjoy the *White Pine Trail.*

CRANKER'S BREWERY

Founded: May 2012
Brewmaster: Adam Mills
Address: 213 South State Street • Big Rapids, MI 49307
Phone: 231-796-1919
Website: www.crankersbrewery.com
Annual Production: 1,000+ barrels
Number of Beers: 6–8 on tap

Staple Beers:
» Bulldog Red Irish Ale
» Dambreaker Brown Ale
» The Local Cal Common
» Professor IPA
» Strongarm Stout
» Torchlight Munich Blonde

Rotating Beers:
» Ambrosia Honey Kölsch
» Fifth Voyage Coconut Porter
» Irish Breakfast Oatmeal Stout
» Oktoberfest
» Old Siberian
» Ploughshare Maibock
» Winter Ale
» expect some oak-barrel aging from time to time

Most Popular Brew: Blonde or Red for the older crowd, with IPA in hot pursuit.

Brewmaster's Fave: "I'm a big fan of the IPA but most proud of the Blonde which I built to be like a Munich Helles but with ale yeast."

Tours? Yes, upon request if he's not busy.

Samples: Yes, 5 four-ounce samplers for about $5.

Best Time to Go: Live music Thursday–Saturday. Open daily at 11AM (Sunday at 1PM). Busier when college is in session.

Where can you buy it? At the bar and in growlers, and in bottles at local stores.

Got food? Yes, appetizers including Saganaki (pan-seared Kasseri cheese with flaming brandy), hummus, gluten-free gnocchi, lager (onion) rings, soft pretzels, flaming sausage plate, sautéed mussels, beer cheese dip. Plus sandwiches, soups, salads, burgers, BBQ entrees, and dinner plates such as cedar-planked salmon, battered cod, steaks, and mac and cheese. Plus a kids' menu and house root beer. There's full diner food at all hours in Cranker's Coney Island next door.

Special Offer: Not participating

The Beer Buzz: Owner James Crank is a Big Rapids native and wanted to offer his community something closer than Mount Pleasant or Grand Rapids. His last name is the origin of Cranker's and he had his first successes with a handful of Crankers Coney Island Restaurants, including one attached to the brewery. With Ferris State University just a few blocks away, a brewery seemed a likely winner as well, but the clientele seem to be as much college-aged as older adults.

Brewer Adam spent 10 years as a teacher working with kids in an "alternative" school setting and loved it. He started homebrewing in 2007 and soon got into beer judging and competition. He volunteered a bit at Arbor Brewing (as did his assistant Bill Gerds) before coming back to Big Rapids. He answered an ad one day in the newspaper for a server position, and in the interview he shared his brewing resume and wound up being hired for more than he expected.

The floor is polished concrete under a high dark ceiling, and with the long tables and benches along the cinderblock walls, the place has the feel of an alternative beer hall. Tables with either short benches or chairs occupy the middle of room. Four 15-barrel serving tanks overlook the hall from a balcony, and a few wooden barrels hang from the ceiling and walls. The tap handles look like gear heads (cranks, right?). Four big TVs are on for sports and such.

Free Wi-Fi. Mug club. Facebook.com/CrankersBrewery

Directions: Both Business US-131 and M-20 pass through the heart of Big Rapids and share the run from north to south on State St. The brewery is on the east side of the street.

Stumbling Distance: The best burger in town is at *Schuberg's Bar* (109 N Michigan Ave, 231-796-5333, schubergsbar.com) plus there's a good beer selection, beer-battered pub fries, walleye, and a lobster bisque that is hard to get hold of but heavenly when it's available.

CHEBOYGAN BREWING CO.

Founded: 2011
Brewmaster: Tim Perry
Address: 101 North Main Street •
Cheboygan, MI 49721
Phone: 231-268-3218
Website: www.cheboyganbrewing.com
Annual Production: 500+ barrels
Number of Beers: 3 on tap

Staple Beers:
» LA CERVEZA (MEXICAN-BOHEMIAN-STYLE LAGER)
» LIGHTHOUSE AMBER (DÜSSELDORF-STYLE ALTBIER)

Rotating Beers:
» HELLES BOCK
» HOPPED UP
» OKTOBERFEST
» WINTER MARZEN

Most Popular Brew: Lighthouse Amber

Brewmaster's Fave: He drinks La Cerveza all day, every day. A man has to stay hydrated.

Tours? Limited availability, for small groups and always by prior appointment.

Samples: Yes.

Best Time to Go: Check website for up-to-date hours, but the tap room is open Thursday through Saturday, less during winter. Growler fills are available during weekday business hours—just call or knock. The Cheboygan Brew House Band plays on Friday nights in summer on the patio.

Where can you buy it? Right here on tap and in growlers, distributed in bottles up into the U.P. to Marquette, throughout Northern Michigan, and down to Lansing.

Got food? No, except some peanuts for sale. Bring your own food or order in.

Special Offer: A Cheboygan Brewery trinket of some sort during your signature visit.

The Beer Buzz: The original Cheboygan Brewery opened in 1882 about a block south of here and survived just over 30 years making German-style lagers. The bottling company still stands but is now a transmission shop. In 2011 the tradition returned and took on the same name. Like its predecessor, the brewery specializes in lagers. They like to switch things up on seasonals, but when they released Summer Cerveza, customer love of the stuff compelled them to keep it on as part of their year-round lineup as La Cerveza.

Brewer Tim once studied pre-med and worked summers in the Frankenmuth breweries, and one summer with Larry Bell when Bell was still brewing in a soup kettle. He is an avid skier and surfer and has traveled the world. Brewing took him to Hawaii at one point. He is Rastafarian and while brewing he plays music according to the task (milling, transferring, bottling, etc.). He's got more than three decades of brewing experience behind him.

The tap room is one part museum, with some nice exhibit-style displays in the corner and a bit of breweriana. The sign bills Cheboygan brews as "The Beer That Made Milwaukee Jealous." The 19th century labels are reproduced in the bar top and on t-shirts. The building was designed specifically for brewing, but within 6 months of opening they had to do an internal expansion to keep up with demand and another not long after that. The tap room has a few tables and chairs, and there is a patio out front with deck furniture as well as a rooftop deck from which you can see down into the brew house through some windows there. The place is family friendly and root beer is served in addition to their lagers.

Free Wi-Fi. Mug club.

Directions: US-23 passes right through Cheboygan and for a block joins Main St/M-27. From that juncture head south on Main Street and the brewery is on the right (west side).

Stumbling Distance: Cheboygan is on an inland waterway and there's a walking bridge to the recreation area across the street. Try *Hoppies Tavern* (7987 Mullet-Burt Road, 231-238-7469, hoppieslanding.com) on Burt Lake for an extensive menu that includes great burgers, perch and local whitefish, and even good Mexican fare. The creative menu over at *Pier 33* (9500 North M-33, 231-268-3336) gets raves too.

SHORT'S BREWING CO. (PRODUCTION BREWERY)

Opened: March 2009
Brewmasters: Joe Short and Tony Hansen
Head Brewers: Curt Guntzviller and Aaron Smith
Address: 211 East C Loomis Drive • Elk Rapids, MI 49629
Phone: 231-498-2300
Website: www.shortsbrewing.com
Annual Production: 24,000 barrels and rising
Number of Beers: 30–35+ styles per year, 5 flagships

Staple Beers:
» Bellaire Brown
» Huma Lupa Licious (American IPA)
» Pandemonium Pale Ale
» Pontius Road Pilsner (With Flake Maize)
» The Soft Parade Fruit (infused rye ale with raspberry, blackberry, blueberry, and strawberry juice—no extracts)

Rotating Beers: (merely a sampling here—many small, limited batches)
» Anniversary Ale (blood orange infused wheat wine with green peppercorns)
» Autumn Ale London ESB
» Black Cherry Porter
» Bloody Beer (Bloody Mary Flavored)
» Controversyale (American IPA With Simcoe Hops)
» Funkin Punkin (Pumpkin Ale)
» Good Humans (Dry-Hopped Double Brown Ale)
» India Spruce Pilsner
» Key Lime Pie
» The Liberator Double IPA (With Citrus Zest)
» Nicie Spicie American Wheat (with lemon and orange zest, coriander, 3 different peppercorns)
» Strawberry Short's Cake

Most Popular Brew: Huma Lupa Licious

Brewmaster's Fave: India Spruce Pilsner, the greatest beer he's ever made, he says.

Tours? By appointment only. Generally Sunday afternoons, $10/person, and with two week advance request. Use the form on their website or email tours@shortsbrewing.com.

Samples: No, but a single pour at the end of a paid tour.

Best Time to Go: Only during your scheduled tour.

Where can you buy it? Throughout Michigan and over at their pub in Bellaire. They do not sell retail beer here at this brewery.

Got food? No.

Special Offer: Not participating.

The Beer Buzz: Why is it that when I think of Short's and this ever-expanding production facility and its often envelope-pushing great beers, I think of Willie Wonka? When their production goals exceeded the capacity of their original Bellaire location (which is still open, by the way),

plans began for a much larger production brewery. They found a vacant building in an industrial zone here in Elk Rapids. The place used to make chain-link fences.

The floor was ripped up for drains in 2008, and by March 2009 they had added a very large cooler. The first bottles came off the line that month.

In July 2012 they brought in more fermentation and conditioning tanks. Tony took over some of Joe's duties as Joe got deeper into many other tasks that come with the larger company. Renovations required the brewery to halt production in June and July of that year. The end product is over 40,000 square feet of production space. And still they wonder how soon they will need more.

Short's is a rather unusual company. They have no plans to distribute outside of Michigan. They have a commitment not just to quality of product but also quality of life. Everyone on the brewing team at this location has the weekends off. Employees are encouraged to get physical with activities such as mountain biking and cross-country skiing. Joe is an avid waterskier. (He attempts to get in at least 3–4 successful back flips on a wake board each summer.) From May to October the staff has a water-ski club, and they meet 2–3 times per week at 5 a.m. and sometimes in the evenings.

Directions: US-31 coming north from Traverse City, passes right through Elk Rapids. On the north side of town you will see the brewery on the right side. Turn right on Loomis Drive to get into the parking lot.

Stumbling Distance: Looking for good food after a tour? Try *Pearl's New Orleans Kitchen* (617 Ames St, 231-264-0530, magnumhospitality.com/ pearls). Be sure to head to Short's in Bellaire. It's about a 30-mile drive from Elk Rapids.

STORMCLOUD BREWING CO.

Founded: June 28, 2013
Brewmaster: Brian Confer
Address: 303 Main St. • Frankfort, MI 49635
Phone: 231-352-0118
Website: www.stormcloudbrewing.com
Annual Production: 400 barrels
Number of Beers: up to 15 on tap, plus one guest cider/mead

Staple Beers:
» B., Sirius Belgian Dubbel
» Birdwalker Blonde
» Silver Lining Saison
» Rainmaker Ale
» Two-Twenty Eight Tripel
» Whiled Away IPA

Rotating Beers:
» Another Day, Another Apocalypse
» Beach Buddha Imperial IPA
» Fun Guv'nr Black IPA
» Goodnight, Porter
» The Handsome Bee
» The Nightswimmer Stout
» 7-Spot Amber
» Strawberry Saison
» Supercell Saison
» Watermelon Saison

Most Popular Brew: Birdwalker Blonde in pints or Whiled Away IPA in growlers

Brewmaster's Fave: "It's a toss up between the Dubbel or the IPA. In fact, I like to blend the two." (In the end, though, it's the Dubbel.)

Tours? Nothing scheduled, but they're happy to show the brewhouse if not busy.

Samples: Yes, 4 four-ounce samples for about $8.

Best Time to Go: Monday–Saturday 11am–11pm, Sunday noon–11pm. Live music in summer Monday & Thursday.

Where can you buy it? Here on tap and in growlers, but watch for distribution soon.

Got food? Yes, flatbread pizzas, soups and salads, some snacks including popcorn, plus meat/cheese/pickle boards.

Special Offer: A free sticker with the signature of the book.

The Beer Buzz: Brian started homebrewing back in about 2005, not as a hobby, but with the full intention of developing recipes to open a brewery someday. He was a commercial photographer before this and he converted his dark room into a brew room. It already had the plumbing and refrigerators. He brewed 2–3 batches per week, all with a Belgian focus. He wanted to be the first Belgian-focused brewery, but Bastone and Brewery Vivant beat him to the punch.

When he was ready to go, business partners Rick Schmitt and Jim Kunz joined him. They found an empty retail building downtown with two empty lots. They remodeled for the brewpub, and brought new construction to one of the empty lots for the brewery.

"A brewery at the end of the sidewalk," Brian calls this. "Drive too far and you are in the lake heading to Wisconsin."

Facebook.com/StormcloudBrewing

Directions: Following M-22 right through town, it comes into Frankfort from the north on Bellows St and from the south on Lake St. From the north just follow Bellows south to Main St and turn right (west) and the brewery is four blocks on the right. From the south turn left on Main St off of Lake St and it's 0.9 mile on the right.

Stumbling Distance: The Lake Michigan beaches are phenomenal. *Alberta Beach* is close; *Sleeping Bear Dunes National Lakeshore* is 10 minutes north. Frankfort has a surprisingly good restaurant scene. *Coho Café* (320 Main St, 231-352-6053, cohofrankfort.com) for one, has great Michigan beer selections on tap.

BIG BUCK BREWERY & STEAKHOUSE

Founded: 1995
Brewmaster: Travis Charboneau
Address: 550 South Wisconsin Avenue • Gaylord, MI 49735
Phone: 989-732-5781
Website: www.bigbuck.com
Annual Production: 500 barrels
Number of Beers: 16 on tap

Staple Beers:
» Antler Ale (Amber)
» Big Buck (American-Style With Corn)
» Black River Stout
» Buck Naked Light
» Doc's Extra Special Bitter
» IPA
» Raspberry Wheat
» Redbird Ale

Gourmet Seasonal Beers:
» Blizzard Warning IPA (Brown IPA)
» Campfire Joe Coffee Stout
» Cascade APA
» Harvest Ale (With Pumpkin)
» Hazelnut Vanilla Brown
» Maple Stout (Oatmeal Stout With Maple Syrup And Brown Sugar)
» Oktoberfest
» Russian Roulette Imperial Stout
» Snow Bunny Blonde (Cranberry Blonde Ale)
» Triple Rye (IPA)
» Winter Warmer
» (And More)

Most Popular Brew: Antler Ale

Brewmaster's Fave: IPA

Tours? Yes, come knock on the brew house window if someone's around and free.

Samples: Yes.

Best Time to Go: Open daily from 11AM through dinner time, and open a bit longer in summer.

Where can you buy it? Only here on tap and to go in growlers and 6-pack bottles.

Got food? Yes, and it is much more than just a steakhouse offering sandwiches and burgers, soups (including beer cheese soup) and salads, pasta, ale battered fish and shrimp, and other entrees, plus kids' and dessert menus.

Special Offer: Not participating.

The Beer Buzz: With a name like Big Buck, you had to expect a wood lodge theme, but the woodwork here is more impressive than most. There are full-sized wood-carved animals near the entrance, and the big four-sided bar was made by a local woodworker who made it to look as if trees are growing up out of the floor to support it. The dining room, with its vaulted ceiling of open wood beams, runs toward the huge copper brew house behind glass in back. Beyond that are big windows to the outside letting in a lot of light and making this look a bit like a cathedral dedicated to beer. The brew system is huge as this was originally designed to be a production brewery. The light fixtures are barrels cut in half, and there are antler chandeliers, as well as a variety of mounted animals on the walls. TVs are spread around the place with one big one occupying a corner. A game room offers a pool table and darts, and there is outdoor seating as well.

Scott Graham of the Michigan Brewers' Guild started this brewery, which is now under different ownership and management. There used to be locations in Auburn Hills and Grand Rapids. Brewer Travis was born and raised in Gaylord and got his start as a homebrewer. He became obsessed with his hobby and spent one month as an intern at Short's Brewing. When he came home, the brewing position just happened to be available.

In addition to the beer, Big Buck also makes its own artisan wines and distillates. The whole line of products is available for sale in the gift shop up front. Free Wi-Fi. Mug Club.

Directions: From I-75 take Exit 282 for M-32/MainSt and head east into Gaylord. Turn right (south) on Wisconsin Ave and the brewery is at the back of a large parking lot on the right (west) side of the street.

Stumbling Distance: Buy some Michigan craft beers for the road at *Otsego Lake Corner Store* (4800 West Otsego Lake Dr, 989-732-8664). The city has an elk herd and the public can see them from near the Elk's Lodge off Grandview at Elk View Park. A free herd wanders about in the 105,000 acres of nearby *Pigeon River State Forest* (989-732-3541).

JAMESPORT BREWING CO.

Founded: 2000
Lead Brewer: Tom Buchanan
Address: 410 South James Street • Ludington, MI 49431
Phone: 231-845-2522
Website: www.jamesportbrewingcompany.com
Annual Production: 360 barrels
Number of Beers: 11 on tap, 28 per year

Staple Beers:
» Altbier
» Dry Stout
» ESB
» IPA
» Scottish Strong Ale

Rotating Beers:
» Amber Steam Style
» Apricot Wheat
» Badger Brown
» Blueberry Wheat
» Dortmunder
» Dunkelweizen
» Hefeweizen
» Kölsch
» Mocha Java Porter (With Local Honey)
» Nitro Stout
» Smoky Porter
» Weizenbock

Most Popular Brew: Altbier

Brewmaster's Fave: Altbier or ESB

Tours? Yes, by appointment recommended, but if you're lucky, on a random walk-in.

Samples: Yes, 5 five-ounce samplers for about $8.

Best Time to Go: Open 7 days a week for lunch and dinner until 11 or so, but closed Sunday/Monday in January and February. Hoppy Hour is 4–6PM Monday–Friday.

Where can you buy it? Only here on tap or in growlers.

Got food? Yes, a full menu (and full bar with a good wine list) including burgers, sandwiches, wraps, soups and salads, fish & chips, lake perch, pastas, and steaks, plus kids' and dessert menus.

Special Offer: Not participating.

The Beer Buzz: "Helping Michigan's economy one beer at a time" is their slogan, and a nod to the obvious: the brewing industry has become a big player in Michigan's economy. This brewery is part of Jamesport Center, a Victorian-Age building with sections dating back to 1890 when this was a saloon and hotel. Back in the logging and Great Lakes sailing days, Ludington was an important port and the traveling workingman—loggers and sailors—needed a place to stay and a saloon to make trouble in. You can still see the 1892 cast-iron columns of what was the Central House Hotel lobby. The brewery's building wasn't completed until 1905 and served as employee lodging for Star Watch Case Co. Since then many businesses have passed through, from butcher shops to bicycle shops and even the State Liquor Control Commission.

The brewery and restaurant are in two storefronts side-by-side with the bar on the left. Breweriana, old canoes, and carrom boards decorate the walls. There's a deck out back for summer dining and drinking. Brewer Tom started homebrewing with friends in 1991. When he and his wife moved to the area he met Michael LeCroix, the brewmaster at now defunct Lighthouse Brewing Company in Manistee. Michael and another brewer consulted in the creation of Jamesport Brewing and Tom came in to help

with the setup. Tom worked his way up to head brewer thereafter. The brewery once won Silver for the ESB and Scottish Strong, and Bronze for the Hefeweizen and Smoky Porter at the Michigan Brewers Cup. They brew Badger Brown for the S.S. Badger, the ferry that crosses Lake Michigan between Ludington, MI and Manitowoc, WI.

See the Ossawald Crumb Tap Room downstairs, which is dedicated to the legendary first resident of Ludington as told in stories and drawings by local industrialist and Saturday Evening Post illustrator, Robert L. Stearns. Reproductions of the illustrations adorn the walls.

Free Wi-Fi. Parking is on the street or in lots in back or across the street.

Directions: Take US-31 to the area and it connects to US-10. Take US-10 west, straight into town as it becomes Ludington Ave. At James St, turn left (south) still following US-10, and the brewpub is 3.5 blocks south on the right (west) side of the street.

Stumbling Distance: Check out *The Mitten Bar* (109 W Ludington Ave, 231-843-7616, mittenbar.com) for all Michigan products including 300+ beers. Named a top beer bar in the US by *Draft* and *Food & Wine* magazines. Enjoy the sunset at the beach; it's typically a stunner. Disc golf enthusiasts know Ludington as the site of the state championships and for being home to 6 courses. Paddlers will also find much to do here between lakes and rivers.

MIDLAND BREWING COMPANY

Founded: 2010
Brewmaster: Dennis Lawrence
Address: 5011 North Saginaw Rd. • Midland, MI 48642
Phone: 989-631-3041
Website: www.midlandbrewing.com
Annual Production: 1,800–2,400 barrels
Number of Beers: 10 on tap

Staple Beers:
» BROTHERS IPA
» COPPER HARBOR ALE
» JENNY'S NUT BROWN ALE
» PINE RIVER PORTER
» RED KEG AMBER

Rotating Beers:
» 3 MILE MARKER HEFE WEIZEN
» DUBLIN ST STOUT
» MIDLAND PALE ALE
» RESPONSIBLY PILSNER
» SMOKE IN THE PORTER
» WHOOPS WHEAT ALE

Most Popular Brew: Copper Harbor

Brewmaster's Fave: Brothers IPA

Tours? Nothing scheduled but if a brewer is around and not busy, sure.

Samples: Yes, 8 four-ounce beers for about $8.

Best Time to Go: Open all week from noon until midnight, later on weekends, 11PM on Mondays. Gets busier after dinner. Live bands Thursday/Friday in fall/winter/spring. Slower in the summer. Come for sports; there are 5 flat screens around the place.

Where can you buy it? Here on tap and in growlers, and on draft in many places around Michigan. Six-pack bottles available on site and select bars and retailers statewide.

Got food? Snacks, some free popcorn, pizza slices, but carry-in is OK and menus are on hand for delivery.

Special Offer: During your signature visit ½ off pints for you and your private party (up to 4 couples).

The Beer Buzz: Business partners Keith Lawrence and Pete Hayes (whose wife worked with Keith) met at a New Year's party. Keith and his brothers were homebrewers, and Pete, a chemistry major, had spent some time as a brewer as well. (He was in Frankenmuth when a tornado took out the brewery there.) Not long after that, they set the idea of a brewery into motion. Brewer Dennis, Keith's brother, retired from GM while still only in his 50s and came on to lead the brewing.

The building dates back to the 1950s or 60s when this was a department store. Then it was a nursery for some time and then a teen night club before becoming a brewery, which is also a sort of nursery. They're selling hops and barley, in a sense. Those are plants. Work with me here.

The walls show some historical photos of Midland and an 1890s drawing. Back then this was a big-time logging center, including Midland, Bay City, and Saginaw. The Dow Chemical Company headquarters are here and started out in a Midland log cabin in 1852. After Prohibition there was a Midland Brewery downtown, but otherwise this is the first (and right now only) brewery in a long time. They make their own root beer and sodas as well. In summer enjoy the outdoor patio.

MBC was the official beer of the 25th Dow Corning Tennis Classic in 2013. Free Wi-Fi. Facebook.com/MidlandBrewingCompany

Directions: From US-10 take Exit 119 and take Stark Rd south to Saginaw Rd. Turn left (east) following it 1.1 miles to the brewery on the right.

Stumbling Distance: Enjoy some minor league baseball: Great Lakes Loons play at *Dow Stadium* (825 E Main St, 989-837-2255) which has Tri-City's Loons Lager on tap. Bike here: the brewery is close to the *Pere Marquette Rail Trail* (lmb.org/pmrt). Get off at the 3-mile marker at Dublin Ave and head north 400 feet to take a left on Saginaw Rd. *WhichCraft Taproom* (124 Ashman St, 989-832-3395, whichcrafttaproom. com) has 40 Michigan beers on tap, plus mead, wine, and eats.

MOUNT PLEASANT BREWING CO.

Founded: 2008
Head Brewer: Kim Kowalski
Address: 614 West Pickard Street • Mt. Pleasant, MI 48858
Phone: 989-400-4666
Website: www.mtpleasantbrew.com
Annual Production: 2,400 barrels in 2012
Number of Beers: Up to 18 on tap; possibly over 100 styles per year

Staple Beers:
» Coal Stoker's Blackberry Ale
» Cow Catcher Red Ale
» Gambler's Golden Ale
» Iron Horse IPA
» Railyard Raspberry Wheat
» Second Wind Wheat
» Steam Engine Stout
» Trainwreck Amber (with local maple syrup and honey)

Rotating Beers:
» Big Apple Beer
» Crazy Train (Black) IPA
» Freight Train Double IPA
» Harvest Ale
» Hobo's Breath Brown Ale
» Maple Ale
» Oktoberfest
» River Bend Bock
» Sacred Gruit
» Wit Dream

Most Popular Brew: Trainwreck Amber

Brewmaster's Fave: Sacred Gruit

Tours? As long as someone is there and free. Big groups need to call for a reservation.

Samples: Yes, 8 four-ounce samplers for about $8.

Best Time to Go: Monday through Thursday from 4–10PM, Friday and Saturday noon to midnight. Live music on Mondays, trivia on Tuesdays. Closed Sundays.

Where can you buy it? Here on tap or in growlers or bottles to go. Around Michigan and northern Indiana in bottles or some draft accounts.

Got food? Yes, a few sandwiches, some soups (typically with beer in them), and chips or soft pretzels. Free popcorn and peanuts.

Special Offer: $1 off the price of your first pint on your signature visit.

The Beer Buzz: This brewery is the result of the success of the beers over at Mountain Town Station Brewing Co. and Steakhouse (thus the train-related beer names). According to Michigan law, a brewpub cannot sell its beer for distribution, so the only way to reach drinkers who loved the stuff was to open a separate brewery. Mount Pleasant Brewing first operated in the back of a garage with just enough room to brew. In 2009 they moved across the street and built this brewery and tap room. It even has windows!

The team is very into experimentation and exploration. In addition to their bigger batches for distribution, they brew perhaps 100 ten-gallon batches of R&D beers throughout the year—and you can only find them in the tap room. If you can't decide what to drink, give the Wheel of Beer Fortune at the bar a spin.

Brewer Kim first brewed in 1998 as an assistant at Lansing's now-defunct Blue Coyote, worked up to head brewer, then managed bottling at also

defunct Michigan Brewing Co. while working at two other breweries on the side. He won medals for his stout at Robert Thomas Brewing (gone!) in Grand Rapids which got him in the door over at Bell's (not gone). He moved to (the city of) Mount Pleasant's Mountain Town Station (still here) and established that brewpub's reputation. When MPBC opened, he was naturally the guy to take the reins.

The building still looks like a sort of car repair garage, complete with a door that opens the tap room up to the outside (with a screen to keep mosquitoes out). In the center is a nice wood bar set before a window looking into the brewery. The room has a fake fireplace, darts, TVs for some sports, and a fridge full of bottles for carry-out.

Free Wi-Fi. Mug Club. On Facebook.

Directions: From US-127, take Exit 143 for M-20. Go right (west) on M-20, which becomes Pickard Rd. The brewery is 2.3 miles along on the right.

Stumbling Distance: Mount Pleasant has a Saturday morning farmers' market in season. Don't miss the sister brewery/restaurant *Mountain Town* here in the book. *Jon's Drive In* (1030 S Mission St, 989-773-9172) lets you order from and eat in your car or sit inside at the café. Fun, simple food experience with nostalgia/novelty, depending on your age. *Max & Emily's Bakery Café* (125 E Broadway, 989-772-7460, maxandemilys.com) is an institution. Busy place with great sandwiches and bakery deliciousness.

MOUNTAIN TOWN STATION

Founded: 1996
Brewers: Laren Avery / Kim Kowalski
Address: 506 West Broadway St. • Mt. Pleasant, MI, 48858
Phone: 989-775-2337
Website: www.mountaintown.com
Annual Production: 1,000 barrels
Number of Beers: 8 on tap

Staple Beers:
» Cow Catcher Red Ale
» Gamblers Gold Ale
» Hobo's Breath Brown Ale
» Iron Horse IPA
» Railyard Raspberry Wheat
» Steam Engine Stout

Rotating Beers:
» Chip River Weizen
» Kölsch
» Oktoberfest
» River Bend Bock
» Winter Warmer

Most Popular Brew: Gambler's Golden Ale

Brewmaster's Fave: "Depends on the season, depends on the mood, depends on the love."

Tours? Yes, if someone is there and available.

Samples: Yes, 6 six-ounce samplers for about $11.

Best Time to Go: Happy hour is 4–6PM weekdays. Summer is a slower time for them and the patio overlooking the river is nice. Open 4–10PM Monday–Thursday, and from 11:30AM on Friday–Sunday.

Where can you buy it? Only here in pints, growlers, table kegs (60 oz.), or half barrels. See also "Mount Pleasant Brewing" for a few of these brews in bottles.

Got food? Yes, this is a premier steakhouse also serving soups, salads, pasta, BBQ, seafood, and burgers/sandwiches. The Brewery Wings are marinated in Gambler's Gold. Gluten-free and kids' menus available.

Special Offer: $1 off one glass of Mountain Town's beer during your signature visit

The Beer Buzz: Back in the late 19th century, railroad tracks to Mount Pleasant were brought in by Lansing, Alma, Mount Pleasant and Northern Railroad (which was bought out two years later by Toledo, Ann Arbor and Mount Pleasant Railway). The depot was brought down by a lightning-strike fire and replaced in 1893. Passenger service ended in 1950. Back in the 1990s, Mountain Town owner Jim Holton visited a brewpub in Illinois, saw the big system and its success, and said, "Wow, I could do that!" And he had just the spot for it back in Mount Pleasant. In 1995, he purchased the old depot along the banks of the Chippewa River and after extensive renovations, created his own restaurant and brew pub. He missed his final exams at university due to the ground breaking.

Brewer Laren says brewing began for him as a joke from his college professor. He was on his 3rd major, Food Admin, and the professor said, Do you like beer? "Who doesn't?" he replied. "Want to brew beer?" said the prof. "Are you kidding me?" And so began his homebrewing. He got his professional start at the sister brewery Mount Pleasant Brewing under Mountain Town's previous head brewer Kim Kowalski. He served as an intern, then went to Durango Brewing in Colorado to hone his skills a bit more. When he was ready to come home, he was taken on as head brewer here. He still helps out Brewer Kim across town. Kim supervises here but lets Laren go creatively.

270 ZONE 3   MT. PLEASANT

The restaurant features a lot of dark wood and has an upscale pub feel to it, though it is a casual place to dine. The copper brew system is behind glass in the center of the restaurant. Right next door is a more intimate space at Camille's on the River (reservations recommended, 989-773-0259) where you can get the same beers (camillesontheriver.com). The Mountain Town complex also has an extensive wine cellar. Free Wi-Fi.

Directions: From US-127, take either Exit 139 or 144 to get onto Business US-127 right through town as Mission St. Turn west on Broadway St and drive 0.7 mile to find the brewery on the right just before you cross the river.

Stumbling Distance: Plenty of good food, beer, and wine here and at *Camille's*, but if you're looking for classic 50s kitsch and a Coney dog with curly fries? Head to *Pixie* (302 N Mission St, 989-772-7494). For fancier fare, try *The Brass Café and Saloon* (128 S. Main St, 989-772-0864, thebrasscafe.com).

BIG O BREWERY (GOOD NEIGHBOR ORGANIC VINEYARD AND WINERY)

Founded: 2011 (winery founded 2007, organic farm 2001)
Brewers: Guest brewers and Dustin Jones
Address: 9825 Engles Road • Northport, MI 49670
Phone: 231-386-5636
Website: www.goodneighbororganic.com
Annual Production: 25 barrels
Number of Beers: 2 on tap

Beers:
» ALWAYS VARYING

Tours? Yes, by appointment, but it's mostly about the wine.

Samples: Yes.

Best Time to Go: Open seasonally from April to November 15. By appointment only during the off season.

Where can you buy it? Only here on tap or in growlers.

Got food? No, but go ahead and bring your own.

Special Offer: 10% off all purchases during the signature visit.

The Beer Buzz: According to the not exactly scientific measure of the research that went into this book, this is the smallest commercial brewery—nanobrewery—in the state of Michigan. This is also the Leelanau Peninsula's first (only, for the moment*) microbrewery, and before that it was the first certified totally organic vineyard. Situated on 67 acres just a mile from Lake Michigan to the west.

Rotating homebrewers have been making the beer here, but Dustin Jones of Ferment back in Traverse City took it on as a regular gig. Ben Crow, another Ferment member, provides the hard ciders. It's run like a coffee shop that sells alcohol. The bar rests on old barrels. There's a gas fireplace in the middle of the tasting room and a moose head up on the wall. Board games are available if you are so inclined. Wines for sale include Gewürztraminer, Pinot Gris, Chardonnay, ice wine, and several fruit wines and hard ciders.

Says winery and brewery owner Stan Silverman, "There's a difference in how beer drinkers act compared to wine drinkers. Wine drinkers come in and ignore each other. Two couples of beer drinkers come in and are socializing after a pint. Wine drinkers look at wine as something to have with food, an experience. Part of the beer experience is to have fun."

Directions: M-22 goes up the east side of Leelanau Peninsula from Traverse City and then down the west side past Sleeping Bear Dunes. From its northernmost point, a right-angle intersection in Northport, drive south on the west side M-22 just 1.9 miles and take a right (west) on Engles Rd. The brewery is 0.4 mile in.

Stumbling Distance: The best fish and chips up here is at *Knot Just a Bar* in Omena (5019 NW Bay Shore Dr, Omena, 231-386-7393, knotjustabar. com). You can't come all the way to Leelanau and not go see *Sleeping Bear Dunes National Lakeshore* (nps.gov/slbe). But *Leelanau State Park* (231-386-5422, leelanaustatepark.com) is a closer option if you want a quiet picnic with fewer tourists.

*Also on the peninsula is *Leelanau Brewing* (leelanaubeer.com). At the time of writing they weren't brewing on site but rather contracting through Jolly Pumpkin's Ron Jeffries. The beer is for sale throughout Michigan.

WILTSE'S BREWPUB & FAMILY RESTAURANT

Founded: 1995
Brewmaster: Dean Wiltse
Address: 5606 F-41 • Oscoda, MI 48750
Phone: 989-739-2231
Website: www.wiltsebrewpub.com
Number of Beers: 5 on tap

Staple Beers:
» AUSABLE WEIZENBIER
» BLUE OX STOUT
» PAUL BUNYAN AMBER ALE
» PREMIUM LAGER OLD

Rotating Beers:
» BELGIAN TRIPEL
» OKTOBERFEST
» AND MORE

Most Popular Brew: Paul Bunyan Ale

Brewmaster's Fave: Paul Bunyan Ale

Tours? Yes, by appointment.

Samples: Yes, five 4-oz. samplers.

Best Time to Go: Open 11AM weekdays, 8AM on weekends. Happy hour weekdays 4–7PM. Closed Mondays in winter.

Where can you buy it? Only here on tap and in growlers.

Got food? Yes, a full menu of soups and salads, appetizers, sandwiches, entrees, and some Mexican fare. Breakfast on weekends.

Special Offer: Not participating.

The Beer Buzz: This family establishment has been around for quite a while considering Oscoda's off-the-beaten-path location and considering it's been brewing craft beer in a sort of not-so-adventurous market since the 1990s. Owner and brewer Dean Wiltse brews the Paul Bunyan-themed beers.

Memorabilia decorates the walls, and the atmosphere is laid back. Locals frequent the place, but in season, travelers find their way in. There is a U-shaped oak bar and a full dining area.

Directions: Coming into Oscoda from the south on US-23, turn left (west) onto F-41 and it will angle northwest. The brewery is 0.9 mile on the right.

Stumbling Distance: Don't miss a paddlewheel riverboat tour on the *Au Sable River Queen* (1775 West River Rd, 989-739-7351, ausableriverqueen. net). Road trippers should see the 22 miles of the River Road Scenic Byway along the AuSable River Valley.

BEARDS BREWERY

Founded: 2012
Brewmaster: Peter Manthei and Ben Slocum
Address: 207A Howard Street • Petoskey, MI 49770
Phone: 231-753-2221
Website: www.beardsbrewery.com
Annual Production: 300 barrels
Number of Beers: 7 on tap, 35–40 style throughout the year

Popular Beers: (always changing)
» BRIMLEY STOUT (OATMEAL STOUT)
» THE LONG STRONG
» POMEGALACTIC
» SERENDIPITY PORTER
» VICTORIOUS PALE ALE

Rotating Beers:
» "LUNA" (CITRUSY WHEAT)
» BLUEBERRY MUFFIN
» BOMBSHELL BLONDE (WITH FLAKED MAIZE)
» CAFE PORTER (SMOOTH COFFEE PORTER)
» CANDY CANE PORTER (ROBUST PORTER WITH PEPPERMINT
   EXTRACT)
» CHOCO MINT PORTER
» CLOVER LAMB (SESSION ALE WITH CLOVER HONEY & SWEET
   ORANGE PEEL)
» DEEZ NUTS (BROWN ALE)
» MALABAR IPA (BLACK IPA WITH MALABAR INDIA COFFEE AND
   CASCADE HOPS)
» MONKEY BUSINESS (BELGIAN-STYLE IPA)
» MOTHER FUGGLE PALE ALE
» NEW SCHOOL AMBER ALE
» RED MYST IRISH ALE
» RYE BYTER
» SADDLED MOOSE (IMPERIAL STOUT)
» SOMETHIN' SOMETHIN' IPA
» TBA IPA (HOP-FORWARD SPICY ALE WITH DRY FINISH)
» THE RABID GOAT (BOURBON-BARREL-AGED IMPERIAL AMERICAN
   BROWN ALE)
» WHEATUS (SWEET CHOCOLATEY WHEAT BEER)

Most Popular Brew: Serendipity Porter

Brewmaster's Fave: "It's quite difficult to nail it down to one beer. Ben and I both have some different styles we like and that helps us to keep a varied tap board. I think between the two of us IPAs and Stouts are well liked."

Tours? Not really—you can see the whole operation through a glass wall, but they love to chat about it when people ask.

Samples: Yes, 4 five-ounce pours for $7.

Best Time to Go: Open 7 days a week. May be closed Monday and Tuesday in winter. Check the website.

Where can you buy it? Here on tap or to go in growlers. Occasional area draft accounts and special events or festivals.

Got food? No, but food friendly—bring your own if you like. Menus on site from area restaurants that deliver.

Special Offer: They'll cut off a length of their keg stickers for you during your signature visit.

The Beer Buzz: Peter has long loved beer and even traveled to Belgium on a pilsgrimage to get some Westvleteren 12. He started brewing while going to school out in Santa Barbara, CA. He helped out a few days a week at Telegraph Brewing Company which is where he got his first brewing knowledge. After graduation, his buddy Ben Slocum flew out to California so they could road trip back to Michigan together. Talk of one day starting a brewery came up on the long drive. Both partners have beards (as do a buzzillion other brewers, it seems) and while they had contemplated Beerds, they decided to skip the pun in the brewery name. (Puns—another thing found in 'apundance' around brewers.)

Peter is into the process of things and brewing in particular fascinated him more, so he bought better equipment. He and Ben decided to see what they could brew. By the end of the summer, they were brewing 10 gallons a week, a surplus their friends and family were only too happy to take care of. The beer was ready, so they made a business plan and set out to raise the funds.

They brew in one-barrel batches for their seven taps, so what's on is frequently changing. Come on in for the 8-bit night, with old school video games projected on the wall, or Vinyl Night when they have a record player going and people can bring in their old LPs. They also have board games for you to play while you knock back a few.

Directions: Follow US-31 right through town, to the east of where it connects with US-131, and find Lake St in front of the Little Traverse History Museum. Go east on Lake St two blocks and turn left (north) on Howard St. The brewery is on the right inside a small arcade.

Stumbling Distance: *Roast & Toast* (309 E Lake St, 231-347-7767, roastandtoast.com) roasts its own coffee and offers great sandwiches, soups, and dinner entrees for economical prices. *Palette Bistro* (321 Bay St, 231-348-3321, palettebistropetoskey.com) and *City Park Grill* (432 E Lake St, 231-347-0101, cityparkgrill.com) are great for dinner. Both carry a good variety of Michigan beers.

PETOSKEY BREWING

Founded: 2012
Brewmaster: Brett Emanuel
Address: 1844 M-119 (Harbor-Petoskey Rd.) • Petoskey, MI 49770
Phone: 231-753-2057
Website: www.petoskeybrewing.com
Annual Production: 10,000 barrels
Number of Beers: up to 18 on tap, 40+ styles per year

Staple Beers:
» Horny Monk Belgian Dubbel
» Mind's Eye Pa
» Morning Fog Mocha Java Stout (On Nitro)
» North 45 Amber Ale
» Tucker's Pale Ale

Rotating Beers:
» Harbor Light Golden Ale
» Hopsessed Double IPA P-Town Brown Ale
» Petoskey Sparkle Summer Wheat Lager
» Red Brick Hard Cider

Most Popular Brew: Horny Monk Beglian Dubbel

Brewmaster's Fave: Hopsessed Double IPA

Tours? Not yet.

Samples: Yes, flights starting at $1.50 for a 4-oz.

Best Time to Go: Open daily at noon.

Where can you buy it? On tap and in growlers to go, and at select bars and liquor stores within about a 100-mile radius of the brewery, mostly western Michigan.

Got food? Yes, soups and salads, sliders, panini, and snacks such as soft Bavarian pretzels and nuts.

Special Offer: A free Petoskey Brewing sticker or equally cool prize during your signature visit.

The Beer Buzz: The modern Petoskey Brewing Co. is actually in the home of the historical brewery of the same name. The building dates back to 1898, and the original brewing company only lasted until 1915. But when

Lou Gostinger and Patrick Dowd wanted to start a brewery and were looking for a good site, they really couldn't have asked for something better than this. The brick walls are over two feet thick on this four-story wonder. But one of the most important factors for beer back in that day, as much as in the present, is good water. This location was originally chosen for its proximity to artesian wells, and the new brewers are taking advantage of that as well. Is it working? Consider that they opened in 2012 and are already looking at expanding capacity for 2014.

Lou worked in the beer wholesale industry, and Patrick had the marketing background—a good combo for the business side, and they found the all-important brewer. Brewer Brett started at HopCat and then spent time at North Peak and Arcadia as a production brewer. Petoskey took him from Arcadia and now he has freedom to do whatever he wants as head brewer. Spent grain goes to local farmers for cattle feed.

Free Wi-Fi. Mug Club. Facebook.com/PetoskeyBrewing and Twitter @PetoskeyBrewing.

Directions: US-31 passes just south of the brewery on the north side of Petoskey. From US-31 take M-119 north 0.7 mile and the brewery is on the right.

Stumbling Distance: Beer has the ingredients to be called liquid bread, but for the crusty variety, check out *Crooked Tree Breadworks* (2264 M-119, 231-347-9574, breadworks.com) down the road. Also don't miss the beautiful *Petoskey State Park* (231-347-2311, michigan.gov/petoskey) right across the street.

BEGGARS BREWERY

Founded: 2013
Head Brewer: Michael B. Rizik, III
Address: 4177 Village Park Drive, Suite C • Traverse City, MI
Website: www.beggarsbrewery.com
Annual Production: 1,500 barrels
Number of Beers: 6 on tap

Staple Beers:
» Boardman Brown Ale
» The Farmhand (American Pale Ale)
» Soothsayer Stout
» The Weight (Dry-Hopped IPA)

Tours? By appointment.

Best Time to Go: Check website for hours.

Where can you buy it? Here and expected regional distribution.

Got food? No.

Special Offer: Not participating.

The Beer Buzz: Owner/brewer Michael grew up just outside of Flint, Michigan, in the suburb of Grand Blanc. He started in film at a university in Queens, but losing interest in the New York state of mind, he headed to Michigan State to study Enology and Viticulture. Then he started homebrewing. Though he ended up as a winemaker in Oregon at one point, Michigan kept calling. Traverse City is a pretty good place for a wine person, truth be told, but the local brews pulled him from the grapes to the grains, so back to school he went. First, Siebel Institute of Technology in Chicago, then The World Brewing Academy in Munich. With the credentials in hand, he came back to TC and started working for Right Brain Brewery before heading out on his own here at Beggars.

The brewhouse is situated in an industrial space on the south side of the city. He tries to get as many of his ingredients locally as possible. Some of his hops come from just a few miles away. Spent grain gets fed to local cattle or composted.

Facebook.com/beggarsbrewery

Directions: Head south out of Traverse City on US-31. Watch for Chums Village Dr on the right. Turn right and it's inside the industrial building at Chums Village and Village Park Dr.

Stumbling Distance: *Brewery Terra Firma* is just about 3.5 miles north of here.

BREWERY FERMENT

Founded: September 2012
Brewmaster: Dustin Jones
Address: 511 S Union Street • Traverse City, MI 49684
Phone: 231-735-8113
Website: www.breweryferment.com
Annual Production: 500 barrels
Number of Beers: 5–10 on tap

Staple Beers:
» Bookstore Bitter ESB
» The 45th Parallale (Pale Ale with local hops)
» The Logger Lager (Pre-Prohibition Style with local corn)
» Mitten Wit (a sour white ale with fresh orange peel/ coriander)
» Old Town Brown
» Worker's Daily Cream Ale
» Worker's Daily And Logger Lager Alternate On Tap

Rotating Beers:
» Cherry Brown Ale
» Cherry Kölsch
» Raspberry Wheat
» Fruit beers in summer, some barrel aging

Most Popular Brew: The 45th Parallale

Brewmaster's Fave: "I have an affinity for hops."

Tours? No, but always happy to chat about beer if available.

Samples: Yes, sampler flights.

Best Time to Go: Open Monday–Thursday 3–10PM, Friday 3–midnight, and Saturday noon–midnight. Closed on Sundays.

Where can you buy it? Only here on tap and in growlers to go, plus some bottle-conditioned beers.

Got food? Yes, but just snack sorts of things such as nuts, hummus, cheeses, pickled eggs, olives and such. Carry-in food is welcome.

Special Offer: Buy one 50-cent pint during your signature visit.

The Beer Buzz: "There are no plans to be traditional here," said Brewer Dustin just before they opened. (Blonde barleywine with morel mushrooms?) So far all is going according to plan. This former bookstore/cottage furniture store in the Old Town neighborhood of Traverse City was turned into a tap room with light, modern interiors, black and white photography and art on the walls, and blonde wood floors and a bar top to match along one wall with its chalkboard beer menu. Check out the white-painted driftwood tap handles by local artist Mindy Morrison.

Brewer Dustin has a culinary background, and his brewing started as a hobby and an inclination to create his own things rather than buying them. It gave him an appreciation of what a person can do, plus he saved a bit of coin and made friends in the process. (Beer brings people together, no?) So he read up on brewing and joined the American Homebrewers Association. His hobby became an addiction and he figured he may as well do it for a living. He moved to Traverse City in March 2012 and at a homebrew supply store saw a handwritten note calling for a homebrewer looking for work. He took a job at The Big O, the nanobrewery for an organic winery up in Northport, and there he met hard-cider maker Ben Crow. They had an idea to start their own place dedicated simply to all forms of fermentation (thus the name was to be simply "Ferment," though they add "Brewery" to the name to clarify). They try to use local hops as much as possible, and along with the tap beers, they offer bottle-conditioned brews. Their first was a Lavender Honey Ale. Expect some ciders (Crow's Hard Cider), meads, wines and more in the future, as well as some concoctions that may blur the lines among them.

Facebook.com/BreweryFerment

Directions: From US-31/MI-37/ Grandview Parkway, head south on Union Street for 0.4 mile and the brewery is on the left (east) side of the road.

Stumbling Distance:

The neighboring *Old Town Coffee* (517 S Union St, 231-933-4200) offers vegetarian wraps, housemade soups, ice cream and more plus free delivery. Open for breakfast and lunch but closed at 5PM every day.

BREWERY TERRA FIRMA

Founded: May 2013
Brewmaster: John Niedermaier
Address: 2951 Hartman Road • Traverse City, MI
Phone: 231-929-1600
Website: www.breweryterrafirma.com
Annual Production: 2,000 barrels
Number of Beers: 12+ on tap, 6 regular beers, over 900 recipes

Staple Beers:
» EBB AND FLOW IPA
» GLADSTONE APA
» MANITOU AMBER ALE
» SLEEPING BEAR BROWN ALE

Rotating Beers:
» ALTAR OF HEAVEN GINGER IPA
» ANCHO CHILI DUTCH DOUBLE CHOCOLATE PORTER
» BLACK BIKINI COCONUT PORTER
» BLACK ORCHID VANILLA BEAN PORTER
» BROWN DONKEY SMASHER WINTER WARMER
» CHOCOLATE ORANGE CREAM STOUT
» DINKELFRITZ BLACK PEPPERCORN RYE MAIBOCK
» FIRE ROASTED SWEET CORN CREAM ALE
» HOODWINK ORANGE MARMALADE WHEAT
» INDIGENOUS IPA (BTF HOP YARD WET HOP)
» JAZZ DEVIL SMOKED BROWN ALE
» LITTLE ITALY HONEY BASIL
» LIZARD KING IPA NOIR
» MACHRIE MOOR SCOTTISH STONE BEER
» MOONCALF ORANGE MARMALADE WHEAT
» SHINSU WASABI CREAM
» SNOWBOUND CHOCOLATE MINT STOUT
» SOMBRA SUMMER WHEAT ALE
» SZECHWAN SEVEN SPICE STOUT
» TEMPLE OF HEAVEN GINGER IPA
» WICKED GARDEN BEET WHEAT

Most Popular Brew: Too soon to tell.

Brewmaster's Fave: "Depends on the environment. If I'm out on the ice, Russian Imperial Stout. At the beach? Sombra."

Tours? Yes, brewery and farm tours by appointment.

Samples: Yes.

Best Time to Go: Open daily. Monday–Saturday 10AM–10PM. Sunday 2–9PM. Check website for evolving hours.

Where can you buy it? On site on tap and in growlers and draft accounts in seven counties surrounding Traverse City.

Got food? Not in the beginning. But they have a kitchen for processing beer ingredients so maybe in the future. Food friendly, so carry-in is OK!

Special Offer: $2 off an empty growler purchase during your signature visit.

The Beer Buzz: Way back in the day there was something called a farm brewery. An immigrant farmer, often German, would brew beer using all the ingredients from his own farm and sell it to the locals. Mount Vernon was such a place. While the beers at this 100-year old 10-acre farm are going to be much more refined and varied than what one could have gotten in the 18th or 19th century, the concept is very similar. The man behind the beer is none other than John Niedermaier, who has quite an impressive local following thanks to the many great beers, often very unusual styles and creations, he brewed when he was at Right Brain. His business partner, an engineer, designed the building to reuse the heat of production, and put in enough space so that future expansions would be possible without a massive new construction project. Spent grain will be repurposed or composted. Hops, wheat, and rye will be grown on site. Varied vegetables, nuts, and herbs—turnips, pumpkins, basil, you name it—will be used to create inventive beers. Waste water will be used for irrigation.

The tap room is a relaxed "human sanctuary." No TVs, no live music. Just people getting together for beer. The microbrewery is starting with draft accounts but expects to expand to bottling by about 2015. Be aware that parking is limited; car pool, take a bus, or hike/bike there when possible.

John started homebrewing in the late 80s after his uncle, a private chef, brought some not so good but intriguing homebrew to the family Christmas party, and it made an impression on him. He was already planning for Terra Firma as he worked 10 years for Traverse Brewing

Co., where a young Joe Short (Short's Brewing Co.) worked for a short time as his assistant. Then he spent 3 years brewing at Right Brain, and brewed over 100 styles just in the first year. When he left, he found the right property. He contacted a broker about some brewing equipment and serendipitously acquired the very same equipment he had first brewed on at Traverse Brewing Co. which had gone out of business. He purchased the brand as well.

He calls himself "a bit of a fanatic." Why? Because he has over 900 beers.

Facebook.com/BreweryTerraFirma

Directions: From downtown Traverse City, take Cass Rd about 3.4 miles south to Hartman Rd and go right (west). Or from US-31/M-72 along the lake it's better to take Division St/US-31/M-37 south to Hartman Rd and go left (east).

Stumbling Distance: It's worth noting that the TART trail, a multi-use path in the Traverse City area, extends almost right to the brewery. For some really nice, housemade and affordable pasta, you can't miss *Spaghetti Jim's* (1133 S Airport Rd W, 231-922-5935, spaghettijims.com).

SPAGHETTI JIM, A TRAVERSE CITY INSTITUTION

THE FILLING STATION MICROBREWERY

Founded: March 2012
Head Brewer: David Cannizzaro
Address: 642 Railroad Place • Traverse City, MI 49686
Phone: 231-946-8168
Website: www.thefillingstationmicrobrewery.com
Annual Production: 450 barrels
Number of Beers: 14 on tap (with room for 20)

Staple Beers:
» BACHARACH GOLDEN
» HUNTINGTON IPA

Rotating Beers:
» ABERDEEN SCOTTISH ALE
» ANTWERP PALE ALE
» D.C. ESB
» DENVER BROWN
» DUBLIN STOUT
» KANSAS CITY ALE
» LOUVAIN FARMHOUSE
» MANHATTAN RYE PALE ALE
» MÄRZEN
» MUMBAI IMPERIAL IPA
» OXFORD IPA
» WELLINGTON WHEAT

Most Popular Brew: Huntington IPA

Brewmaster's Fave: Manhattan Rye Pale Ale

Tours? Not really, but if David is around and not busy, doesn't hurt to ask.

Samples: Yes, "trains" of four-ounce samplers—4 for about $6, 5 for about $7, 6 for about $8.

Best Time to Go: Open daily from noon to 11PM, or midnight on weekends. Watch for occasional live music. The patio is nice on summer evenings.

Where can you buy it? Only here on tap or in growlers to go.

Got food? Yes, flatbread pizzas from a wood-fired oven, plus a few salads and kids' items. They also serve Michigan-made Wild Bill sodas.

Special Offer: $1 off your first pint on your signature visit

The Beer Buzz: Situated in a former train station with a view of Lake Boardman, the Filling Station offer Ales by the Rails. But it could also be ales by the trails as the T.A.R.T. bike trail runs right past and the Boardman Lake Trail circles the lake. (The TART trail also connects to Brewery Terra Firma making for a nice brew ride between the two.)

The beers are listed on the Beer Schedule behind the small bar and are numbered like tracks in a station. Make your order and take it to either some tables of barn beams and glass tops behind you, or into the next room with tables and high cocktail tables in a brightly lit room. Outside seating is at picnic tables on a covered patio (a train platform really), and the train tracks run right past. While there is some food on offer (and good food, at that), they are still primarily focused on the beer experience, they say. But it would be crazy not to take notice of the wood-fired oven encased in some large stones from northern Michigan, and to try one of the flatbread specialty pizzas.

Brewer David went to culinary school, got married, and opened a bakery in Vermont. His father-in-law suggested they make the move to Traverse City and set up this brewery. David brews big batches on a 10-barrel system, but a 3-barrel system—made in Belding, Michigan—allows him to try a lot of different beers that come and go. His sister-in-law Amanda manages the place, and other in-laws are part of the show as well: uncles, cousins, siblings—it's a group effort. Huntington IPA is named for the brewer's hometown in Vermont.

Facebook.com/thefillingstationmicrobrewery

Directions: From US-31/M-72 coming from the west, go right (south) on Cass St to 8th St and go left (east). Take a right (south) on Railroad Ave and it takes you right to the former railway station. From the east, stay on Front St even as US-31/M-72 continue on a right curve; there are traffic lights here so you can cross that oncoming traffic and go straight into downtown. As soon as you've made that crossing, watch for Franklin St on the left, turn, and then immediately take the soft angle left onto Railroad Ave and follow it right to the brewery.

Stumbling Distance: Right next door is *The Soup Cup,* a micro-souperie with 8 different soups daily (231-932-7687, thesoupcuptc.com). Sandwiches and fries are also served. Don't forget the paved 10.5-mile *T.A.R.T. bike trail* (traversetrails.org) is here for walking and riding.

JOLLY PUMPKIN BREWERY & DISTILLERY (MISSION TABLE RESTAURANT)

Opened: 2009
Master Brewer/Distiller: Mike Hall
Address: 13512 Peninsula Drive, Old Mission Peninsula • Traverse City, MI 49686
Phone: 231-223-4333
Website: www.jollypumpkin.com
Number of Beers: 11 on tap

Jolly Pumpkin Beers:
» Bam Biere
» Bam Noire
» Oro De Calabaza
» La Roja

North Peak Beers:
» Diabolical IPA
» Majestic Wheat
» Siren Amber Ale
» Vicious Wheat IPA

Most Popular Brew: Oro de Calabaza

Best Time to Go: Open daily from 11AM until 9PM (10PM Friday and Saturday). Tasting room 11AM–6PM; Mission Table Restaurant after 5PM.

Tours? On occasion, but by appointment only.

Samples: Yes, beer flights of 5 samplers.

Where can you buy it? Here on tap and to go in bottles, and throughout Michigan and much of North America.

Got food? Yes, gourmet starters, salads, sandwiches, entrees, and artisan pizzas.

Special Offer: Not participating.

The Beer Buzz: Old Mission Peninsula is quite an extraordinary wine destination, jutting out into and dividing Grand Traverse Bay from Traverse City. But this Jolly Pumpkin complex adds great beer to the mix and a distillery. Set in a 19th century mansion—which is allegedly haunted, by the way—Jolly Pumpkin is a restaurant/bar, brewery, winery and distillery all rolled into one. Though many varieties of Jolly Pumpkin beer are on tap or in bottles here, the beers themselves are actually being produced by Ron Jeffries down at the expanded Jolly Pumpkin brewery in Dexter, along with the bulk of the North Peak beers. Internationally recognized Master Brewer Mike Hall oversees operations here. With the move of major beer production to Dexter, he is now focused more on the distillery and some specialty beers.

How to summarize Brewer Mike in a small paragraph? The Nova Scotia native started brewing with his dad when he was 13; he got his first training under Peter Austin at Ringwood Brewery in the UK. Halifax, Amsterdam, Berlin, Somerset—he brewed far and wide and opened a brewery with Austin in Russia before becoming a Master Brewer in the International Brewers' Guild. As a consultant and trainer he's helped start loads of breweries including Bastone, North Peak, Grizzly Peak, and Blue Tractor. He even trained the master sour ale maker, Ron Jeffries, founder of Jolly Pumpkin. In 2009, he joined Northern United Brewing Co., which encompasses North Peak and Jolly Pumpkin beers, several brewpubs, and Civilized Spirits.

Mission Table makes a nice place for dinner on a summer evening or as an end to a day of touring wineries out here on the Peninsula. Come early and enjoy the tasting room as well.

Directions: From Front St (US-31/M-37/M-72) in Traverse City, take Garfield Ave (M-37) north onto Old Mission Peninsula. Stay on M-37 for 9.9 miles then keep straight on Seven Hills Rd where it breaks from a curve on M-37. Turn left (west) on Devil's Dive Rd. Continue 0.7 mile and turn left on Peninsula Dr. Jolly Pumpkin is on your left at 0.1 mile.

Stumbling Distance: Spend part of the day with grapes instead of grains: *Wineries of Old Mission Peninsula* (wineriesofoldmission.com) has an 8-winery Wine Trail map you can download.

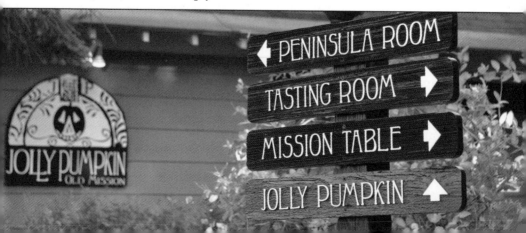

MACKINAW BREWING CO.

Founded: 1997
Brewmaster: Mike Dwyer
Address: 161 East Front Street • Traverse City, MI 49684
Phone: 231-933-1100
Website: www. mackinawbrewing.com
Annual Production: about 600 barrels
Number of Beers: 7 on tap (6 staples plus 1 seasonal)

Staple Beers:
» BELGIAN WHITECAP
» G.T. GOLDEN
» HARVEST MOON OATMEAL STOUT
» PENINSULA PALE ALE
» RED 8 ALE
» WEST BAY IPA

Rotating Beers:
» CHERRY HERITAGE LAGER (DURING CHERRY SEASON)
» SUMMER LOVE AMERICAN WHEAT

Most Popular Brew: West Bay IPA or Harvest Moon Stout, but Summer Love in summer

Tours? By appointment.

Samples: Yes, 7 five-oz. samplers for about $12.

Best Time to Go: Open daily from 11AM–midnight (noon–9PM on Sunday). Busy like crazy in summer.

Where can you buy it? Here on tap and to go in growlers.

Got food? Yes, barbecue options, seafood, sandwiches, soups and salads, and a kids' menu. Dishes of interest might be the French onion soup with oatmeal stout, smoked mac and cheese, smokehouse wings, or some Great Lakes whitefish.

Special Offer: Not participating.

The Beer Buzz: This was the first brewpub to open in downtown Traverse City. Owner Rod Langbo is also the head chef and a big fan of barbecue. Brewer Mike is originally from town and does his magic in the basement. He is also a local musician.

The brewpub is located inside the John T. Beadle building which dates back to 1892 when it was a harness shop. The brick walls are 18 inches thick. The smell of smoky barbecue wafts through the place. Make reservations if you want to eat during summer at typical mealtimes because the place gets packed. It is very family friendly. There are tables up front in the bar area, and booths in back as well as a small outdoor terrace.

Mug club membership is for life and you'll get your name in brass on the wall. Facebook.com/Mackbrew

Directions: From Grandview Parkway (US-31/M-37/M-72) right along the lake on West Bay, turn south on Cass St and drive 2 blocks. It's on the corner of Cass and Front St.

Stumbling Distance: Check out the best beer bar in town (and a contender in any town) *Seven Monks* (128 S Union St, 231-421-8410, 7monkstap. com) which is run by a certified Cicerone and features 46 taps including Belgian and Trappist ales and various Michigan craft brews. A nice pub menu as well.

7 Monks Taproom, an excellent beer bar in Traverse City

NORTH PEAK BREWING CO.

Founded: 1995
Brewmaster: Dave Hale
Address: 400 West Front Street • Traverse City, MI 49684
Phone: 231-941-7325
Website: www.northpeak.net/np.html
Annual Production: 1,250 barrels
Number of Beers: 7

Staple Beers:
» DIABOLICAL IPA
» LEINSTER IRISH-STYLE LAGER (RED ALE UNDER NITROGEN)
» MISSION POINT PORTER
» NORTHERN LIGHT
» SHIRLEY'S IRISH STOUT
» SIREN AMBER
» PLUS TWO SPECIALTY BEERS AND A CASK ALE

Most Popular Brew: Diabolical IPA

Brewmaster's Fave: Porter

Tours? No.

Samples: Yes, $6 for 5 four-ounce samplers plus $1.50 for each specialty beer.

Best Time to Go: Happy hour Monday–Friday from 3–6. Live music on the deck on summer weekends.

Where can you buy it? Here on site and in growlers, plus distributed throughout Michigan and parts of Ohio.

Got food? Yes, a full menu with seafood, steaks, sandwiches, soups, salads, and hearth-baked pizzas.

Special Offer: Not participating.

The Beer Buzz: Located in a refurbished brick candy factory at the west end of downtown Traverse City, the brewpub spent its first 10 years developing good business with their beer and food offerings. In 2008, founders Jon Carlson and Greg Lobdell hooked up with Ron Jeffries of Jolly Pumpkin and formed Northern United Brewing Co. Brewmaster Mike Hall joined the team, and about a year later bottling of the flagship beers began.

The brick building shows the brewhouse under glass out front and offers a large, high-ceiling dining room with the bar area at center. Don't miss the Irish-themed Kilkenny's downstairs, which also offers house brews. The North Peak bottled beers are produced at the at the Jolly Pumpkin facility in Dexter, but the draft beers here are brewed on site.

Brewer Dave attended Western Michigan University in Kalamazoo in the 90s. His roommates were on the bottling line over at Bell's and got him into homebrewing. Then he graduated with a public administration degree and couldn't find work. As he traveled he always sought out the brewpubs and breweries and simply fell in love with the industry and art form. In 1995 he studied at the American Brewers Guild in California. It was the only fermentation science program in the US (hassled by government for brewing on campus). He helped open a brewpub in upstate New York, then came back to Michigan, put in time in Pontiac, as well as at Bell's and Arcadia, and now here at the brewpub.

"We don't make our own schedules. The beer rules what we do." He prefers the small batches because they are more hands-on. He does open fermentation using plastic wrap to cover the fermenters.

Mission Management of Grand Rapids oversees the operations of North Peak, Jolly Pumpkin up in the Old Mission Peninsula (not brewing there), and Northern United Brewing Co. which bottles North Peak's beers (also Bastone, Blue Tractor, Grizzly Peak, Jolly Pumpkin, and Royal Oak).

Lifetime mug club membership.

Directions: From Grandview Parkway (US-31/M-37/M-72) right along the lake on West Bay, turn south on Union St and go one block to get to Front St. Turn right (west) and the brewery is one block farther on the right at Front and Hall Streets.

Stumbling Distance: Right downstairs, featuring live music, food, and more house brews, is *Kilkenny's Irish Public House* (400 W Front St, 231-941-7527, kilkennyspub.com). It's also a good place to shoot some pool.

RARE BIRD BREWPUB

Founded: 2013
Brewmaster: Tina Schuett
Address: 229 Lake Avenue • Traverse City, MI 49684
Phone: 262-719-2298
Website: www.rarebirdbrewpub.com
Annual Production: around 1,000 barrels
Number of Beers: 8–10 house brews, and 25–30 rare beers

Beers:
» Various American-Style Ales

Brewmaster's Fave: American Pale Ale

Tours? Yes, free tours whenever requested, but best to call in advance.

Samples: Yes.

Best Time to Go: Open noon to midnight Monday–Thursday, noon to 2AM Friday–Saturday. Closed Sundays, but check web to be sure. Happy hour is 4–7PM weekdays. Live music some nights. Watch them on Facebook.

Where can you buy it? Only here on tap and to go in growlers.

Got food? Yes, simple dishes with as much local and beer-focused ingredients as possible.

Special Offer: Get a Rare Bird sticker and either $1 off a pint or sampler flight or $2 off a growler fill.

The Beer Buzz: Brewery founders Tina Schuett and Nate Crane saw the need for a brewpub that not only offered their own beer but also fine beers from around the world and a full bar including liquor, specialty cocktails, wine, and cider. They found a home in this old brick building in the heart of Traverse City. This was once a potato warehouse, standing next to the old Traverse City Iron Works which has now been replaced by the new River's Edge-Midtown neighborhood. The building is divided into offices; Rare Bird is the most recent renovator of this space.

The brewery name came about from Nate and Tina's connection in rare birds: Tina has done research on kiwis in New Zealand, and Nate is a respected area birder. Tina started homebrewing in college. After working as a park ranger and a children's health researcher, she decided brewing was her true calling. She got her start over in Wisconsin at Sand Creek Brewery in Black River Falls, before coming to work at another brewery in Traverse City where she met Nate.

Mug Club. On Facebook and Twitter @RareBirdBrewpub

Directions: From Grandview Parkway (US-31/M-72/M-37), go south on Cass St for 0.4 mile and turn left (east) on Lake Ave. The brewery is on the left 200 feet from the corner.

Stumbling Distance: You can hop on the *Boardman Lake Trail* not far from here and bike/walk to *The Filling Station Microbrewery*. It's about 0.8 mile (the walk via streets is only 0.5 mile).

COURTESY OF RARE BIRD BREWPUB

RIGHT BRAIN BREWERY

Founded: December 2007
Head Brewers: Russ Springsteen with Nick Panchame and Mike Wooster
Address: 225 East 16th Street • Traverse City, MI 49684
Phone: 231-944-1239
Website: www.rightbrainbrewery.com
Annual Production: 3,000 barrels
Number of Beers: 15 to 50 on tap

Staple Beers:
» Black Eye PA
» CEO Stout
» Dead Kettle IPA
» Flying Squirrel Brown Ale
» Northern Hawk Owl Amber Ale
» Satisfaction ESB
» Shadow Watcher Stout
» Willpower Pale Ale

Rotating Beers:
» Debauchery Wheat Wine
» Fat Lad Russian Imperial Stout
» Irish Goodbye (Red Ale)
» Kelapa Porter (Collaboration Brew With Paw Paw Brewing)
» Looping Owl (Barrel-Soured Amber)
» Magical Mystery Pale Ale
» Mangalista Pig Porter
» Midnight Rendezvous (Experimental Black Ale)
» Naughty Girl Stout (With Mint)
» Pecan Pie Whole (With Actual Pies)
» The 2nd Coming Imperial IPA
» Strawberry Fields (Strawberry Ale)

Most Popular Brew: Northern Hawk Owl Amber Ale, CEO Stout, and Dead Kettle IPA.

Brewmaster's Fave:
    Russell: Willpower Pale Ale
    Mike: Midnight Rendezvous Black Ale
    Nick: Chubby Squirrel

Tours? By appointment.

Samples: Yes, 6 six-ounce pours for $15.

Best Time to Go: Open Monday–Wednesday 1–10PM, Thursday 1–11PM, Friday–Saturday 11AM–midnight, Sunday noon–8PM. Happy Hour runs Monday–Friday from 3–6PM. Euchre on Monday nights, Trivia on Tuesdays, Pint Night on Wednesday. Watch their Facebook page for live music dates.

Where can you buy it? On tap here or in growlers or kegs (24 hr notice) to go. Draft accounts throughout Michigan.

Got food? Only a few snacks: hummus and tortilla chips, pretzels, potato chips, and popcorn. Carry-in allowed.

In addition to serving a selection of locally made wines and ciders, they also have soda pop from Northwoods Soda.

Special Offer: Not participating.

The Beer Buzz: The first time I walked into Right Brain was at their previous location downtown, and I thought their long and creative beer menu was a bit crazy. That was nothing. When I stopped in the new place, owner/founder Russ Springsteen showed me a frozen pig's head that was going into the next brew. That's been about how things roll around here.

Russ got his start out in Boulder, Colorado… cutting hair that is. But surrounded by craft beer as he was, he developed a passion for it. So when he moved to Durand, MI to help his father in real estate, he found there wasn't much to be had. Solution: make your own. He homebrewed and went on a mission to start a brewery. To raise funds he flipped houses. When he was ready, his financial advisor told him to skip the food and focus on the beer. And so he did, but no one said anything about the hair; he opened an attached Salon Saloon. He hired John Niedermaier (now at Terra Firma) to do the brewing, whipping out over 100 recipes in his first year. John and Russ parted ways and the brewery was closed for a short time while this new location was being remodeled.

The brewery occupies an old warehouse on the south side of Traverse City with a high industrial ceiling, cinderblock walls, and glass-block windows. It's a huge space with tables and chairs and a long bar at the back end with plenty of perches. The name Right Brain comes from a high school experience where a teacher had all students take a test for whether they are left-brained or the generally creative right-brained. Russ was the only one in class; the teacher said he must have taken the test wrong. Maybe not. Try the beer.

Facebook.com/RightBrainBrewery

Directions: From Grandview Parkway (US-31/M-37/M-72) right along the lake on West Bay, turn south on Cass St and drive 1.1 miles. Turn left (east) on 16th St and the brewery is on the left half a block down.

Stumbling Distance: The best beer bar in town, with three Cicerone-certified beer servers on staff, is *7 MonksTaproom* (128 S Union St, 231-421-8410, 7monkstap.com). Make a point to get over here between brewery visits and try a few of their 46 beers on tap (including Trappist beers, other imports, and a lot of Michigan craft brews).

THE WORKSHOP BREWING CO.

Founded: 2013
Brewmaster: Corey Wentworth
Address: 221 Garland Street, Suite A • Traverse City, MI 49684
Phone: 231-421-8977
Website: www.traversecityworkshop.com
Annual Production: under 100 barrels for 2014
Number of Beers: 7 on tap plus seasonals (up to 15 taps possible)

Staple ("Journeyman") Beers:
» BALLPEEN ESB
» COLD CHISEL (BIERE BLANCHE)
» PRY BAR PORTER (USUALLY ON NITRO TAP)
» THE SICKLE (SAISON)
» 10 LB SLEDGE ENGLISH IPA
» TENPENNY AMERICAN BLONDE ALE
» THE UNCAPPER (STOCK ALE WITH A BIT OF LOCAL HONEY)

Rotating Beers:
» BASTARD RASP RASPBERRY BLANCHE
» BENCH VISE OUDE BRUIN
» MONKEY WRENCH BELGIAN DUBBEL
» PIPE WRENCH BELGIAN TRIPEL
» SCYTHE BIÈRE DE GARDE
» SPIRIT LEVEL CHESTNUT BROWN
» TAP AND DIE OKTOBERFEST
» 20-LB SLEDGE ("JOHN HENRY") TRIPLE PALE ALE (NITRO)
» WRECKING BAR BOURBON BARREL IMPERIAL PORTER (NITRO)

Most Popular Brew: 10 lb Sledge English IPA

Tours? In planning, check the website for times.

Samples: Yes, four 6-oz. pours for $10.

Best Time to Go: Open 11AM–10PM weekdays, and until midnight on weekends. Happy hour runs 3–5PM weekdays. Watch for live music.

Where can you buy it? On tap in 6-, 12-, and 16-ounce pours, and to go in growlers.

Got food? Yes, one-hander sandwiches, named like the beers (7), paired with the brews. $3–$5. Snacks, salads, daily specials. Duck poutine on occasion.

Special Offer: Not participating.

The Beer Buzz: Founder Pete Kirkwood decided he liked Traverse City. He'd been taking his vacations here all his life and finally just figured he'd move his family here and save all the driving. Pete helped run a brewpub in Pennsylvania called Shawnee Craft Brewing, and with Traverse City's thriving beer community, opening another brewery in town just made sense. The Workshop occupies the original location of Right Brain Brewing but has been totally redesigned. Some old church pews inside offer seating, while a garage door opens to an outdoor patio. The brewery name prompted all the references to tools and the room itself has an industrial feel: old table saws are just tables now. A full stage will feature a lot of live music.

This is a near-zero waste facility. The spent grain goes to area cattle, and they are pretty intensive with their composting and recycling. Brewer Corey works on a 7-barrel system and produces beers which are 90% or more organic. Watch for their Master Series barrel-conditioned beers.

Facebook.com/traversecityworkshop and Twitter @WorkshopBrewing

Directions: From Grandview Parkway (US-31/M-37/72) turn south on Hall St. Go half a block and turn left (east) on Garland St.

Stumbling Distance: If you are looking for some Cornish pasties, stop in at *Cousin Jenny's* (129 S Union St, 231-941-7821).

The Traverse City Ale Trail

Obviously, this book strongly supports the practice of making a pils-grimage. Traverse City's brewing and beer scene has exploded in recent years, and now TC makes a very fine destination—so much so that they have designed their own Ale Trail. Pick up one of the free passports at any of the breweries, the City Visitor Center, many restaurants, or even your hotel, and then set off getting each brewer's unique stamp. Complete the trail and you receive a commemorative pint glass. Follow the instructions in the passport to claim it.

tcaletrail.com

ZONE 4

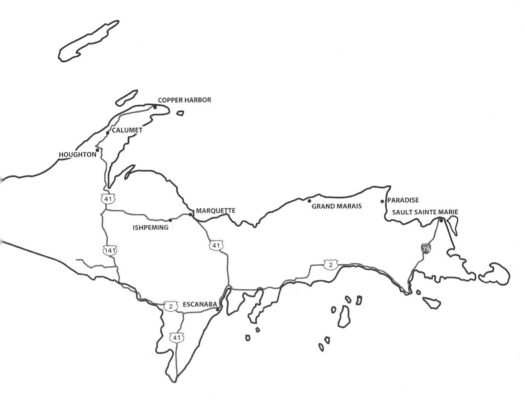

RED JACKET BREWING CO. (MICHIGAN HOUSE CAFE)

Founded: 2005
Brewmaster: Tim Bies
Address: 300 Sixth Street • Calumet, MI 49913
Phone: 906-337-1910
Website: www.michiganhousecafe.com
Annual Production: 50 barrels
Number of Beers: 3 on tap plus a guest tap

Staple Beers:
» APPLE/JUNIPER BERRY ALE
» COLD-HEARTED ALE (AMERICAN PALE ALE WITH WHEAT)
» DOWNTOWN BROWN
» OATMEAL EXPRESS STOUT

Most Popular Brew: Oatmeal Express Stout

Brewmaster's Fave: Oatmeal Express Stout

Tours? Not really, but if someone is free, you might talk beer with them.

Samples: Yes.

Best Time to Go: Open from lunch through dinner. Closed Wednesday.

Where can you buy it? Only here on draft or in growlers.

Got food? Yes, a full menu with a full bar and wine list. Burgers, wraps, paninis, pasta, steaks, soups and salads. Lake Superior trout, the famed walnut burger from Trempeleau Hotel in Wisconsin, and a really nice French onion soup. 75+ other beer choices are available in bottles plus a housemade root beer. Try the oatmeal stout ice cream.

Special Offer: $4 off your first house draft beer on your signature visit.

The Beer Buzz: Back in 1864 when Calumet was founded, it was known as Red Jacket, named for a chief of the Seneca tribe. The boom of copper mining brought everyone here. By the 1920s, demand dropped, but not to worry—many migrated to Detroit for the growing auto industry. What could go wrong?

A hotel has been on this site since the 1890s, taking on the name Michigan House and Hotel in 1895. In 1905 a local brewery, Bosch Brewing, razed that structure and built the current one. The air of its long history permeates the place. Step in through the screen door in front and find a booths-and-tables restaurant, with hand-pieced tile floors, filled with antiques and a few mounted hunting prizes. A big old-school bar is backed by two large mirrors, an antique cash register, and stained-glass cabinet doors on either side. A mural of a beer picnic, done on canvas inside the barrel ceiling above the bar, was painted by the Milwaukee Artists' Association in 1906. There are burgers on the menu, including one for the Gipper. George "The Gipper" Gipp worked as a waiter at the Michigan House back around 1912. Book one of the rooms upstairs and stay a night. Free Wi-Fi.

Brewer Tim started out in 2005 making 10 gallon batches on a SABCO half-barrel system, but since 2010 has been using a 3.5-barrel system. The small production leaves the risk of running out of beer, but it also allows him to experiment a lot. He says, "I wish I had more time for just that." He puts 13 double shots of espresso in at the end of the boil for each half-barrel batch of Oatmeal Express Stout.

Trivia: Calumet has the only natural ice curling facility in the country.

Directions: US-41 passes right through Calumet. Turn north-northeast on 6th St and follow it about 7 blocks and the pub is on the right on the corner of 6th and Oak St.

Stumbling Distance: Take a tour of the 1899 *Calumet Theatre* (340 Sixth St, 906-337-2610), the oldest municipal theatre in the US. Many other old Lake Superior brownstone buildings and a number of art galleries are worth checking out. Visit the *Coppertown Mining Museum* (25815 Red Jacket Rd, 906-337-4354) part of the *Keweenaw National Historical Park* (nps.gov/kewe) and *Keweenaw Heritage Center* in the former St. Anne's Church (25880 Red Jacket Rd, 906-337-4579 pasty.com/heritage).

BRICKSIDE BREWING

Founded: June 9, 2012
Brewmaster: Jason Robinson
Address: 64 Gratiot Street • Copper Harbor, MI 49918
Phone: 906-289-4772
Website: www.bricksidebrewery.com
Annual Production: 400 barrels
Number of Beers: 8 on tap, 6 in bottles

Staple Beers:
» FINE DAY PALE ALE
» PARK BENCH PORTER
» STONE SHIP STOUT
» SUPERIOR WIT
» U.P. IPA
» WALTERS WEISSEN

Rotating Beers:
» CHAINBREAKER DOUBLE IPA
» MOSQUITO LAKE PALE ALE
» SNAPPING TURTLE IPA

Most Popular Brew: U.P. IPA

Brewmaster's Fave: "I tend to prefer IPAs or a stout."

Tours? Yes, if he's there and not in the middle of something.

Samples: Four 4-oz. samples for about $4.

Best Time to Go: In summer, open daily about 3–11PM; in winter, Wednesday–Saturday. Phone first! Migratory bird fest in May, 4th of July (one of Michigan's best fireworks shows), Copper Harbor Trails Festival in September.

Where can you buy it? Right here on draft and in growlers or 22-oz. bottles. Distributed in the Keweenaw Peninsula for starters and moving toward Marquette, but solely the U.P. for now.

Got food? Just some snacks. Carry-in is allowed. There's a simple market across the street.

Special Offer: 10% off Brickside glassware or t-shirts during signature visit.

The Beer Buzz: Brewer Jason and his wife Jessica run this little operation at the northernmost bit of Michigan on the shores of Lake Superior.

Jason got the brewer's itch when his sister-in-law bought him an Ale Pail homebrewer's kit. They sat around nights (those are long nights in winter in the U.P.) brewing and drinking, and thinking, "Wouldn't it be cool to start a brewery?" They ran some numbers, and while the beery idea became a sober reality, location was going to be an issue. Jason is originally from brew city Milwaukee, and as a Coast Guard brat he bounced around a lot until ending up in Calumet where he met Jessica. As a volunteer firefighter and first responder, he has become part of the Copper Harbor community. Jessica was finishing her nursing degree further tying them to the area, but most brewery options would have required them to move.

Jason took on some distance learning with the American Brewers Guild, did some hands-on training and lab work in Vermont, and then worked some short-term jobs including a 5-week stint at Jolly Pumpkin in Dexter, MI. In the end, they got the licensing approval and little Copper Harbor put its pin on the brewery map. Everything is bottled and labeled by hand.

The original name of this building—unofficially—was Brickside. This is some seriously small-town Michigan, and a delivery guy showed up one day looking for the address: "the brick-sided building." From 1945 it was a grocery store and later added a gas station. In fact, Jason used to work here. The beer names have regional significance. Mosquito Lake was the original name of Lake Mendora in the 1920s, but proved a difficult sell for the real-estate market. Stone ships were built as public work projects during the Great Depression. There were three originally, and one can still be seen on the way to Copper Harbor along US-41 in Kearsarge. Free wifi. Copper top bar in the tap room.

Directions: Kinda hard to miss. Take US-41 all the way up to Copper Harbor. Turn right on Gratiot (still US-41, actually) and go 4.5 blocks and it's on your right. Wi-Fi

Stumbling Distance: Mountain bikers enjoy the *Copper Harbor Trails*. Rent some bikes, canoes, or kayaks from *Keweenaw Adventure Kayak* (906-289-4303, keweenawadventure.com). The *Isle Royale Queen* departs from here making the crossing to the incredible island state park nearly in Canadian waters far into Lake Superior. For eats you have *Harbor House* (77 Brockway Ave, 906-289-4502, harborhaus.com), a sort of German-themed restaurant, or *Fitzgerald's* ("The Fitz") in Eagle River (5033 Front St, Eagle River, 906-337-0666, eagleriverinn.com) with over 100 beers and a huge list of whiskeys.

HEREFORD & HOPS STEAKHOUSE & BREWPUB

Founded: December 1994
Brewmaster: Mike Sattem
Address: 624 Ludington Street • Escanaba, MI 49829
Phone: 906-789-1945
Website: www.herefordandhops.com
Annual Production: 500 barrels
Number of Beers: 8–10 on, 40+ styles throughout the year

Staple Beers:
» CLEARY RED
» REDEMPTION IPA
» WHITETAIL ALE

Rotating Beers:
» BLACKBIRD OATMEAL STOUT
» CRANBERRY PUMPKIN SOUR ALE
» DORTMUNDER
» HEFEWEIZEN
» KOELSCH ALE
» MEXICAN SOLEIL WHEAT
» NUT BROWN ALE
» OKTOBERFEST
» PINTAIL PILSNER
» RAZZBERRI ALE
» SCHWARZBIER
» SOUR ALES (VARIOUS)
» STOUTS (MILK, COFFEE, AMERICAN)

Most Popular Brew: Redemption IPA

Brewmaster's Fave: Any of his sours (Cranberry Pumpkin Sour, his first)

Tours? Yes, if the brewer is around.

Samples: Yes, $1 each.

Best Time to Go: When you're hungry! Happy hour is 3–7PM Monday–Friday featuring cheaper pints and free popcorn.

Where can you buy it? Only here, on tap, in growlers, chubbies (gallon jugs), and pigs (2.25 gallons).

Got food? Yes, this is a grill-your-own steak restaurant but also offers a full menu of burgers, sandwiches, pizza, seafood, pasta, salads, cheddar ale soup. Award-winning ribs. Peel-and-eat IPA-steamed shrimp. Butcher's Challenge: eat a 48-oz. top sirloin with salad, baked potato and toast in 75 minutes and win a gift certificate, hat, and the notoriety you'd expect. Beer pairing suggestions are on the menu.

Special Offer: Happy hour prices for the book owner and group during the signature visit.

The Beer Buzz: Escanaba sits on the west side of Little Bay de Noc, which opens out to Lake Michigan. The port access made the city key to the lumber and iron ore industry. In 1914 this building was the site of the Delta Hotel. The restaurant offers an unusual experience in that you may grill your own steak on an indoor grill. There are two main dining rooms: the casual one in front and a more formal room toward the back. The bar is in a separate room off to the side, and you can see the copper brew kettles through glass windows opposite the bar. In the very back of the bar is a game room as well. CJ's Lounge in the basement has some cool historical photos on the walls, but it is commonly only reserved for private parties. The food is good and the wait staff is trained to talk about the beers.

In high school, Brewer Mike was a co-op student for one of the owners. An All American wrestler, he also liked beer. When the previous brewer took ill, Mike helped out. He caught on and took over—a self-taught brewer. The beers have garnered some awards: Cleary Red and Schwarzbier took bronzes at the Great American Beer Festival. At the World Beer Championship, Whitetail and Schwarzbier took gold, Blackbird Oatmeal Stout nabbed a bronze.

Directions: US-2/US-41 from the west comes right into town on Ludington Ave. Stay on it and the brewery is downtown on the left at the corner of Ludington and 7th St. From the north, come in on US-2/US-41/M-35 (which is Lincoln Rd) and turn left (east) on Ludington Ave.

Stumbling Distance: *Pacino's* at the Best Western (2635 Ludington St, 906-789-0712, pacinosfoodandspirits.com) has great food and a very good beer selection. Beer selection is first-rate at *Kobasics' Sav-Mor* (306 Stephenson Ave, 906-786-4222), and there's some build-your-own six-pack selections. Best pasty in town: *Dobber's Pasties* (827 N Lincoln Rd, 906-786-1880, dobberspasties.com).

LAKE SUPERIOR BREWING CO.

Founded: 1994
Brewers: David Beckwith and Robert Nyman
Address: N 14283 Lake Avenue • Grand Marais, MI 49839
Phone: 906-494-2337
Website: www.grandmaraismichigan.com/lsbc
Annual Production: 250 barrels
Number of Beers: 6 on tap

Staple Beers:
» BLUEBERRY WHEAT
» CABIN FEVER ESB
» GRANITE BROWN
» HEMATITE STOUT
» LONESOME POINT IPA
» PUDDINGSTONE WHEAT

Rotating Beers:
» SAISON
» AND OTHERS

Most Popular Brew: Whatever is hoppiest

Brewmaster's Fave: IPA

Tours? Sure. "If someone actually wanted one. It's small."

Samples: Yes, about $1.75 for each five-ounce sampler.

Best Time to Go: "Noon until the last person leaves." Closed the first three weeks in April.

Where can you buy it? Only here, on tap or in growlers.

Got food? Yes, a full menu and some pizza. They sell "a ton of whitefish."

Special Offer: Not participating.

The Beer Buzz: Originally from Brighton, MI, founder Chris Sarver was a disgruntled mechanical engineer working for the auto companies. Needless to say, business wasn't so good. Then the brewpub law changed in 1992. The economy was bad, so he figured "may as well brew beer." So he opened one of the very first brewpubs in Michigan.

Step inside this brewpub just a stone's throw from Lake Superior and witness a taxidermist's representation of what's in the woods next door. The floor, ceiling, and walls show the gleaming hardwood common in northern taverns. The bar is a 1946 Brunswick—yes, the bowling people also made bars—and tables are made out of repurposed barrels. Agate slices hang in the windows. An addition to the building gave more room to the brewers, but there is also a bit of seating in that long hall in back. From the outside it looks like an old saloon and a sign on the side even says Dunes Saloon. August is their busiest time, and they may run out of some of their beers, in which case they'll put someone else's on tap. Founder Chris is also into wine and has a 37-acre pinot noir vineyard out in Eugene, Oregon.

Directions: Coming in from the south on M-77 or from the west on CR-58 just take it to where the two roads intersect near the lake in Grand Marais.

Stumbling Distance: If you're up here, you must visit *Pictured Rocks National Lakeshore* (www.nps.gov/piro) and *Au Sable Lighthouse*. Plenty of places to camp around here, but beware they fill up fast in summer. Here in town check out *West Bay Diner & Delicatessen* (E21825 Veteran St, 906-494-2607) a 1949 Paramount diner with food as notable as the wait.

KEWEENAW BREWING CO.

Founded: 2004
Brewmaster: Tom Duex
Address: 408 Shelden Ave • Houghton, MI 49931
Phone: 906-482-5596
Website: www.keweenawbrewing.com
Annual Production: 10,000 barrels
Number of Beers: 9 on tap, 40+ style per year, 6 canned for distribution

Staple Beers:
» Lift Bridge Brown Ale
» November Gale Pale Ale
» Old Ore Dock Scottish Ale
» Pick Axe Blonde Ale
» Red Jacket Amber Ale
» Widow Maker Black Ale

Rotating Beers:
» Empress Hefeweizen
» Keweenaw Belle
» Let It Go Stout
» Many, Many More At The Pub

Most Popular Brew: Pick Axe Blonde Ale on tap, Widow Maker in cans

Tours? Yes, just stop in at the production brewery during business hours on a weekday. No tours at the pub unless totally by chance.

Samples: Yes, 5 four-ounce glasses for about $4.

Best Time to Go: Open daily, but not until 3pm on Monday–Wednesday.

Where can you buy it? On site on tap, in growlers, half- and quarter-barrels, and six-pack cans for carry out. Throughout the UP and the rest of Michigan and parts of Wisconsin and Minnesota.

Got food? Plenty of roasted peanuts to go with that beer. You can also carry-in or have food delivered.

Special Offer: Not participating.

The Beer Buzz: Not far off of Lake Superior on the Keweenaw Peninsula, Houghton once was a star in the copper-mining industry. Though the last of the mines closed in the late 1960s, you still can find some copper over at Keweenaw Brewing Co—copper brewing tanks, that is. Keweenaw occupies two old buildings side by side and connected to each other, with old wood floors, reclaimed barn wood, and exposed brick walls. There is a bar on either side made of polished concrete. A gas fireplace in back and some couches make a comfortable hangout in winter time, while the back patio overlooks the ship channel and features a big mural on the next building. (The mural depicts what you would be able to see of the bridge and water if the building didn't exist.)

Keweenaw Brewing Co., or KBC as fans know it, is the creation of Paul Boissevain and Michigan Tech grad Dick Gray. Dick just wanted an excuse to come back to his old stomping grounds while Paul was enamored of the mighty Lake Superior and the beauty and charm of the area, not to mention that they both loved beer.

Folks from the big cities will likely be thrilled by the low prices for a pint. This is the U.P. after all. The 16-barrel copper and stainless steel brewhouse is right where you can see it.

Free Wi-Fi on site and board games for patrons to play.

In 2007, KBC opened a production facility with a 50-barrel brewhouse just outside town in South Range (10 Fourth St, 906-482-1937).

Directions: Sheldon Ave is one-way, heading west. Come into Houghton on US-41 or M-26 and they meet in downtown on the south side of the bridge. Coming from the east, US-41 hits a fork in downtown (the left fork goes to M-26) and you take the right fork into Sheldon Ave, the brewery is on the right. From the west, follow M-26 into town and stay straight on Montezuma Ave. Take a left at Huron St and go one block to Sheldon Ave and turn left.

Stumbling Distance: It's the U.P., so don't miss a chance to try a signature food item: the pasty. *Roy's Pasties & Bakery*, 901 W Sharon Ave, 906-487-6166) should work. Visit *The Library*, right down the street and around the corner. Trust me: it's not how it sounds (see the next brewery in the book).

THE LIBRARY RESTAURANT & BREWPUB

Founded: 1998
Brewmaster: Bob Jackson
Address: 62 Isle Royale Street • Houghton, MI 49931
Phone: 906-487-5882
Website: www. librarybrewpub.com
Annual Production: barrels
Number of Beers: 8–10 on tap plus guest taps

Staple Beers:
» AMBER LAGER
» COPPER TOWN ALE
» KEWEENAW GOLDEN ALE
» MINER'S IPA
» RABBIT BAY BROWN ALE
» REDBRICK RYE
» SHAFTHOUSE DRY STOUT
» WHITEOUT WHEAT

Rotating Beers:
» BUMBLETOWN ALE
» KOWSIT LATS BARLEYWINE
» PICK AXE PORTER
» PORTAGE PREMIUM LAGER
» ROCK HARBOR LIGHT ALE
» SCOTTISH ALE

Most Popular Brew: Copper Town Ale

Tours? Yes, by chance or by appointment.

Samples: Five 4-oz. pours for about $4.

Best Time to Go: Pints are cheap during happy hour, 4–6PM Monday–Thursday.

Where can you buy it? Only here on draft or in growlers.

Got food? Yes, a full menu that includes pan-seared ahi tuna, brown ale battered mushrooms, local whitefish, sometimes trout. Tuesday is sushi night with fresh seafood from Hawaii.

Special Offer: Not participating.

The Beer Buzz: This is that place a college kid loves: "I spend a lot of time at The Library, Mom." The Library has been an institution since the 1960s, and locals remember a somewhat dark and dingy place with dancing upstairs at night. It was the first restaurant to have Bell's on tap (which it often still does). It suffered a fire in 1996, and when it reopened in 1998, it added the brewhouse. The walls and beams are the originals. Books along the walls and bar are more decoration than reading material, and a beer can collection is also spread throughout the place. The view out the back is over the water.

The establishment is very active in the community and does Michigan Tech tailgate parties with food and beer. Owner Jim Cortright is as passionate about the beer as Brewmaster Bob is. Bob's beer has won awards—for the IPA, Barleywine, and Porter—but the food is worth noting as well with its abundance of fresh seafood. Parking is free in the lot behind the building.

Directions: Sheldon Ave is one-way, heading west. Come into Houghton on US-41 or M-26 and they meet in downtown on the south side of the bridge. Coming from the east, US-41 hits a fork in downtown (the left fork goes to M-26) and you take the right fork into Sheldon Ave. Take a right on the next street, Isle Royale, and the brewery is on the left at the end of the block. From the west, follow M-26 into town and stay straight on Montezuma Ave. Take a left at Isle Royale St and it snakes for one short block and then crosses Shelden Ave. The Library is on the left.

Stumbling Distance: Learn a bit about the industry that made this region boom: *Quincy Mine* (49750 US Hwy 41, Hancock, 906-482-3101, www.quincymine.com) offers guided tours from early May to late October. A lot of Finns settled in the area back in the early 1900s. For either traditional Finnish items or just a good breakfast, visit *Suomi Home Bakery & Restaurant* (54 Huron St, 906-482-3220).

JASPER RIDGE BREWERY

Founded: 1996
Brewmaster: Grant Lyke
Address: 1075 Country Lane • Ishpeming, MI 49849
Phone: 906-485-6017
Website: www.jasperridgebrewery.com
Annual Production: 350 barrels
Number of Beers: 8 on tap, 15 styles, plus root beer

Staple Beers:
» BLASTIN' BLUEBERRY WHEAT
» COPPER KÖLSCH
» JASPER BROWN
» OLD ISH IPA
» RED EARTH PALE ALE
» ROCKIN' RASPBERRY WHEAT
» ROPE'S GOLDEN WHEAT
» STOUT

Rotating Beers:
» MAIBOCK
» OKTOBERFEST
» PAULDING LIGHT PILSNER
» PORCUPINE PORTER
» SULLY'S STRONG ALE
» WINTER WARMER

Most Popular Brew: Blueberry Wheat or Golden Wheat

Brewmaster's Fave: Old Ish IPA

Tours? Yes, by appointment.

Samples: $1 each. Sampler tray available.

Best Time to Go: Happy hour 3:30–6 Monday through Friday. Open daily for lunch and dinner.

Where can you buy it? Here on tap or in growlers to go.

Got food? Yes, a full menu and full bar. Burgers, sandwiches, wraps, pizzas, salads, cheese and beer soup, ale-battered mushrooms, Friday fish fry, and housemade cudighi (a form of Italian sausage created by immigrants and rarely found outside the U.P.).

Special Offer: Get 50% off a single pint of house beer during your signature visit.

The Beer Buzz: Jasper Knob is a bare-topped hill made entirely of jaspilite in the center of Ishpeming. Locals claim this to be the largest semi-precious gem in the world. You don't need to be a geologist to appreciate the beauty of this rare rock make of very red jasper banded together with dark hematite. The name of the brewpub plays off that name and around town it is known affectionately as "The Ridge."

Jasper Ridge opened as a family business and remains so. This is a brewpub with a resort license meaning they can still be a brewery and offer a full bar according to Michigan state law. (Normally brewpubs can only offer their own products.)

Years ago Brewer Grant was at a party and the host offered him some of his phenomenal homebrewed stout. Grant was hooked immediately. His father had been making wine at home, but it had never occurred to him to try beer until that moment. Grant brewed his first batch in 1990. In 1996, he was hired at The Ridge and has brewed every batch here since.

The bar does beer blends. A customer once suggested mixing their stout with the blueberry wheat. It was so good it ended up on the menu as a Black and Blue.

This establishment stands in its own parking lot and is part of Country Village Resort with the Jasper Ridge Inn next door. There are two sides to the place: a long lounge area with the bar and cocktail tables, and the family-style restaurant. The brewery is behind glass and set between the two rooms. Check out the old bottles from U.P. breweries of the past; they are in a glass case under the windows looking into the brewhouse.

Free Wi-Fi and a Mug Club. Facebook.com/JasperRidgeBrewery

Directions: From US-41/M-28 passing right through Ishpeming, turn north on Country Lane (next to the BP gas station a block east of McDonald's) and drive in two blocks. The brewpub is across a parking lot on the left.

Stumbling Distance: Not far from here, just across US-41, is the *Cliffs Shaft Mine Museum* (501 W. Euclid St, 906-485-1882) which is a collection of historical and geological artifacts. You can't miss the tower-like head frames as you look out over the city. Marquette and its breweries are just another 20 minutes east of Ishpeming.

BLACKROCKS BREWERY

Founded: December 28, 2010
Brewers: David Manson, Andy Langlois, Andrew Reeves, and Christopher Hott
Address: 424 North 3rd Street • Marquette, MI 49855
Phone: 906-273-1333
Website: www. blackrocksbrewery.com
Annual Production: 440 barrels
Number of Beers: 8 on tap; 250 styles in 2011

Beer Examples:
» Bramber (Brown Amber)
» Creamsicle (Orange Cream Ale)
» Drunk Yoda (Hop-Forward Amber)
» Honey Lavender Wheat
» Willie O'ree Ale
» Plus various IPAs (primarily galaxy hops-based) and Pale Ales

Most Popular Brew: Check their "Brewquests" posted at the bar: a list of beers that people vote on.

Brewmaster's Fave: "That'd be like picking your favorite kid!"

Tours? Sure, but more like the down-and-dirty in five minutes.

Samples: Yes.

Best Time to Go: When they're open. Wednesday–Sunday 5–10PM, except Saturday 12–10PM. Earlier on Saturday in summer. Live music on Sundays, open mic on Thursdays.

Where can you buy it? Right here on tap or in growlers.

Got food? No, but carry-in is welcome and menus are on site for ordering in.

Special Offer: Take 50 cents off your first pint on your signature visit.

The Beer Buzz: As Brewer David told me, "We like to play." He ain't kidding. That's not a typo above—they brewed 250 different beers their first year. "Here's a stout. Let's add chipotle."

Brewers David and Andy brewed in their basements for 4.5 years, always dreaming of going pro. Both worked in pharmaceuticals, and when "reductions" were announced, they decided it was time. Andy lost his job.

The pair found an empty 1910s house, gave it a paint job, found some outside money, and started brewing. Good thing, because then David's job was next on the chopping block.

The name comes from the Black Rocks of Presque Isle, a park in town. Jumping off the cliff there into Lake Superior is a local rite of passage. The brewers started on a one-barrel system, which is still in the basement for one-offs ("Basement recipes"). Tap handles include a bicycle gear, hockey stick, golf club head, and a ski pole. Inside are tall benches with footrests that make one feel like they're getting a shoe shine. Outside seating in the yard or on the front porch give it a neighborhood house-party sort of feel. Every night at the house ends with a thank you toast to the loyal clientele.

They have a mug club and free Wi-Fi.

Directions: At the center of downtown Marquette, US-41 hits a traffic roundabout to make a right angle turn west or south. Head north (lake on your right side) 0.8 mile on Front St and turn left on Michigan St. The brewery is on the corner on the left a block later at 3rd St.

Stumbling Distance: *The Pasta Shop* (824 N 3rd St, 906-228-6620, thepastashop.com) just down the street serves fresh, housemade dishes for very reasonable prices. No pretense; like eating at your Italian grandmother's. *Vango's Pizza & Cocktail Lounge* (927 N 3rd St, 906-228-7707, vangospizza. com) offers a good cudaghi sandwich and waffle fries. *Jean Kay's* (1635 Presque Isle Ave, 906-228-5310, jeankayspasties.com) near the dam at Presque Isle for a good pasty.

ORE DOCK BREWERY

Founded: May 24, 2012
Brewmaster: Nick VanCourt
Address: 114 Spring Street • Marquette, MI
Phone: 906-228-8888
Website: www.ore-dock.com
Annual Production: 850 barrels
Number of Beers: 10 on tap

Staple Beers:
» Belgian Blonde
» Dream Weaver Belgian (With Citrus And Chamomile)
» Saison (7.2% ABV)
» Gluten-Free With Sorghum
» Radler

Rotating Beers:
» Belgian IPA
» Dark American Wheat
» Dark Saison
» Double IPA
» ESB
» Snow Day IPA
» Summer Saison
» Superior Supper Stout
» Winter Wit Bier
» and more...

Most Popular Brew: Dream Weaver.

Brewmaster's Fave: On the Belgian style side the Belgian Blonde, on the American style side the Session Pale Ale

Tours? Free scheduled tours. See website.

Samples: Flights of 5 samples for just under $10.

Best Time to Go: Happy hour is Tuesday–Friday from 5–7PM with discounts on select pints. Closed Mondays. Open noon–11PM, or midnight Thursday–Saturday.

Where can you buy it? Growlers and kegs for now; cans and bottles to come.

Got food? No, but carry-in is allowed and there are menus for ordering in.

Special Offer: Get a $1 pint and a free sticker for getting your book signed.

The Beer Buzz: The building that houses this brewery once stood in the shadow of a trestle of an ore dock, a massive structure used to run trains out over the water, high above the ore ships coming to port to pick up loads of taconite. You can still see a couple ore docks here in Marquette; the closest one is defunct and stands just offshore, a few minutes walk from the brewery. The mining company once brought in vehicles to be serviced in this 100-plus-year-old building.

The downstairs has a bar and a posted menu of what's on tap plus a few TVs around the place, some board games, and a serious cribbage board carved from a tree stump. And you can see the brewery through windows in back. A garage door opens in season and allows for some outside sun and air to get to the drinkers. The upstairs has a bit of a beer hall feel and loads of space but doesn't open until the evening. An ore-dock-sized bar wraps around the center of the building and serves both sides. This area was actually a Model T showroom and later storage for Chevy. When the partners purchased it, 30 cars filled the upstairs and had to be brought down the steep ramp. The building received a "vigilante carpentry" makeover: everything inside has been reclaimed and refashioned—the floor, old barn boards from Wausau, WI.

Brewer Nick grew up in Daggett, MI, and used to take sips of his grandfather's imported German lagers. Like many, he discovered Bell's, the gateway drug to the craft beer world. He ventured to Madison, WI,

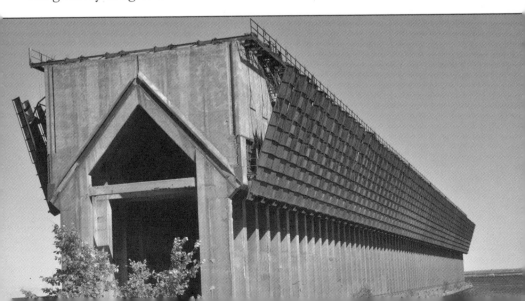

where he put in some time at the Great Dane Brewpub. He earned an International Diploma in Brewing Technology from the World Brewing Academy which had him studying and practicing in Chicago and Munich. He came back to the States after a European brewery pilsgrimage and worked at Milwaukee Brewing Co. and then Tyranena in Lake Mills, WI. Then he made the move home to Michigan. His focus is on Belgian beer styles.

For starters, Ore Dock Brewery is brewing for local consumption, but ultimately they want to be a distribution brewery. Three of the five partners are homebrewers and have brewed with the folks over at Blackrocks, and one is cousin to the brewer at Vierling. Because the brewery is right off the city's 16-mile paved bike path, it has become a popular hangout for cyclists.

Plenty of parking nearby. Free Wi-Fi on site.

Directions: At the center of downtown Marquette, US-41 hits a traffic roundabout to make a right-angle turn west or south. Head north (lake on your right side) on Front St and go three blocks and turn left (west) on Spring St. and the brewery is on the right.

Stumbling Distance: All brewers in Marquette are within walking distance of each other. It's a bit of Beervana or the Brewmuda Triangle. *Lawry's Pasty Shop* (2164 US Highway 41 W, 906-226-5040, lawryspasties.com) is the place to go for the quintessential U.P. meal. Cyclists have much to do here. Mountain-bike enthusiasts should check out the *Noquemanon Trail Network* (noquetrails.org) and the *Marquette South Trails*, with over 40 miles of premier trails.

THE VIERLING RESTAURANT & MARQUETTE HARBOR BREWERY

Founded: 1985 (1995 brewery)
Brewmaster: Derek "Chummly" Anderson
Address: 119 South Front Street • Marquette, MI 49855
Phone: 906-228-3533
Website: www.thevierling.com
Annual Production: 360 barrels
Number of Beers: 9 on tap, up to 15 styles each year

Staple Beers:
» BLONDE ALE
» BLUEBERRY WHEAT
» HONEY WHEAT
» PALE ALE
» RED ALE
» STOUT

Rotating Beers:
» CHUB'S DOUBLE PALE ALE
» COCO BROWN ALE
» HONEY PILSNER
» IPA
» PEACH WHEAT
» PINE MOUNTAIN PALE ALE
» PORTER

Most Popular Brew: Blueberry Wheat

Brewmaster's Fave: All of them!

Tours? By appointment.

Samples: Yes, nine 4-oz. pours for about $10.

Best Time to Go: Monday through Saturday from 11AM–10PM or 11ish on weekends.

Where can you buy it? Only here, on tap or in growlers to go.

Got food? Yes, a full menu for lunch and dinner, and a great selection of fresh Lake Superior whitefish from Thill's, the fishmonger across the parking lot behind them.

Special Offer: A free pint glass with book signature.

The Beer Buzz: The Vierling Saloon and Sample Room dates back to 1883, while the modern restaurant came into being after a 9-month remodeling project in 1985. Inside you can see old photos and city maps along the walls. Check out the painting of monks playing chess, then find it in one of the old black and white shots. The artist, Lundmark, used to bet his works during poker games. The sunny back room has dining tables and a nice view out to Lake Superior. A tasting room usually only open for overflow or private events is set apart from the rest of the restaurant and features a large copper kettle the owners found in a field. (It was originally used for cheese making, though it's not uncommon for dairy equipment to be repurposed for brewing beer.)

The brewery is down in the restaurant's basement, which, because of the sloping street, actually looks out onto the sidewalk in the back of the building. Brewer Chummly started working in the kitchen back in 1987. When brewpubs became legal in Michigan in 1992, it was suggested he learn how to brew. He skipped the typical homebrewer step and just started reading anything he could get his hands on. He considers himself a "scholarly" brewer and has a keen interest in the science of the process. Brewing equipment arrived from Budapest. "The installers brew a few test batches before they leave. That was my training." They left him a phone number, which he called a few times in the beginning. Then he traveled

to Milwaukee to visit Lakefront and Water Street Breweries to do some research. Everything else was learned by experience. His cousin is a partner over at Ore Dock Brewing, and he's good friends with the guys over at Blackrocks—they used to buy their homebrew supplies from him. He even used to commute to Tahquamenon Falls Brewery for a couple years.

Free Wi-Fi on site. Parking is easier in the evening in lots or on the street; during the day street parking meters must be fed.

Directions: At the center of downtown Marquette, US-41 hits a traffic roundabout to make a right-angle turn west or south. Head north (lake on your right side) on Front St and go five blocks to find The Vierling on the right on the corner of Front and Main St.

Stumbling Distance: *Donckers' Restaurant* (137 W Washington St, 906-226-6110, donckersonline.com) offers hand-dipped chocolates, an old-fashioned soda machine experience, and a restaurant upstairs. Since 1896! It's not often you get authentic Thai this far into the northwoods, but try out *Sai Uwa Thai Bistro* (102 West Washington St, 906-228-8424, saiuwa. com). Look for the Quonset hut down by the old ore dock to find *Thill's Fish House* (250 E Main St, 906-226-9851). Try some of their smoked fish with a stout.

TAHQUAMENON FALLS BREWERY & PUB

Founded: 1996
Brewmaster: Lark Ludlow
Address: Upper Falls Drive, M-123 • Paradise, MI 49768
Phone: 906-492-3300
Website: www.tahquamenonfallsbrewery.com
Annual Production: 260 barrels
Number of Beers: 4 on tap, 12 style per year

Beers:
» BLACK BEAR STOUT
» BLUEBERRY ALE
» FALLS TANNIN AMERICAN RED
» HARVEST WHEAT ALE
» LUMBERJACK BLONDE LAGER
» PORCUPINE PALE ALE

Most Popular Brew: Lumberjack Blonde Lager or Wheat Ale

Brewmaster's Fave: Falls Tannin Red and Black Bear Stout

Tours? No one can go behind the bar for a tour, but she is happy to chat about brewing.

Samples: Yes, four for $5 or $1.25 each.

Best Time to Go: Open 7 days a week, 11AM–8:30PM, but beware that though this is a four-season brewery, it does close for a short time in the shoulder periods between winter and not winter: Closed 1–3 weeks in April, and from the 3rd Sunday in October until mid-December.

Where can you buy it? Only here on tap or in growlers to go.

Got food? Yes, a full menu that includes some regional items such as a local buffalo burger, local whitefish, beer soup with Wisconsin cheddar, wild rice soup, pasty, and deep-fried pickle spears.

Special Offer: $1 off one glass of house beer during your signature visit.

The Beer Buzz: Though it may seem like this is a brewpub in the middle of a state park, it isn't actually on state park land. Its two-acre patch of private land, however, is indeed surrounded by the park, requiring one to pay the park fee to get to the beer. Do it; it's worth it.

The brewpub is part of Camp 33, named for a logging camp for the Barrett Logging Co. Jack Barrett had the replica built as an eating and rest stop for visitors, and in the 1990s, his grandchildren Lark and Barrett Ludlow spruced it up and created this brewpub, restaurant, and gift shop. Designed like a northern wood lodge with high peaked ceilings, the brewery's walls are adorned with stuffed animals—both the toy and the hunted variety. The tanks are right behind the long bar with its railroad rail footrest. Lark had spent 20 years in upstate New York, but she moved to "Paradise" to work with her brother to put a brewpub out here in the middle of the Michigan Northwoods. Some places have to close down in winter for lack of business, but she interviewed people who came to see the falls in the "off season" and found there was a market—and not just for indoor dining. There are fireplaces inside and outside. Snowmobilers can hang around outdoors with their food and drinks rather than coming inside and overheating in their heavy clothing.

Lark wanted to go to some kind of brewing school, but she simply didn't have the time. She ended up getting training from the folks from California who installed the equipment. The equipment came from Hungary and lacked a parts manual, so when it breaks down she has to have parts made from scratch. Despite the challenges, she does an impressive job.

Directions: Follow M-123 to Paradise and continue on it as it turns west away from Lake Superior. The park entrance is on the left 4 miles from Paradise along M-123.

Stumbling Distance: *Tahquamenon* (tah-KWA-men-on) *Falls* are the main attractions up here, and the state park has an abundance of hiking (including the *North Country National Scenic Trail*) and paddling opportunities, and camping with a total of 260 modern sites and 36 rustic. The Upper Falls are the 2nd biggest east of the Mississippi (after Niagara): 50 feet high and 200 feet across. Don't miss the *Great Lake Shipwreck Museum* at Whitefish Point (18335 N. Whitefish Point Rd, Paradise, 888-492-3747, shipwreckmuseum.com) which has the bell from the Edmund Fitzgerald, an 1861 iron-pile lighthouse, and much more, about 15 miles from here, north of Paradise. *Oswalds Bear Ranch* (13814 County Rd 407, Newberry, 906-293-3147, oswaldsbearranch.com) is 20 minutes south and offers a walkabout experience with a couple dozen bears! Open Memorial Day through September.

SOO BREWING CO.

Founded: March 2011
Brewmaster: Ray Bauer
Address: 223 West Portage Avenue • Sault Sainte Marie, MI 49783
Phone: 906-632-4400
Website: www.soobrew.com
Annual Production: 368 barrels produced, before spillage and sampling. 50+ varieties: "Sometimes we repeat, sometimes we don't."
Number of Beers: up to 10 taps plus root beer

Beers:
» Goldilocks Blonde Ale
» Laker Gold
» Maggie's Monthly
» Rotation Of IPAs
» Soo Brew (session ale with UK ingredients)

Rotating Beers:
» Blue Spruce IPA
» Braveheart Stout
» Harmony Health Food's Manic Organic Pale Ale
» Hop The Border IPA
» Maggie's Irish Red
» Noel Divine Biere De Garde
» Northern German Altbier
» O Tannenbaum
» Punkin' Drublic
» Ray's Dry Rye
» Slowhand IPA
» Soo Grand Cru
» Sooper Yooper IPA
» Tabellenerbauer Bavarian Black
» Trinity Belgian Tripel
» The Yooper Forklift Double IPA

Most Popular Brew: GoldiLocks Blonde Ale

Brewmaster's Fave: "My beers are like my kids they are wonderful in their own unique way." The trilogy of lagers is his favorite if you had to pin him down. And you would have to.

Tours? Not really, but Ray will chat with you about brewing. The law says you can't step behind the bar.

Samples: Yes, 4 four oz. $6.

Best Time to Go: Cheap growler refills on Mondays.

Where can you buy it? Just right here, pints and growlers.

Got food? Free peanuts and pretzels on hand. Bring your own food or order in with menus on site.

Special Offer: A free Soo Brewing Co. pint glass on your signature visit.

The Beer Buzz: From about the late 1800s into the 1940s (with a pause for Prohibition) there was a Soo Brewing Co. Some of that Soo Brewery's breweriana made it into this modern Soo Brewery. You'll see some of the old bricks worked into the bar and old Soo bottles functioning as tap handles.

A college friend bought Ray a homebrew kit in 1990 and he gave it a go. But at first he was unhappy with the results and the amount of work. But then his father died, and at his funeral his cousin Willy spoke nostalgically of family homebrewing before the turn of the last century (Ray's grandparents were born in Germany). At any family gathering—someone home on military leave, first communions, weddings—they'd set up big homemade tables in the yard and bring out the homemade beer and wine. Ray was inspired to revisit his heritage and went back to brewing with a mission. As a homebrewer he was more into brewing it than drinking it, so he'd have people over frequently. In so doing, he created a buzz before he opened the brewery years later. Success was so good in his first year, he kept running out. He added fermenters in summer of 2012 so he could keep up.

Ray encourages community. A neighbor made the tables for the place, and patrons sit in old church pews, about ten people to a table. This is a family-oriented place (kids can join a root beer mug club for a lifetime fee) and there are board games available. The mug club votes on what Ray should make for the next specialty brew, a challenge he loves. Once a year Ray brews something called The Legend, a secret recipe. That's as much as you or I know. Under a blue awning in an old storefront, the somewhat plain tap room is sparsely decorated under pressed-tin ceilings. A beer can collection lines up along one wall, as does a collection of growlers from other Michigan breweries. It's all about the beer and hanging with friends here.

Free Wi-Fi. Mug Club. Facebook.com/SooBrew

Directions: From I-75 coming in from the south, take Exit 392 for Business I-75 (becomes Ashmun St). Take that all the way into town and take a left on Portage Ave. The brewery is on the left at the end of the first block.

Stumbling Distance: Watch from the Visitor Center as Great Lakes ships as long as 1000 feet traverse the *Soo Locks* (906-253-9290, 9AM to 9PM mid May to mid-October)—just across the street from the brewery. *The Antlers Restaurant* (804 E Portage Ave, 906-253-1728) not only has great food (burgers, whitefish, salads, steaks, etc), but the name is just a hint at the incredible amount of taxidermy you'll find, er, stuffed into this place. *Plaza Motor Hotel* (3901 I-75 Business Spur, 906-635-1881, plazamotormotel.com) is a good place to crash for the night just off of I-75 at the southern edge of town.

HOP(S) ON THE BUS BREWERY TOURS

Sometimes it's easier to just go along for the ride and focus on the beer rather than sorting out your own designated driver. Join a brew tour!

MOTOR CITY BREW TOURS

On foot, by bike, or by bus, not a bad route to go. They have a calendar of scheduled tours or you can set up your own private one.

motorcitybrewtours.com, info@motorcitybrewtours.com

PARTY BUS DETROIT

Gather a group and rent a comfortable party bus ride. They cover the greater Detroit area (that's a lot of breweries within striking range) as well as Ann Arbor.

www.partybusdetroit.com, 248-630-5605, info@partybusdetroit.com

WEST MICHIGAN BEER TOURS

Generally they stick to beer destinations in western Michigan, but occasionally they draw outside the lines.

westmichiganbeertours.com, 269-205-4894, info@westmibeertours.com

GLOSSARY OF BEERS

Ale—Short answer: beer from top-fermenting yeast, fermented at warmer temperatures.

Altbier means "old" beer—as in a traditional recipe, not a brew that's gone bad. It's a bitter, copper-colored ale.

Amber is that funny rock-like stuff that prehistoric bugs got trapped in and now makes great hippie jewelry or that pretty girl you were sweet on in middle school. But here I think they're just talking about the color of a type of American ale that uses American hops for a balanced bitter, malty, and hoppy flavor.

APA (American Pale Ale) is a pale ale using American hops. The hops flavor, aroma and bitterness are pronounced.

Barley wine is like precious gold wherever it's brewed. This ale jumps off the shelves or out of the tap. It is strong, sweet, a bit aged, and those who know are waiting to pounce on it.

Bitter is part of the family of pale ales, cousin perhaps to the IPA. Like folks in a small Michigan town, all beer is related in some way, I guess. This brew has a wider range of strength, flavor and color than the IPA. See "ESB." You'll be back.

Blonde or Golden Ale is a lighter form of pale ale usually made with pilsner malt. It's a popular Belgian style and gentlemen prefer them.

Bock is a strong lager darkened a bit and brewed in the winter to be drunk in spring. Monks drank it during the Lenten fasting period because it had substance to it, you know, like liquid bread? The name comes from the medieval German village of Einbeck. So, no, it does not mean Bottom of the Keg or Beer of Copious Kraeusening. (What IS kraeusening anyway?) Bock means goat in German. Thus the goats on so many of the labels and the popularity of headbutting at fraternity bock parties.

Brackett (also called braggot) is the first form of ale and a sort of beer and mead hybrid. It was first brewed with honey and hops and later with honey and malt—with or without hops added.

Cream Ale is a smooth and sweet American ale often containing some corn.

Measure for Measure

A **growler** is a half-gallon jug, refillable at your local brewpub. Many brewers sell them to you full for a few dollars more than the refill.

One **US barrel** (1 bbl) is two kegs or 31 gallons or 248 pints, so you better start early.

A **keg** holds 15.5 gallons – this is the legendary half-barrel of the college party fame

A **Cornelius keg** is a pub keg, similar to one of those soda syrup canisters and holds 5 gallons.

A **can** = 12 oz. = generally an improper beer of the mass-produced variety, but not always.

A **US pint** = 16 oz. = a proper US beer. (Also defined as 1/8 of a gallon)

A **UK pint** = 20 oz. (lucky chumps) and there are laws protecting the drinker from improperly filled pints! Look for that little white line on the pint glass.

A **firkin** is a small cask or barrel, usually the equivalent of a ¼ barrel or about 9 gallons (34 liters)

Getting confused yet? I gave up at "pint" and drank one.

And don't even get me started on the whole metric vs. Imperial gallon vs. US gallon vs. 10-gallon hat conundrum.

Doppelbock see "Bock" and read it twice. Seriously, just a bock with a stronger punch to it though not necessarily double.

Dunkelweiss is a dark wheat beer, a German style. "Dunkel" means dark.

Eisbock if you say it out loud it is probably easier to guess. No, it's not beer on the rocks. Take a bock, freeze it, take the ice out, and you have a higher alcohol content bock.

ESB (Extra Special Bitter) see "Bitter" and add some more alcohol. Isn't that what makes beer extra special?

Gruit or **Grut** is a mixture of herbs that beer makers used to use before hops came into favor. It added bitterness and in some cases preservative qualities, and the unique blends offered a variety of flavors for beers. Some brewers might do unhopped beers and use things like juniper berries, chamomile, heather or other things that sound like lawn clippings.

Hefeweizen (German Wheat Beer) is supposed to be cloudy—it's unfiltered. Don't make that face, drink it. That's where all the vitamins are and stuff. See also "Weisse" et al.

Imperial Stout see "Stout." The Brits originally made this for the Russian imperial court. It had to cross water as cold as our frozen tundra so the high alcohol content kept it from freezing. Expect roasted, chocolate, and burnt malt flavors and a strong left hook.

IPA (India Pale Ale) is what the Brits used to send to India. The long journey spoiled porters and stouts, and so this recipe calls for lots of hops. Did you read that part yet? About hops as a preservative? You can't just skip parts of the book. I'll catch you. And there will be a quiz. Don't say I didn't warn you.

Irish-style Stout is a dry version of stout, typically served under nitro for the creamy special effect. However, it's very dark and thus too difficult to dye green on St. Patty's Day.

Kölsch is just an excuse to use those little dot things—"What is an umlaut?" for those of you looking to score on Jeopardy—and a difficult-to-pronounce-and-still-retain-your-dignity name for a light, fruity ale that originated in Cologne... the city in Germany, please don't drink your aftershave no matter how nice it smells.

Lager—Short answer: beer with bottom-fermenting yeast, fermented colder than ale.

Lambic—let's just call this the Wild One. It's a Belgian ale with wheat and it uses naturally occurring yeast, the kind that's just floating around out there. The brew is tart and may have a fruit element added such as raspberries or cherries.

Low alcohol—See "Near Bear."

Maibock is not your bock and if you touch my bock, there's gonna be trouble. This is the lightest of the bocks and is traditionally brewed to be drunk in May, but we're not always hung up on tradition and it is often around whenever you want it.

Märzen takes its name from March, the month in which this lager is typically brewed so it can age in time for Oktoberfest when it magically becomes Oktoberfest beer.

Mead is honey fermented in water. It ain't beer but it's good. And there's plenty of honey in Michigan to make it. The word "honeymoon" comes from a tradition of gifting a newlywed couple a month's worth of mead to get things off to a smooth start. From this you can guess why we say "the honeymoon's over" with such lament.

Near Beer—Let's just pretend we didn't hear this and move on, shall we?

Nut Brown Ale uses roasted malt, and a bit of hops brings some bitterness. The color and a nuttiness bring the name.

Oktoberfest is Märzen after the 6–7 month wait as it ages a bit.

Pilsner is a style that comes from Plzen, a Czech version of Milwaukee. Dry and hoppy, this golden lager is hugely popular and most of the mass-produced American light versions fail to imitate the Czech originals. Best to try a handcrafted version at your local—or someone else's local—brewpub. Also a term I use to describe residents of Moquah, Wisconsin, which is also the Township of Pilsen where my grandparents lived.

Porter is a fine, dark ale made with roasted malt and bitter with hops.

Rauchbier is made with smoked barley malt. It may be an acquired taste, but if you like bacon…

Rye beer substitutes some malted rye for some of the malted barley. Remember in that "American Pie" song, the old men "drinking whiskey and rye?" Yeah, that's something else.

Sahti is an old Finnish style of beer, herbal in its ingredients, typically employing juniper berries but not always hops.

Saison is French for "season" (those people have a different word for everything it seems) and this beer was intended for farm workers at the end of summer. It's Belgian and the yeast used ferments at a higher ale temperature. It's generally cloudy and often has something like orange zest or coriander in it. While it was originally a low-alcohol brew so the workers could keep working, many American revivals of the style are packing a bit of a punch.

Saké—This is more of a trivia note than anything. It's not wine or rice wine; it's actually a Japanese rice beer. Odds are you won't see it brewed here but remember this to impress your friends next time you have sushi.

Schwarzbier is the way they say "black beer" in Germany. This lager is black as midnight thanks to the dark roasted malt and has a full, chocolatey or coffee flavour much like a stout or porter.

Scotch Ale or Scottish-style Ale is generally maltier than other ales and sometimes more potent. The FDA insists it be labeled "Scottish-style" as it is not actually from Scotland if brewed here in Michigan. Fair enough.

Sour Ale is a variety of beer that uses wild yeasts and bacteria to get a brew that makes you pucker a bit. Beer can become unintentionally and unpleasantly sour when bacteria infect it. This is different; it's intentional and when done traditionally, it's kinda risky. A lambic fits the category. It may be a last resort when you find a wine drinker who swears they don't like any types of beer.

Stout is black ale most smooth, with dark roasted barley and lots of hops. It can be bitter, dry, or even sweet when it's brewed with milk sugar (lactose). Often brewers add oatmeal for a smoother and sweeter ale and you have to start wondering if there is something to that saying, "Beer, it's not just for breakfast anymore." Some brewers add coffee or chocolate. Imperial Stout is a strong variation on the recipe first done up by the English exporting to the Russians in the 1800s. The real fun of it is when it is on a nitrogen tap or beer engine. Look that up!

Tripel is an unfiltered Belgian ale that has a very high alcohol content. The combination of hops and large amounts of malt and candy sugar give a bittersweet taste to this powerhouse. Many brewpubs will only allow you to drink one or two glasses to make sure you can still find the door when you leave.

Wheat Beer is beer made with wheat. You didn't really just look this up, did you? Dude.

Witbier, Weisse, Weizen, Wisenheimer—three of these words are simply different ways of saying white wheat beer that originated in Belgium. They are sometimes flavored with orange peel and coriander and are mildly to majorly sweet. The fourth word describes the kind of guy that would write that Wheat Beer definition.

INDEX

SIGNATURES

51 North Brewing Company (Lake Orion)

_____ DATE: _____

57 Brew Pub & Bistro (Greenville)

_____ DATE: _____

Arbor Brewing Company (Ann Arbor)

_____ DATE: _____

Arcadia Ales (Battle Creek)

_____ DATE: _____

Arcadia Ales (Kalamazoo)

_____ DATE: _____

Atwater Brewery (Detroit)

_____ DATE: _____

Bad Brewing Company (Mason)

_____ DATE: _____

Barn Tavern, The (Grand Ledge)

_____ DATE: _____

B.A.R.T.S. Brewery (Bay City)

_____ DATE: _____

Bastone Brewery (Royal Oak)

_____ DATE: _____

Batch Brewing Co. (Detroit)

DATE:
_____

Beards Brewery (Petoskey)

DATE:
_____

Beggars Brewery (Traverse City)

DATE:
_____

Bell's Brewing Co. (Production) (Galesburg)

DATE:
_____

Bell's Eccentric Café & Brewery (Kalamazoo)

DATE:
_____

Bier Camp (Ann Arbor)

DATE:
_____

Big Buck Brewery & Steakhouse (Gaylord)

DATE:
_____

Big Lake Brewing (Holland)

DATE:
_____

Big O Brewery (Northport)

DATE:
_____

Big Rapids Brewing Co. (Big Rapids)

DATE:
_____

Bilbo's Pizza (Kalamazoo)

DATE:
_____

Black Lotus Brewing Company (Clawson)

_____ DATE: _____

Blackrocks Brewery (Marquette)

_____ DATE: _____

Blue Tractor BBQ & Brewery (Ann Arbor)

_____ DATE: _____

Boatyard Brewing Co. (Kalamazoo)

_____ DATE: _____

B.O.B. Brewery, The (Grand Rapids)

_____ DATE: _____

Bravo! Restaurant and Café (Portage)

_____ DATE: _____

Brewery Becker (Brighton)

_____ DATE: _____

Brewery Ferment (Traverse City)

_____ DATE: _____

Brewery Terra Firma (Traverse City)

_____ DATE: _____

Brewery Vivant (Grand Rapids)

_____ DATE: _____

Brickside Brewing (Copper Harbor)

_____ DATE: _____

Cheboygan Brewing Co. (Cheboygan)

_____ DATE: _____

Chelsea Alehouse Brewery (Chelsea)

_____ DATE: _____

Copper Canyon Brewery (Southfield)

_____ DATE: _____

Corner Brewery (Ypsilanti)

_____ DATE: _____

Cranker's Brewery (Big Rapids)

_____ DATE: _____

Dark Horse Brewing Co. (Marshall)

_____ DATE: _____

Detroit Beer Co. (Detroit)

_____ DATE: _____

Dragonmead Microbrewery (Warren)

_____ DATE: _____

Eaglemonk Pub & Brewery (Lansing)

_____ DATE: _____

Elk Brewing (Grand Rapids)

_____ DATE: _____

Falling Down Beer Company (Warren)

_____ DATE: _____

Fenton Winery & Brewery (Fenton)

_____ DATE: _____

Fetch Brewing Co. (Whitehall)

_____ DATE: _____

Filling Station Microbrewery, The (Traverse City)

_____ DATE: _____

Fletcher Street Brewing Co. (Alpena)

_____ DATE: _____

Fort Street Brewery (Lincoln Park)

_____ DATE: _____

Founders Brewing Co. (Grand Rapids)

_____ DATE: _____

Frankenmuth Brewery (Frankenmuth)

_____ DATE: _____

Gonzo's Biggdogg Brewing (Kalamazoo)

_____ DATE: _____

Grand Rapids Brewing Co. (Grand Rapids)

_____ DATE: _____

Granite City Food & Brewery (Troy)

_____ DATE: _____

Great Baraboo Brewing Company (Clinton Township)

_____ DATE: _____

Greenbush Brewing Co. (Sawyer)

DATE:

Griffin Claw Brewing Co. (Birmingham)

DATE:

Grizzly Peak Brewing Company (Ann Arbor)

DATE:

Harmony Brewing Company (Grand Rapids)

DATE:

Harper's Restaurant & Brewpub (East Lansing)

DATE:

Hereford & Hops Steakhouse & Brewpub (Escanaba)

DATE:

Hideout Brewing Co., The (Grand Rapids)

DATE:

Hometown Cellars Winery and Brewery (Ithaca)

DATE:

HopCat (Grand Rapids)

DATE:

Jaden James Brewery (Grand Rapids)

DATE:

Jamesport Brewing Co. (Ludington)

DATE:

Jasper Ridge Brewery (Ishpeming)

_____ DATE:

Jolly Pumpkin Artisan Ales (Dexter)

_____ DATE:

Jolly Pumpkin Brewery & Distillery (Traverse City)

_____ DATE:

Keweenaw Brewing Co. (Houghton)

_____ DATE:

Kuhnhenn Brewing Co. (Production) (Clinton Township)

_____ DATE:

Kuhnhenn Brewing Co. (Warren)

_____ DATE:

Lake Superior Brewing Co. (Grand Marais)

_____ DATE:

Latitude 42 Brewing Co. (Portage)

_____ DATE:

Lexington Brewing Co. (Lexington)

_____ DATE:

Liberty Street Brewing Co. (Plymouth)

_____ DATE:

Library Restaurant & Brewpub, The (Houghton)

_____ DATE:

Lily's Seafood Grill & Brewery (Royal Oak)

DATE:

Livery, The (Benton Harbor)

DATE:

Mackinaw Brewing Co. (Traverse City)

DATE:

Michigan Beer Cellar (Sparta)

DATE:

Midland Brewing Company (Midland)

DATE:

Midtown Beer Company (Lansing)

DATE:

Millking It Productions (Royal Oak)

DATE:

Mitten Brewing Co., The (Grand Rapids)

DATE:

Motor City Brewing Works (Detroit)

DATE:

Mountain Town Station (Mt. Pleasant)

DATE:

Mount Pleasant Brewing Co. (Mt. Pleasant)

DATE:

New Holland Brewing Co. (Production) (Holland)

_____ DATE: _____

New Holland Brewing Co. (Pub) (Holland)

_____ DATE: _____

North Peak Brewing Co. (Traverse City)

_____ DATE: _____

Odd Side Ales (Grand Haven)

_____ DATE: _____

Old Boys' Brewhouse (Spring Lake)

_____ DATE: _____

Olde Peninsula Brewpub & Restaurant (Kalamazoo)

_____ DATE: _____

Ore Dock Brewery (Marquette)

_____ DATE: _____

Original Gravity Brewing Co. (Milan)

_____ DATE: _____

Osgood Brewing (Grandville)

_____ DATE: _____

Our Brewing Company (Holland)

_____ DATE: _____

Patchwork Brewing (Decatur)

_____ DATE: _____

Paw Paw Brewing Co. (Paw Paw)

DATE:

Perrin Brewing Company (Grand Rapids)

DATE:

Petoskey Brewing (Petoskey)

DATE:

Pigeon Hill Brewing Co. (Muskegon)

DATE:

Pike 51 Brewing Co. (Hudsonville Winery) (Hudsonville)

DATE:

Quay Street Brewing Company (Port Huron)

DATE:

Rare Bird Brewpub (Traverse City)

DATE:

Red Jacket Brewing Co. (Calumet)

DATE:

Redwood Brewing Co. (Flint)

DATE:

Right Brain Brewery (Traverse City)

DATE:

Rochester Mills Beer Co. (Rochester)

DATE:

Rochester Mills Beer Co. (Production) (Auburn Hills)

DATE:

Rockford Brewing Company (Rockford)

DATE:

Round Barn Brewery & Public House (Baroda)

DATE:

Royal Oak Brewery (Royal Oak)

DATE:

Rupert's Brew House (Kalamazoo)

DATE:

Saugatuck Brewing Company (Douglas)

DATE:

Schmohz Brewing Co. (Grand Rapids)

DATE:

Sherwood Brewing Co. (Shelby Township)

DATE:

Short's Brewing Co. (Pub) (Bellaire)

DATE:

Short's Brewing Co. (Production) (Elk Rapids)

DATE:

Soo Brewing Co. (Sault Sainte Marie)

DATE:

Sports Brewpub (Wyandotte)

DATE:
_____

Stormcloud Brewing Co. (Frankfort)

DATE:
_____

Sue's Coffee House (St. Clair)

DATE:
_____

Sullivan's Black Forest Brew Haus & Grill (Frankenmuth)

DATE:
_____

Tahquamenon Falls Brewery & Pub (Paradise)

DATE:
_____

Tapistry Brewing Co. (Bridgman)

DATE:
_____

Traffic Jam & Snug (Detroit)

DATE:
_____

Tri-City Brewing Company (Bay City)

DATE:
_____

Unruly Brewing Co. (Muskegon)

DATE:
_____

Vander Mill Cider Mill & Winery (Spring Lake)

DATE:
_____

Vierling Restaurant & Marquette Harbor Brewery (Marquette)

DATE:
_____

Villa Brew Pub & Grille (Middleville)

_____ DATE: _____

Walldorff Brewpub & Bistro (Hastings)

_____ DATE: _____

White Flame Brewing Co. (Hudsonville)

_____ DATE: _____

Wiltse's Brewpub & Family Restaurant (Oscoda)

_____ DATE: _____

Witch's Hat Brewing Co. (South Lyon)

_____ DATE: _____

Wolverine State Brewing Co. (Ann Arbor)

_____ DATE: _____

Woodward Avenue Brewers (Ferndale)

_____ DATE: _____

Workshop Brewing Co., The (Traverse City)

_____ DATE: _____

COPPER HARBOR

CALUMET

OUGHTON

MARQUETTE

ISHPEMING

GRAND MARAIS

PARADISE

SAULT SAINTE MARIE

ESCANABA

CHEBOYGAN

PETOSKEY

GAYLORD

NORTHPORT

BELLAIRE

ELK RAPIDS

FRANKFORT

TRAVERSE CITY

OSCODA

LUDINGTON

BIG RAPIDS

MT. PLEASANT

MIDLAND

BAY CITY

WHITEHALL

ITHACA

FRANKENMUTH

LEXINGTON

MUSKEGON

SPARTA

GREENVILLE

ROCKFORD

FLINT

PORT HURON

SPRING LAKE

GRAND HAVEN

GRANDVILLE

GRAND LEDGE

LAKE ORION

AUBURN HILLS

ROCHESTER

SHELBY TWP

ST. CLAIR

GRAND RAPIDS

LANSING

FENTON

HOLLAND

HUDSONVILLE

DOUGLAS

MIDDLEVILLE

EAST LANSING

BIRMINGHAM

ROYAL OAK

SOUTHFIELD

TROY

CLINTON TWP

HASTINGS

MASON

BRIGHTON

SOUTH LYON

DEXTER

PLYMOUTH

CLAWSON

WARREN

FERNDALE

DETROIT

GALESBURG

BATTLE CREEK

CHELSEA

KALAMAZOO

PAW PAW

ANN ARBOR

YPSILANTI

LINCOLN PARK

WYANDOTTE

BENTON HARBOR

PORTAGE

MARSHALL

DECATUR

MILAN

BRIDGMAN

BARODA

SAWYER

ABOUT THE AUTHOR

Kevin Revolinski is an amateur beer snob and born-again ale drinker with a writing habit. A Wisconsin native with some U.P. roots (he grew up on homemade pasties), he has written for a variety of publications including *The New York Times, Chicago Tribune, Wisconsin State Journal* and many postcards to his grandmother. He once sampled beers on *The Today Show* with Al Roker at Lambeau Field in Green Bay. His other travel books include *Wisconsin's Best Beer Guide, Best Easy Day Hikes Grand Rapids, Camping Michigan, Backroads and Byways of Wisconsin, 60 Hikes Within 60 Miles of Madison, Best in Tent Camping Wisconsin, Paddling Wisconsin, Insiders' Guide Madison,* and *The Yogurt Man Cometh: Tales of an American Teacher in Turkey.* Check out his website and blog, The Mad Traveler at www.TheMadTravelerOnline.com. Or look for him at your local brewpub. (It's more likely he's at one of his own local brewpubs in Madison though.) Follow The Mad Traveler on Facebook and Twitter @KevinRevolinski